THE

Cutter's Practical Guide

TO CUTTING

All Kinds Of Ladies' Garments

MADE BY TAILORS

Bibliografische Information der Deutschen Nationalbibliothek:
Die Deutsche Nationalbibliothek verzeichnet diese Publikation
in der Deutschen Nationalbibliografie; detaillierte bibliografische
Daten sind im Internet über www.dnb.de abrufbar.

Reprint of the original from 1900
© 2025
Republished by Sven Jungclaus

Verlag:
BoD · Books on Demand GmbH, Überseering 33, 22297 Hamburg,
bod@bod.de
Druck:
Libri Plureos GmbH, Friedensallee 273, 22763 Hamburg
ISBN: 978-3-7693-2402-0

THE CUTTER'S

PRACTICAL GUIDE

TO THE CUTTING OF

LADIES' GARMENTS,

EMBRACING

All the New and Current Styles

OF

Every Class and Style of Ladies' Garment,

Now being made in the best Tailoring Firms.

REVISED EDITION UP TO DATE.

BY W. D. F. VINCENT.

LONDON:

PUBLISHED BY THE JOHN WILLIAMSON COMPANY LIMITED, 93 & 94 DRURY LANE, W.C.

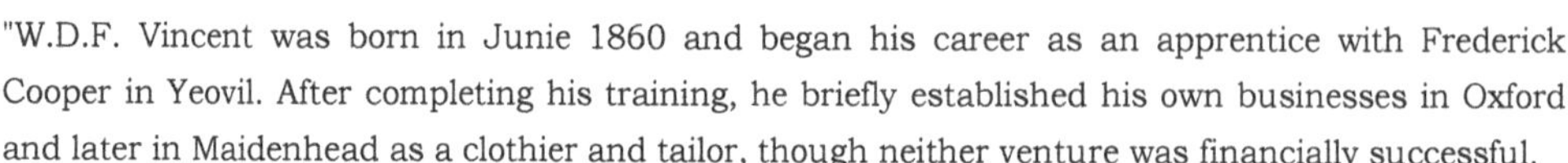

"W.D.F. Vincent was born in Junie 1860 and began his career as an apprentice with Frederick Cooper in Yeovil. After completing his training, he briefly established his own businesses in Oxford and later in Maidenhead as a clothier and tailor, though neither venture was financially successful.

While in Maidenhead, Vincent won an essay competition on tailoring, which was open to all members of the National Federation of Foremen Tailors, titled "The Great National Work on Trouser Cutting, or Defects in Trousers." He submitted his entry under the pseudonym "Oxonian" and won the first prize. This success led him to secure a position with The Tailor and Cutter magazine. In the early years, Vincent contributed numerous articles on tailoring methods and techniques to the magazine. However, due to the terms of his employment, these articles were published without attribution to him.

By the 1890s, Vincent became a leading tailoring authority. His books, such as The Cutter's Practical Guide to the Cutting & Making of All Kinds of Trousers, became standard reference work. By 1917, Vincent referred to himself as a journalist. He died in June 1926.

The Tailor and Cutter magazine and academy were operated by John Williamson & Co Ltd. In the 1950s and 1960s, many tailors displayed their Tailor & Cutter Academy Diplomas, signed by W.D.F. Vincent, as the Chairman of Examiners, as a centerpiece in their shop windows. One such example can still be seen on display at the Museum of Welsh Life at St. Fagans in South Wales."

(cf. https://vincents.org.uk/family-history/w-d-f-vincent-tailor; 15.12.2024)

This edition is a reprint of the legendary 'Cutter's Practical Guide' series; the first book in a series of thirteen was published in 1890. The entire text has been meticulously read, and the images have been carefully cleaned and edited to ensure the highest quality.

Part 1   – Juvenile Garments
Part 2   – Body Coats
Part 3   – Trousers, Breeches & Knickers
Part 4   – Livery Garments in all their varieties
Part 5   – Overcoats
Part 6   – Ladies' Garments
Part 7   – Defects, Remedies, Trying on
Part 8   – Economical Cutting
Part 9   – Lounges, Reefers, Norfolk, Sporting & Patrol Jackets
Part 10 – Waistcoats for Gentlemen, Ladies, Military & Naval Officers, Livery
          Servants, etc.
Part 11 – Shirts, Undergarments, Collars, Cuffs, Aprons and Speciality Clothing for
          Various Occupations
Part 12 – Clerical Dress
Part 13 – British Military Uniforms

PUBLISHER'S PREFACE

I t is now about three years since we added a new part to "The Cutter's Practical Guide Systems" in the form of a Work on ladies' tailor-made garments. Not only has a large Edition been disposed of, but a number of the styles which were then popular are now out of date. In preparing this new Edition, a number of what are now regarded as old styles are deleted, and the new and popular styles of the period take their place.

The Work is based on the "Guide" System, and was originally prepared to meet a two-fold want or demand — an instructor and guide to the production of all the new and popular styles in tailor-made garments; and also the demand for such a work by the Practical Guide System.

The Work itself will bear testimony to its scope, and the way in which every current, as well as new style of Ladies' Tailor-made Garment is treated and illustrated. Here we have the systems for producing the garments, each illustrated by beautifully engraved diagrams; and there is, further, the finished garments, illustrated upon artistically engraved figures. The Work thus presents a completeness which renders it an invaluable acquisition to the ladies' cutter. Should the inexperienced or timid cutter hesitate to use his own productions by these systems, our arrangements for supplying Special Cut Patterns of any style of ladies' garment — if the style can be conveyed to us — at a very nominal price, will meet the difficulty, at the same time allow him to compare our pattern with his own production.

We doubt not but this new and latest Work will fully sustain the character we have already attained by the Works now being published at the TAILOR AND CUTTER Office.

THE JOHN WILLIAMSON COMPANY LIMITED.

PREVIOUSLY PRINTED BY THE JOHN WILLIAMSON COMPANY LIMITED,
93 & 94 DRURY LANE, LONDON, W.C.

https://www.becomeatailor.com

Content

CUTTER'S PRACTICAL GUIDE

TO CUTTING

All Kinds of Ladies' Garments

MADE BY TAILORS.

The object we set before us in this work, is the preparation of a Complete Instructor and Guide in the production of all Ladies' Garments, which may be classed as "tailor-made", not only as regards the cut, the fit and the making, but embracing also all the new, the current and popular styles, in all their different classes and departments — an Instructor to the inexperienced and a Guide to the experienced cutter. While tailoring has been largely augmented during recent years by Ladies' Garments, this comparatively new branch is capable of very considerable further development, which can only be accomplished by cutters generally setting themselves to study and acquire the Art of Cutting and getting up Ladies' Garments — an art in most respects widely different from the production of gentlemen's garments, and which must receive special and attentive study before success can be possible. This work will supply the necessary materials in every detail for such study. Starting at the beginning, with anatomy of the female figure we proceed step by step till we embrace every point connected with the production of Ladies' tailor-made garments, in all their styles and varieties, so that by application and perseverance, any cutter of ordinary tact and intelligence, can find the foundation for his study, and which by practical application in daily experience, will enable him to master this art, and, as cutter, to take any position in a high-class trade; or, as master, to develop his trade by the making of ladies' garments, turned out with such fit, taste and style as will be well-nigh certain to ensure success.

Such, briefly, is the aim and object of this work. There must be a continuous study on the part of the cutter, for fashions change so rapidly, onestyle succeeds another so speedily, that unless he is on the alert, he will soon drop back into the second rate; for it is well known that ladies make a study of dress; they not only know what is the latest style, but they also understand every appli-cation of art, and very often some of the laws of science. They will often tell you where the seams of their garments should be placed, and they know the effect certain styles of ornamentation will have on the body; and woe to the reputation of the man who leads them in the wrong direction; and although we do not wish to impute that, with all ladies, dress is the one end and object of their life, yet they study it, they read about it, they write about it, they talk about it, they think about it, they attend public institu-tions to look at it, they work for it, aye, and often deny themselves the common neces-saries of life to procure it. Our object in mentioning these facts is to show the cutter who hopes to become first-class at this branch of tailoring, the necessity there is for application and study, to become acquainted with science in all its teachings, so as to apply it to his calling; to thoroughly under-stand the application of art in all its fine studies, so as to utilise its lessons to the adorning of the female form; to understand the phases of practical tailoring, which enables form to be introduced into what was before flat and lifeless. We might proceed almost indefinitely to show how know-ledge was power in this direction, but we will take the various phases in their order, and leave the

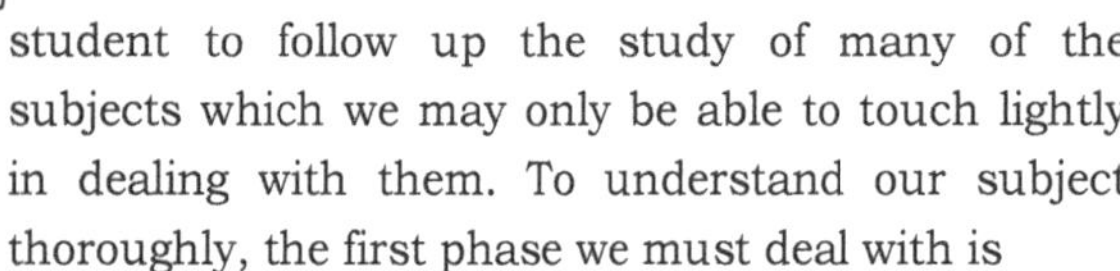

student to follow up the study of many of the subjects which we may only be able to touch lightly in dealing with them. To understand our subject thoroughly, the first phase we must deal with is

Anatomy,

A subject deserving of more attention from tailors than it receives. It is a study which recalls to us the laws of our Divine Creator when he fashioned our bodies. It is not necessary that our readers should spend months or years acquiring the name of all the bones of the human figure; what we want them to understand is, that a bone of such a shape is in such a position, and that its movements are in certain directions; that is surrounded by certain muscles which develop in certain directions; and, having acquired this knowledge, the cutter will be able to distinguish between the possible and im-possible in nature, and so lay the foundation for formulating sound systems. It will enable him to understand the outline of the form he has to clothe, independent of such artificial appliances as bustles, crinolines, &c, &c.

It teaches the symmetry of the body, and shows how the left side is an almost exact reproduction of the right only in reverse.

It teaches where growth is possible and where impossible; how certain bones always remain near the surface of the skin, and how, when the body develops either fat or muscle, where the increment is placed and how it affects the surrounding parts. mmIt teaches the movements of limbs, where the three different joints are to be found, viz., * the gilding, the universal or ball socket and the hinge joint.

But the study that applies more particularly to thiswork, is what we may term comparative anatomy, by which we may realise the difference between the male and female form, and as we have treated of Anatomy in Part 1 of the "Cutter's Practical Guide", we will suppose the readers of this work have made themselves, to a certain extent, acquainted with the general anatomy of the male form. On

Figure 1

The female skeleton is illustrated, and on figure 2 the male. By comparison we at once notice the smallness of the ribs and the largeness of the hips,

whilst the space between the chest and pelvis (hips) is much wider in woman than in man. The collar bones are weaker in woman than in man, and are differently shaped, which remark applies to all the bones of the superior extremities *.

The ribs of the female are not so arch-like nor so strong as in the male.

When the bones are quite characteristic, the male are more arched than the female ribs, especially between the fifth and ninth on either side. It is there that the female ribs are flattened, and it is in this situation that the female waist exists. In man, when strongly formed, the ribs continue fully arched, much lower down, placing his waist between the last rib and the top of the haunches.

In man the back is strong; in woman the loins.

But probably the part where the tailor will learn the best lesson is the hips, as it will soon force itself to his notice in practice how very much more the hips are developed in the female form than the male. Another reference to figure 1 and 2 will readily illustrate this; of the male pelvis we shall not particularise, but of the female we wish to call attention to the fine oval form it presents as com-pared with the male, the great breadth of the haunch bones, &c. It is this great breadth of the hips in woman, that the ladies' tailor has to observe and make provision for, and which, together with the other peculiarities of the female skeleton, will open his eyes to the reason for many of the effects he has to deal with. Important as is the study of anatomy as a foundation upon which to build up a scientific and practical knowledge, we do not wish to overlook the undisputed fact, that the skeleton bears but an indistinct resemblance to the outside, the muscle and flesh formation having much to do with that. But a little study will soon inform us where and how these muscles develop, and as we know the bones never really alter their actual forms (though they seem to do so by the condition of the surrounding muscles) and consequently a know-ledge of the skeleton formation is the very best foundation we can possibly have. In

Figure 3 and 4

we have illustrations showing the proportions of man and woman, taken from a manual of artistic anatomy by Robert Knox, M.D., F.R.S.E., which

---

* These are fully described in Part 1 of the "Cutter's Practical Guide".

*Scapula clavicle, humerus, radius, ulna, carpel, meta-carpel and digital bones.

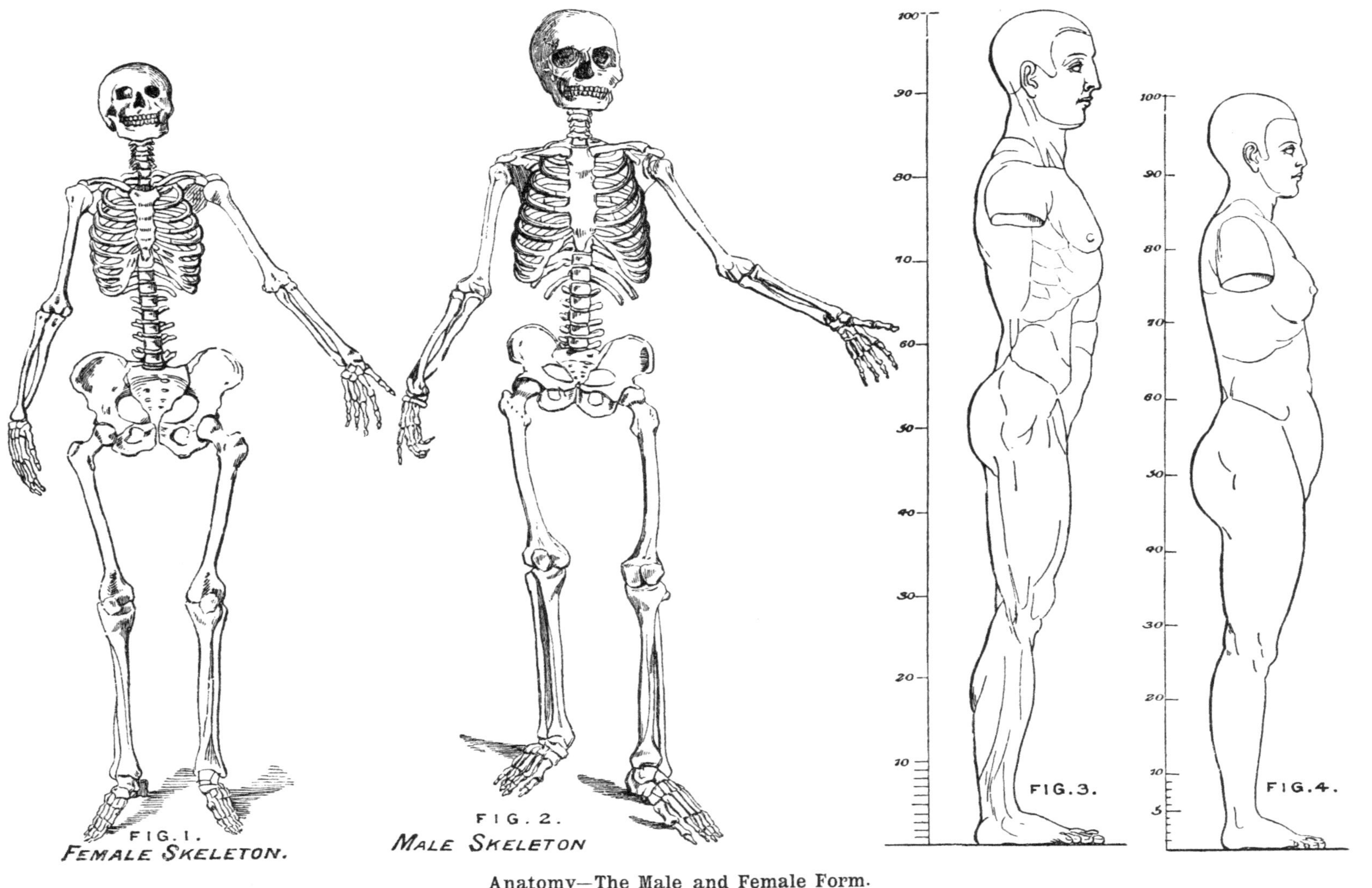

Anatomy—The Male and Female Form.

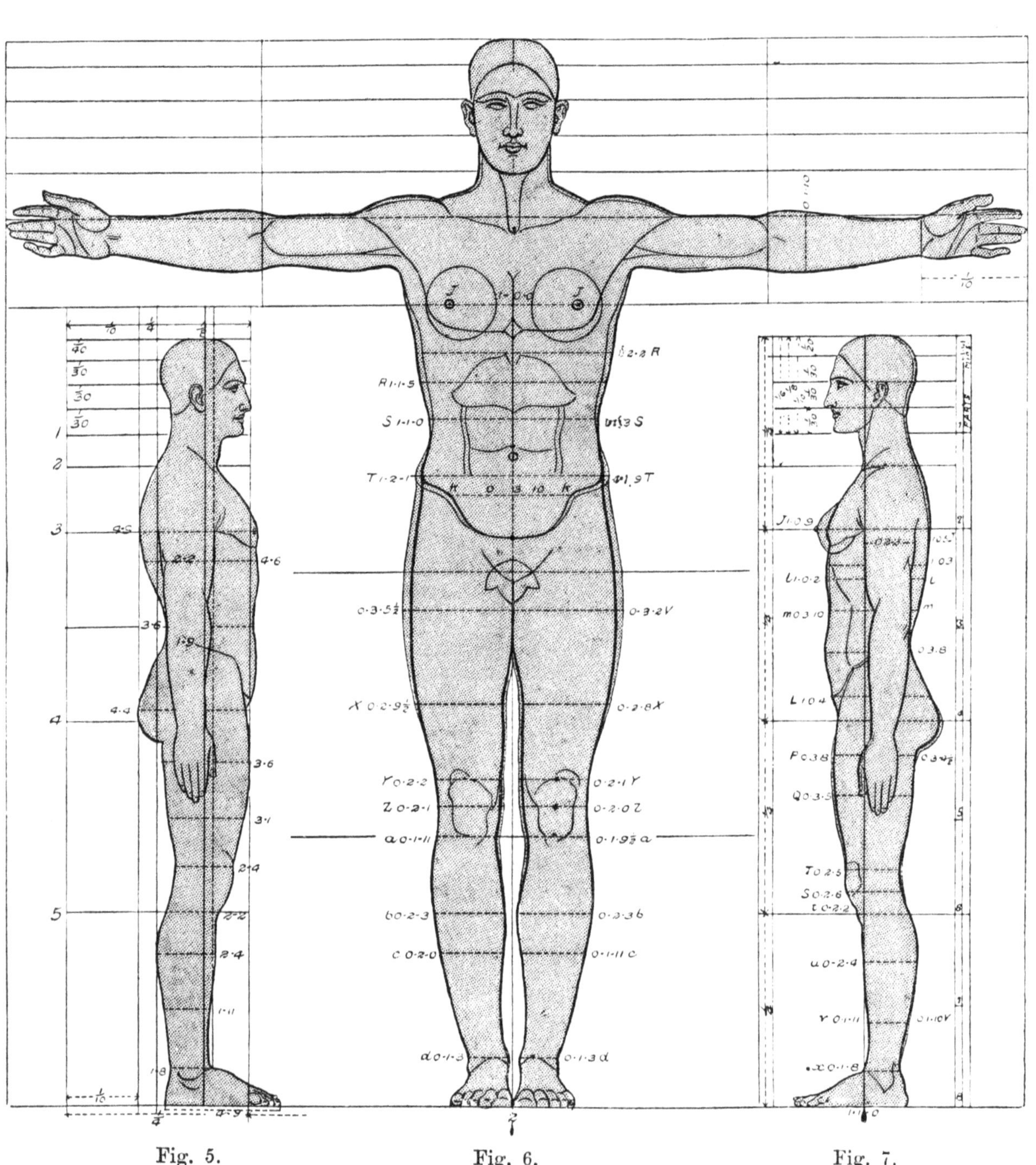

Fig. 5. Fig. 6. Fig. 7.

Anatomy—Difference between Male and Female.

still further emphasises the lessons we learnt from the skeleton. The shoulders are small, the circumference of the chest is increased by the development of the breasts, the extra size of the hips and thighs, and lastly, the softness of outline, which seems to hide every trace of the skeleton, and even tones down, and in many cases altogether hides the muscular development which is so clearly marked in man.

We cannot close this section on anatomy without referring to one of the best works published in modern times; it is by J. Bononi, F.R.A.S., M.S.B.A., entitled, Proportions of the Human Figure, and from which the following diagrams and quotations of relative proportions of the human figure are taken. Amongst the various difficult questions which are always cropping up in connection with our art is: What is proportion? and on this topic we give the definition of proportion as laid down by Virtrivius. "Proportion is the commensuration of the various constituent parts with the whole, on the existence of which symmetry is found to consist". As, for instance, the human frame is divided into four equal parts by very distinctly marked divisions in its structure and outward form. See,

Figure 5

Firstly. From the crown of the head to a line drawn across the nipples, as at 3. Secondly. From the nipples to the pubis as from 3 to 4. Thirdly. From the pubis to the bottom of the petella, as from 4 to 5. Lastly. From the bottom of the petella to the sole of the foot, as from 5 to 6. Again, four measures equal in themselves, and likewise equal to those just described, and as well marked in the structure of the human body, are seen when the arms are extended horizontally, as in

Figure 6

From the tip of the middle or longest finger to the bend of the arm is one-fourth of the height of the person, and from the bend of the arm to the pit of the neck is another fourth. Again, with regard to the face and hands. From the tip of the forehead to the chin is a tenth, and from the tip of the middle finger to the wrist is also a tenth. The face is also divided in three parts as shown, but this is not of so much importance to us as the relation the head bears to the body. It has so often been asserted that the head bears the relation of one-eighth of the total height of the body, that it will be as well if we examine this assertion thoroughly. For, although it undoubtedly is somewhat near the mark, yet at the same time, its reliability is open to question in many cases, so we will take the relation this part bears to the body in some of the most noted statues, and in doing so, we divide the figure in the same manner as is done by artists, &c., and which is illustrated on

Figure 7

viz., heads, parts and minutes; the head is the distance from the crown of the head to the chin, as at I. The parts are obtained by dividing the head into four equal divisions, and the minutes are obtained by dividing one of those divisions into twelve equal parts, and in this manner the true relation that each portion bears to the other is obtained. For example, let us suppose the head measures 9 inches, each part would be 2¼ and each minute three-sixteenth of an inch. It would be as well for the student to note this, as we shall have occasion to refer to this later on, but for the present will deal with

The Eight Heads Theory.

The Apollo Sauroktonos, it is said, would be seven heads and nine minutes if he stood upright; thus it will be seen in this case the height of the figure is three parts three minutes short of this standard; or taking our division of inches as just worked out, would be over 7 inches short of eight heads. The Apollino of Florence, is said to be seven heads, three parts and five minutes high, thus, he only wants six minutes to complete the eight heads, or as we have been calculating ¼⅛ inches short. The Achilles of the Louvre is said to be seven heads, one part and eleven minutes; thus he wants nearly 4¾ inches to reach this standard. The Venus de Medeci is said to be seven heads, three parts and ten minutes, thus she only requires 2 minutes or ⅜ of an inch to complete eight heads. The Venus of the Capitol is said to measure seven heads, one part and four minutes; thus, she wants two parts and eight minutes, or six inches according to our calculation, to complete the eight heads, so by this test the eight heads theory fails, for these are the statues which have charmed the world for ages, and have been looked upon as masterpiece of art, or in other words

The Highest Ideals of Proportion

That sculptors have ever produced, and as every one of these fall short of the standard thus fixed, and in some cases by as much as 6 or 7 inches, it will be seen that from 7½ to 8 heads would be nearer the mark, certainly well inside the 8, as in no case do they reach eight heads. Again, the "length of arms equal the height" is equally erroneous, for out of 84 persons measured by Bononi, 54 were found to be long armed, 24 short armed, and 6 only whose arms were exactly equal to the height when extended. The greatest excess was in the case of a carpenter, whose arms exceeded height by 5 inches. The greatest excess of height was in the case of an architect, whose height exceeded the distance of his extended arms by 4 inches. Figure 6 shows the proportion of the male figure according to Bononi, whilst Figures 6 and 7 shows

The Relation of the Male and Female Forms.

The male figure is represented by the thick lines, and the measurements referring to it are placed on your right hand, whilst the female is represented by the fine lines, and the measurements on the left. The measurements are all calculated by heads, parts and minutes, and as marked represent the width in profile. The measurements of length, according to Virtrivius and Leonardo da Vinci, are relatively the same in both sexes, and are expressed in long horizontal lines running through both the front and profile figures; the letters by the side of the figures refer to the proportions of the relative parts, and which will be of value to the tailor in helping him to obtain measures, which, for some reason or the other, he is unable to take direct on the figure.

To get the circumference of any part, add the width in profile (as given on figure 5 for the male, and figure 7 for the female) and width in front (as illustrated on figure 6, the figures on the left side representing the female, and those on the right the male), together multiply them by 1½ and the result will give approximate circumference. Example: male thigh profile, 3 parts 6 minutes, 3 parts =6¾, 3 minutes =$\frac{9}{16}$ =7$\frac{5}{16}$ front, 3 parts 2 minutes, 3 parts = 6¾, 2 minutes =⅜ =7⅛, 7$\frac{5}{16}$ plus 7⅛ =14$\frac{7}{16}$, one and a-half times 14$\frac{7}{16}$ =21$\frac{11}{16}$ thigh. Other parts may be treated in the same way.

The following list of measurements of the

Venus de Medicis,

as compared with those of a modern beauty, will prove most interesting, and to the tailor who has a difficulty in getting certain measurements, they will prove most useful. Some papers have been printing facts about the "perfect woman" physically considered. An artist supplies the comparative measurements of a modern beauty and the Venus de Medicis, two types of the ancient and modern worlds. The height of these two beautiful women, the one in flesh and blood, and the other in marble, happens to be the same, viz., five feet and seven inches. Hence the two may be taken as illustrating the difference of ideal physical proportions between the ancient and the modern.

	Modern Beauty.	The Venus.
Height	5 ft. 7 in.	5 ft. 7 in.
Across the shoulders	15 inches.	16½ inches.
Bust	36 inches.	38 inches.
Arm	12 inches.	12 inches.
Thigh	24 inches.	24 inches.
Calf	12 inches.	12 inches.
Neck	12 inches.	13½ inches.
Hips	45 inches.	42 inches.
Length of Leg	28 inches.	32 inches.
Waist	26 inches.	—
Length of Arm	26 inches.	28 inches.
Ankle	8 inches.	9½ inches
Foot	8 inches.	—
Face	7½ inches.	—

Doubtless there are millions of beautiful women who do not come very close to either, but taking the nineteenth century type of beauty, it appears that the modern runs less to the shoulders and more to the hips than the woman of antiquity. The ancient has also a decided advantage in the length of legs and arms, and the size of neck and ankles. On the whole, the modern woman appears to be less muscularly and more voluptuously formed than the ancient. It would be very easy to note a series of coincidences in these measures, such as the neck, arm and calf being the same size, but they would be of little value, as one part develops independently of another, so we pass on to deal with

The Principles which Govern the Fitting of Garments,

and which must form the foundation on which all

systems are built. Putting these briefly, they consist of two, viz., size and form; but inasmuch as that is rather indefinite, we prefer to classify them under seven heads, viz.: (1) Length. (2) Width. (3) Height and size of neck. (4) Location and size of scye. (5) Provision for prominence and depressions, such as blades, chest, &c. (6) Provisions for muscular developments. (7) Attitude. We will briefly touch on the principal features to be noted in dealing with these. That length should govern length, and width govern width, seems such a common-sense rule, that we can hardly realise any other plan being adopted, and yet many cutters of the present day cling to the relic of a bygone age, fixing every point of the garment by division of width. Of the fixed points in the body, two stand out prominently as starting points of great value to the cutter. These are the centre of back and the centre of front, and it will be well for every cutter to realise that at these parts the body is hollow, that is, there are decided depressions; and to fix these points in their proper relation to each other is of great importance in the garment. The only measure necessary to do this is the size, or, if you will, the width round body, plus an allowance for seams, ease, &c., and which for an ordinary garment made from medium material would run about two inches. Of the length, the nape is the starting point, it is the first prominence that shows itself at the back of the neck (the seventh vertebræe), and from which the hollow of waist and full length is obtained. In these two we have all that is contained in size; but in form we have to provide for all the local prominences and depressions. Let us take

The Height and Size of Neck.

Here we have one of the most puzzling parts of the garment, or, at least, it is so to a large number. Why? Simply because they try to provide for it either by divisions of the breast, or divisions of the length, both being erroneous — we were going to say equally, but this is hardly so, for certainly a division of the length is preferable to a width, although it is far from reliable, for we occasionally find tall people square shouldered, and *vice versâ*; whilst there is still another feature to be borne in mind, viz., the thickness of the body at that part, for if the shoulders are largely devoloped in the front, the same or almost the same provision must be made as for square shoulders. Then there is still another

feature, viz., that with short-necked figures the thickness of the neck from side to side is more than would be the case with the normal figure, whilst with the long-necked figure the diameter is less. This we account for in the following way :— In the short neck the muscles go up from the shoulder to the neck more suddenly, and so increase the diameter from side to side, and *vice versâ*. Hence, the only mode of fixing the correct amount of height of neck in all cases is by direct measure, division of length or width being both erroneous, and will lead the cutter who trusts in them astray.

The Location and Size of Scye.

This may either be done by measuring from the centre of back, or the centre of front; either method is reliable, though, for our part, we prefer measuring from the centre of front, as it is not affected by any variation in the allowance for making up or ease. But important as is the location of the front of scye — and it is one of the most important in the garment — there is another part which claims an equal share of attention, viz., the bottom, or what is usually termed the depth of scye. This may be done in two ways: either by measuring from waist line upwards, or by getting a true horizontal line round the figure level with the bottom of scye with a tape, or by means of a square. We prefer the latter method, as the run of waist is often out of the true horizontal, and liable to be disturbed by fashion, such as when prominent bustles were worn, the length of waist was shortened behind. We do not consider the one-third of the circumference used in connection with a quantity for the height of neck equal to this direct measurement method, as the arm develops in various ways, and when the muscles develop it forms anything but a circle, and consequently such a method would provide too much length in the back section.

Provision for Prominence and Depressions.

This is made either by suppression, or what is equivalent, drawing in and pressing the fulness away. In practical tailoring there are three relative lengths: the hollow, the straight, and the round; and if we remember the effect of those on the adjoining parts, we shall be materially helped in fitting the various forms. Thus, if we cut a hollow back seam, it will fit very snug down the centre; but as it will be brought to a straight line when on the figure, it will throw fulness over the blades, and if there are no sideseams, fulness round the back of scye. It is well to remember that any deviation from the straight line for either back or front, must be made to provide for prominence or depression, the hollow giving extra room, the straight being normal, and the round producing shortness on all the surrounding parts. Thus, it will be seen, there are no figures that require a round front edge to their garments, as there is a development of breast to be provided for in both male and female figures; though if darts are not permissible, the round front edge may be cut, but it must always be manipulated back to the straight line if a proper fitting garment is desired. There is one principle we must specially call attention to, viz., suppression at one part causes fulness both above and below, and the greater the suppression the greater the fulness, hience the waist must be suppressed with the view of providing for the prominence of blades, breasts, &c. Closely allied to this question of provision for prominence, is

Provision for Muscular Development.

This can only be successfully met by a series of short sectional measures, starting from fixed points, and going along those parts where the muscles are likely to develop. In cutting from block patterns, provision may be made for this by the insertion of wedges, but it should be understood that the insertion of the wedge at any part will have a purely local effect, and, indeed, it is in this feature that its greatest value consists.

In attitude we have a principle of the greatest importance, for unless the attitude of your customer is duly considered, it will be impossible to produce a fit. Many cutters meet this successfully by the aid of a trained eye; but that takes some time to acquire. We prefer taking such measures as will of themselves indicate the relative lengths of back and front, which really constitute the balance. The attitude of the figure indicates whether they stoop or stand erect, and as every cutter knows what would fit the one would not fit the other, it becomes necessary to make it one of the special points to be observed, regulating in each case the relative lengths of back and front in accordance with the customer's requirements. These few ideas on principles must suffice.

SECTION TWO.

Art in Relation to Ladies' Garments. Fashion Designing. Plate 3.

There is a general desire on the part of ladies to have original styles, and whilst we are reminded again and again there is no new thing under the sun, and that fashion periodically returns, yet the reverse of this is equally true, viz., that as no two leaves are exactly alike, so with the combination of form, colour, and material, each costume may be quite distinct and fresh. Let us assume a lady comes to order a costume, and as she does so, we show her a number of Plates, she is much taken with the one in particular, and wishes us to adapt Figure A in a somewhat similar style to some of the others, for instance, she prefers the vest should fasten right up to the throat, and wishes the bodice to fasten at the waist with a much fuller skirt below, the braiding to be retained, together with a little braiding on the skirts, as on Figure A.

The sleeves are to be of the same style as shown, but with fancy cuffs, and the back of the skirt being finished in a large double box pleat, as shown on Figure B. It is, of course, not to be expected that these details will be arranged without a good deal of conversation, and as the cutter may be appealed to a great many times during the progress of discussion, it will be necessary for him to be thoroughly conversant with

The Laws of Beauty.

Fashion is often far from beauty, and it is necessary for us to modify those that would not suit our customer, if a stylish and beautiful garment is to be the result. It must be obvious to the most superficial observer that one style would not suit all classes of figures, the short and stout must be specially catered for as well as the tall and thin, and there are few customers who are more alive to this fact than those ladies who are a little out of proportion.

But not only must the style be adapted to the prevailing fashion, and the customer's peculiarities, but there must be unity, order and proportion in the design. For instance, if it is a Costume, the skirt must have something about it to show its connection with the bodice, and the trimming is a very fruitful means of providing this, and so in like manner order must be introduced, a something to show there has been a designer at work, and that order has been

Fig. A.   Fig. B.

A LESSON IN FASHION DESIGNING.

carefully arranged. The proportion of the various parts must be harmonious; and if, as was the case a few years ago, there is a tendency to extra large sleeves, well, the only plan is to modify them as far as possible.

Colour

Must also receive proper attention; not only should the material and trimmings harmonise together, but both must blend with the complexion, &c.

First of all, then, we would remind our readers that all colours depend upon light; without light there is no colour, but with light we get all the varying shades of the rainbow.

The light as it streams down to flood the earth appears to us to have no colour, though we usually consider pure light to be white, from the simple fact that white reflects the light as nearly as possible the same as it comes down from the great luminary. In reality there is in that light every possible colour we can conceive, and to prove this, we prepared a darkened room (see Diagram top of Plate), in such a way that the only light that enters it comes through a hole in the door or window, and this we so arrange that it is only out about the size of a pencil. We now take a prism, and by these means we make a

Division of Light.

We find that the single ray of white light is passed on to the wall in seven colours. Starting from darkness we get violet, indigo, blue, green, yellow, orange and red; the seven prismatic colours. The proportion in which they exist in white light is shown on Diagram at side which gives blue 8 parts, red 5 parts, yellow 3. The intervening colours produced by the prism are what is known as secondaries or binaries, from the fact that they are produced by the overlapping of two primaries thus, in the centre diagram we have blue, red and yellow, as the basis, with orange composed of a combination of yellow and red. Green is a mixture of yellow and blue, and purple the blending of blue and red; thus, in white light the division of orange and blue would be — orange 1 part, and blue 8 parts; with red and green it would be — red 5 parts, and green 11 parts. With purple and yellow it is 13 parts purple, and 3 parts yellow; these proportions we have indicated by the colums in the right hand top corner, as well as the circles at the bottom.

There is still another class of colours which are known as Tertiaries, and these are illustrated on the outer edge of the circle in the centre, viz., olive, citrine, and russet; in each of these all three primaries are used, but not in the same proportions as form white light; thus, russet is a mixture of red, blue and yellow, with red preponderating. Citrine has yellow as its principal constituent, and olive is made up most largely of blue.

So far we have not referred to the neutral tints, viz., black, grey, and white, these are merely reflections of all parts of white light. Thus, white reflects all parts, grey reflects portions of all parts and absorbs the other, and thus occupies a mild position between black and white.

So far, then, we have very briefly sketched the science of colours, and our readers may be desirous to see its

Application to Tailoring,

And we now proceed to do this. For our purpose we roughly divide our customers into blondes and brunettes, and in like manner we divide our colour into two classes — 1, blues; 2, red and yellows. Now, those of our customers who come under the description of blondes, are best suited when their garments have a preponderance of blue, whilst brunettes are set off to the best advantage when dressed in red and yellows. But whilst this is so, every part of the costume should be so arranged as to present a perfect harmony, each colour lending its quota to the general effect.

Of course, we do not mean that every customer should be attired in dresses composed of red, blue and yellow, though in effect that is the first principle; but, as Ruskin tells us, the best effects are always produced by the most indefinable shades, so primary colours can only be used sparingly. This leads us to a study of

The Harmony of Contrast,

Which the great French authority (M. Chevreul) on colours states to be of the first importance. The harmony of contrast consists of the combination of two colours, which in themselves make up the complement of white light; thus we have blue and orange, since the colours left when blue is taken awayare red and yellow, and these blended together make orange. Now, blue never appears to such good advantage as when placed side by side with

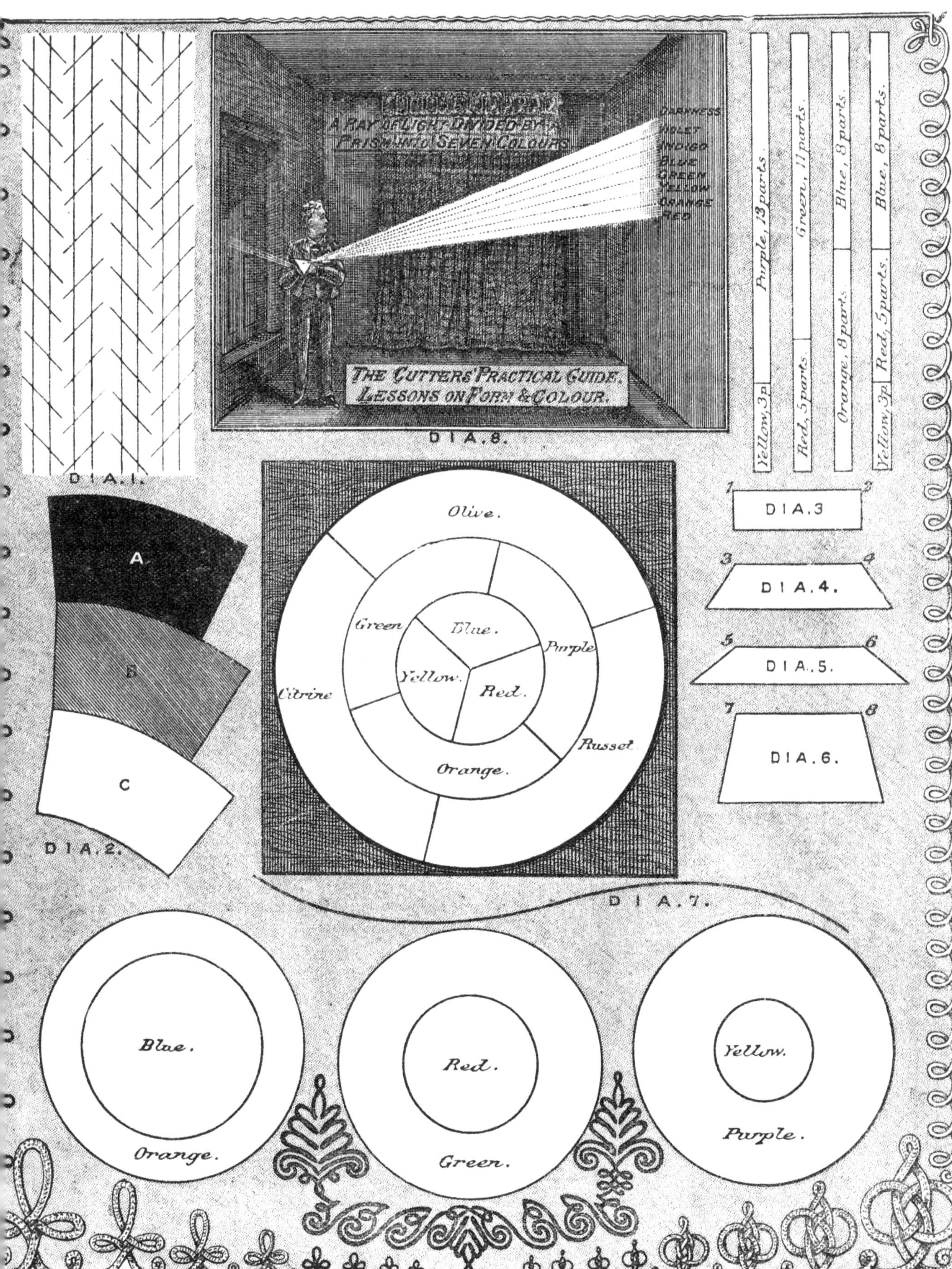
DIA.1.

A
B
C

DIA.2.

A RAY OF LIGHT DIVIDED BY
PRISM INTO SEVEN COLOURS

DARKNESS
VIOLET
INDIGO
BLUE
GREEN
YELLOW
ORANGE
RED

THE CUTTERS' PRACTICAL GUIDE.
LESSONS ON FORM & COLOUR.

DIA.8.

Olive.
Green
Citrine
Blue.
Yellow.
Red.
Purple
Orange.
Russet

Purple, 13 parts.
Yellow, 3p.
Green, 11 parts.
Red, 5 parts.
Blue, 8 parts.
Orange, 8 parts.
Blue, 8 parts.
Yellow, 3p. Red, 5 parts.

1   3
DIA.3

3   4
DIA.4.

5   6
DIA.5.

7   8
DIA.6.

DIA.7.

Blue.
Orange.

Red.
Green.

Yellow.
Purple.

orange, red never looks so bright as when placed in the midst of green. Nature recognises this complementary arrangement, for if the eye gazes steadily at any colour, say red, for a minute, and the gaze be then transferred to a blank wall or ceiling, the same form will be observed but in the complementary colour, thus showing that the eye gazing on any bright colour tires, and seeks to find rest by creating the complementary.

These combinations produce some excellent effects, and are worthy of the most careful study in connection with dress. But in addition to the harmony of a primary and a binary, there is also the harmony of a binary and a tertiary, thus harmonious contrasts are found in green and russet, orange and olive, and citrine and purple; and as the binaries and tertiaries are softer in effect, the result is often considered more artistic.

The harmony of analogy also finds full scope in the matter of dress, this being none other than the harmony of similars. Thus the varying shades blue or brown blended together give very good results, as is so often seen in the combination of Oxford and Cambridge blues. It may be as well here to observe that all colours start in white and lose themselves in black, thus the yellow may be so fair as to be scarcely distinguishable from white, and yet may be so deep as to eventually become lost in black. The harmony of analogy consists in blending these various shades together.

We have not yet noted that

Black, White, and Grey

Are suitable for all complexions, though not for all figures; small people are set off to the best advantage when dressed in white or light grey, the stout ones, when their clothing is made from black or dark grey, for the simple reason that the latter shades absorb the light, and so make them appear smaller, and the former reflect the light, and so make them appear larger; but as far as complexion is concerned both black, white, and grey are suitable for all, and though, of course, inferior in effect to some of the colours formerly dealt with, yet they are safe.

Further, these shades are useful in separating colours that do not of themselves blend satisfactorily; but the effect they have in this way must not be overlooked. White has the effect of brightening everything it is associated with, whereas black deadens it. Grey brightens or deadens as it approaches white or black. It must not, however, be assumed that white has the same effect as the complementary; for instance, white placed beside red brightens it considerably, whereas green placed beside red intensifies it and makes it appear redder. This is useful in many ways for trimming, window dressing, &c., and those of our readers who care to study this further will find it a most profitable one.

Colour and Sentiment.

It is well known that certain colours have an effect on the sentiments of the beholder or wearer. The waving a red flag in front of a bull has always been the signal to call forth his rage, and it will be found each colour has its suggesting sentiments.

White suggests purity and brightness.

Black	guilt and despair.
Grey	retirement, quiet, &c.
Red	licence, life, and daring.
Blue	calmness, peace, &c.
Yellow	glory and grandeur.
Green	gentleness, amiability, freshness.
Orange	violence, sourness, &c.
Purple	inflated wealth and melancholy.

A careful consideration of this phase of our subject will repay the student. There is a very great deal more in it than appears on the surface. We will now briefly consider the subject of

Form and Pattern.

And here again we find an almost unlimited field for study, so that we may clothe our customers in that form of garment most becoming. The effect that can be produced in the matter of form is certainly startling, clearly illustrating the difficulty there is in believing one's own eyes.

For instance, let us look at Diagram 1. Here we have a number of parallel lines intersected by short cross lines, running at opposite angles, with the apparent result that some of the lines converge at top, and others at the bottom, or in other words, the orange stripe appears narrower at bottom than the top, and others appear narrower at top than bottom, whereas there is no difference whatever.

Take again Diagram 2, the three spaces A, B and C, and although they are all the same size, B certainly appears larger than A, and C in turn appears larger than B, yet this is quite an illusion. Examine Diagrams 3, 4, 5 and 6, the upper line as

1, 2; 3, 4 ; 5, 6; 7, 8, are equal, and yet they all appear of varying lengths, thus illustrating the effect produced by surrounding parts.

Our object in taking these simple examples is to impress our readers with the importance of making a study of form, so that it may be adapted to our customers' requirements. We think they will find that loose-fitting garments give the figure a shorter appearance than close-fitting ones.

Long garments make people appear taller than short ones. Garments with numerous vertical lines of braiding, seams, or pattern of material, make the figure taller.

Costumes that have light terminations, that is top and bottom, also give height by calling attention to the extremities of the figure.

Lines and Curves

Also call for a little comment, and we cannot do better than repeat that the beautiful in outline is the curve. In Diagram 7 we have what Hogarth, the celebrated painter, was pleased to call the Line of Beauty, which takes the form of a prolonged S, and our readers will find it profitable to notice how often this line is repeated in the human body — the arm, the side and hips, the leg, &c., all partake of this; indeed, in the whole body it will be difficult to find a decided angle, or even a straight line; so in our garments we shall do well to avoid the introduction of straight lines in the finished garment. This does not necessarily mean that in cutting there should be no straight lines (though there should not be many), but rather that when the garment is finished there should be a graceful curve; thus it is with the front edge, we believe in cutting it straight, but when finished, the suppression at the darts, &c., has formed it into a decided curve. In the matter of sideseams to bodices both extremes should be avoided, that is, the very straight and the very curved; the former takes away all form from the back, and makes it flat and lifeless, and the very curved gives the figure a round-backed appearance that is not generally approved, so that the best effect is produced by a modified curve, more after the style of Diagram 7.

It may also be well to notice that the angular line has greater length than the vertical, hence, in placing the darts in the front of a lady's bodice, &c., they are arranged to run forward at waist, thus giving the appearance of greater length between the breast and waist, an effect now generally desired.

Thus, again, the question of lines and curves opens up a most useful study for the cutter, and we trust these hints may be helpful in directing the mind to that which is most profitable.

In addition to these there are several incidental issues which need explanation from an artistic standpoint, such as the

Effect Produced by Materials

Of different finish. Rough surface cloths generally make the figure appear larger than those dressed in plain-surfaced materials; but, on the other hand, polished surfaces, such as satin, superfine, &c., give the figure a larger appearance than those with a dull surface. The reason for this is that the dull surface absorbs the light, whereas the polished surface reflects it; this, of course, is intensified by the shade, and here we had better notify that when it is desired to make a figure appear larger or smaller, the material should be chosen not only in regard to its colour, but also as to its finish, as it is well-known that both have their effect, inasmuch as a white material with polished surface reflects more light than white with a dull surface, and *vice versâ*. Thus, for small figures use light colours with polished surfaces, and for stout figures use dark colours with plain surfaces. We must also notice the effect produced by

Patterns of Materials,

Such as stripes, checks, &c.

As a general rule stripes are more suitable for dress materials than checks, especially, when they are arranged to run vertically, that is up and down the figure, though there is great need for discrimination in this particular.

It is obviously out of all good taste to dress a very tall thin figure in a striped dress, neither is it good taste to dress a short stout figure in a material the leading features of which is a very prominent stripe. For all stout figures the aim must be to avoid everything that directs special attention to the figure, so that when using a stripe, which is decidedly the correct thing to do, let it be of such a moderate character as to be unobtrusive.

Stripes always add apparent length to the direction in which they run; thus, if the stripes run vertically, they make the figure appear taller, if horizontally, that is round the figure, they give the appearance of extra width or circumference; hence it is very seldom ladies adopt striped materials with the pattern running round the figure.

It is always as well to bear in mind that a very similar effect to a stripe can be produced by seams, braid, or even rows of buttons or stitching; hence it is the more usual custom to finish all kinds of jackets, bodices, &c., plain along the bottom edge, so as to avoid anything which apparently cuts the figure short, and gives width rather than length. Whenever a trimming of any kind is put round the bottom of a skirt, it ought never to be darker than the upper part, but rather lighter, for the simple reason that at a little distance the figure would end at the commencement of the darker part.

Checked Goods.

Are seldom advantageous, for various reasons. In the first place a check adds width to the figure without increasing the height, and this can only be borne by tall well-built figures. In the second place, if the material is well woven, the danger is that any discrepancy in the two sides at once becomes apparent; and if, as too often is the case, the checks are not woven true, then the figure is made to appear one-sided, when there is no discrepancy in the figure itself.

This applies mostly to when the lines of the check are arranged to run in the true vertical and horizontal on the figure; but many of the defects can be overcome by arranging the pattern of the material to run on the bias, hence the popularity of this method with ladies.

There is no doubt that on a tall well-built figure, a costume made from a bold checked material, has a very dashing effect, and some exceedingly smart results are thus achieved; but as tailors we have to cater for all classes, and we shall do well to remember these points if we are to suit the deformed as well as the proportionate, the little people as well as the fully developed.

In draping costumes it is always well to introduce contrasts wherever possible in the materials as well as colours. For instance, a bright silk facing on a dull surface cloth, or a velvet trimming on a bright silk dress, introduces relief which makes the garment attractive. So with the buttons and trimmings the same rule holds good, and if contrast in colour is added to contrast in material, the effect is heightened.

Ornamentation.

The laws of ornamentation may be reduced to five, viz., Repetition, Alternation, Symmetry, Progression, and Balanced Confusion, each of which has a secondary form which admits of an infinite variety of combination.

Thus, to repetition belongs consonance, to alternation belongs contrast, to symmetry belongs radiation, to progression belongs gradation, to balanced confusion belongs deliberate complication. We have endeavoured to illustrate the application of these by designs of braiding round the border. Thus, on the right-hand side we have repetition, a style of braiding largely used both on ladies' and gentlemen's costumes and uniforms. It is simple, but nevertheless effective. Consonance, the secondary of this, consists in the repetition of idea which brings out a dominant harmony. Thus, in the case of flaps to a garment that agree in outline with the fronts, the idea is repeated rather than the actual reproduction. Bernardo de Saint Pierre says: "It is very remarkable that the most beautiful harmonies are those which have the most consonance."

On the left-hand border we have a good illustration of

Alternation,

Which is a happy blending of repetition and variety, a succession of two different objects recurring regularly in turn, in this case of the eye and the crow's toe. The seasons in their regular return is a good example of this from nature. The secondary of this principle is contrast, such as night and day; the succession of a square and a circle, a combination of what appears conflicting into a suitable harmony, and thus producing a splendid effect.

Symmetry is illustrated by the design at bottom just below red and green circle; here we have a design which is divided into two parts, the one being an exact reproduction of the other, but in reverse. In radiation we have a heightened form of symmetry. Thus a daisy illustrates in its white corolla a good example of radiation which can be easily adapted to the dress of ladies.

Progression comes next on our list, and that is illustrated by the overlapping Austrian knots and crow's toes along the bottom. Perspectives are highly attractive examples of progression, which give charms to nature as well as work of art, and is often used in braidings and other forms of ornamentation of ladies' garments. The difference between progression and gradation is best illustrated by the figures 1, 3, 5, 7, 9, as example of progression, and 2, 4, 8, 16, 32, as an example of gradation.

Balanced confusion is not often used in dress ornamentation; the best illustration we can give of that principle is when sleeves are covered in braid without any definite design; the balance is introduced by the outline of the sleeve, and is thus kept in its place, otherwise the ornamentation would be very questionable. Its secondary, deliberate confusion, does not lend itself to ornamentation in dress; it needs a wider field. The heavens present to us the appearance of deliberate confusion, yet that may probably be only from our point of view; we certainly know there is unity and order, and so we have to leave it, realising that the ornamentation of the heavens is on a scale too grand to lend itself to be applied to wearing apparel.

SECTION THREE.

Measuring. — Taking the Order.
Plate 5.

In taking the order for any kind of garment, two things must be clearly kept in view; the first is to get a clear grasp of the customer's wishes, and the second is to obtain a correct measure of the customer's form. The former of these is frequently a harder matter than the latter, and every aid that can be brought to bear in this direction will be of service. A specimen garment is often the best help, and, those trades that cater largely for the tailoring trade, devote a good deal of time and attention to their preparation of models for this purpose. Messrs. Redfern, for instance, at their West-end establishment, have a number of such garments prepared and arranged on dummies placed in recesses so as to be shown off to the best advantage.

Materials often appear so very different when made up, that a finished garment is often a great help, the seams and outline of the garment modify the patterns very considerably; and when ornamentation in form of braid and buttons is introduced, is still more noticeable.

This plan, however, is far too expensive for the majority of trades to adopt, and so an excellent substitute is found in

Fashion Plates.

Some firms have these sketched from their own finished garments, while others depend on such productions as the *Ladies' Tailor* Plates, which, as our readers know, are got up in excellent style.

In presenting these to ladies, it will generally be found they have a great desire for originality, and will often endeavour to combine altogether unsuitable features. This must be carefully guarded against, or the costume will lack that unity of design which is so necessary an element in all truly beautiful attire.

It will often happen that the customer will only be able to tell what she does *not want* from Fashion Plates, and though such help is of a very negative style, yet it is of service to the cutter to know what to avoid, though even in this ladies are not always consistent, frequently condemning the same features in one garment that they commend in another. Having obtained the details of style required by the customer, the next requisite is to enter them in

The Order Book.

Nothing should be left to memory. Details of style, finish, material, trimming, time to try on and finish, being noted here. We would emphasise this as of the utmost importance, and a point upon which many fail; the order is so clearly before the cutter's mind when the customer is present that it sometimes appears absurd to note every little detail in pen and ink, and yet what appears superfluous then is very quickly realised as a necessity when some comparative trifle has been overlooked, and the garment is returned to correct in this and many another detail, but for this particular would not have been thought of.

Our experience goes to prove that customers pay more attention to little details (which in our eyes may appear as trifles) than they sometimes do to the more important matters of fit and general style, and any neglect in these particulars they are apt to interpret as carelessness, which does not facilitate our reputation with them, so we emphasise, "make records of all your customers' wishes down to the

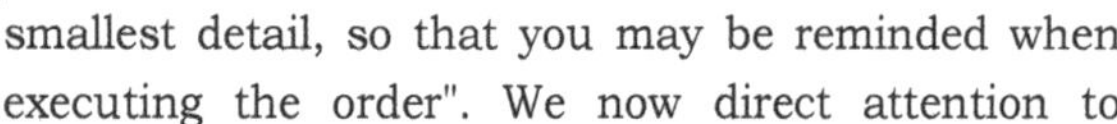

smallest detail, so that you may be reminded when executing the order". We now direct attention to

Measuring.

We have obtained a clear idea of what we are to measure for, and now take a *clean* tape and proceed to measure.

Have a regular order for taking your measure, and always adhere to it,

Master your method, and so avoid all hesitancy, as if you were wondering which was the next measure to take.

Practise taking these measures frequently, so as to acquire a graceful style. Clumsiness is a serious fault.

Use your eyes as well as your tape; ladies are often one-sided, and have abnormalities quite as much as gentlemen.

If you think an extra measure will be beneficial, do not hesitate to take it; for instance, a lady expresses a decided taste in the matter of sleeve width, and it will be far better to take an extra measure here to guide the judgment than to leave it to guess work.

Our Method.

(1) Take chest measure rather loosely, close up under the arms, as indicated by level of 1, Figure 1.

(2) Take waist measure very tightly, as indicated by 2, Figure 1.

(3) Take hip measure about 7 inches below waist, as 3, Figure 1.

(4) Find level of bottom of scye on back; this may either be done by putting square close up to the bottom of scye, and marking front and back by it, as Figure 3, or the tape may be put saddle-fashion over the shoulders and brought back under the arms, and so find level of bottom of scye on the centre seam, as Figure 2. This latter plan requires practise in order for it to be done accurately. Having found point B, measure from A to B, Figure 4.

(5) Continue from A to C, Figure 4.

(6) Continue to full length of garment desired, A to D, Figure 4.

(7) Measure width of back, E to F, Figure 5; this is best done with the arm resting at the side.

(8) Raise arm as Figure 5, bend arm forward, and continue measure, E to G.

(9) Continue last measure full length of sleeve, as from E to H, Figure 5.

(10) Measure across chest from arm to arm as from I to I, Figure 6.

(11) Measure from front of scye to front of scye, taken over prominence of bust, as from J to J, Figure 6.

(12) Next follows a series of measures from L, Figure 7; the neck from L, Figure 7, to K, Figure 6.

(13) The front shoulder measure from L, Figure 7, to level of bottom of scye M, Figure 8.

(14) Over shoulder, measure starting from B, Figure 7, and going over the shoulder as indicated by N, Figures 7 and 9, to KKlevelKK of bottom of scye point M, Figure 9.

These measures are necessary to the working of the system, and in addition to these we recommend a measure from A, Figure 4, to prominence of bust E, Figure 10, from A to waist level C, Figure 10, and on to bottom of fronts D, of Figure 2.

From these measures a really first-class garment may be drafted. We advise our readers to carefully practise the taking of these measures, when they will be ready to proceed with the next stage.

If thought advisable, these measures may be supplemented by the width of shoulder, the size of the sleeve, &c. These measures apply to all body garments, though it may be well to point out that for

Jackets and Habits

It may be desirable to take the fashion waist as indicated by the buttons just below B of Figure 10, and then on to the full length C in harmony with the style required or customer's taste.

Vest Measures. — Figure 12.

Are the same as above, but in addition, the opening desired as from A to B, Figure 12, and the full length from A to D.

Ulster Measures. — Figure 14.

These are as before. Chest, waist, hips. Depth of scye, natural waist, A to B, fashion waist, A to C, and full length, A to D. Width of back, continue to elbow and cuff, across chest, across breast, neck, front shoulder and over shoulder. In measuring for an ulster it should be ascertained if it is to be worn over bodice only, or over a jacket; if the

THE MEASURES AND HOW TO TAKE THEM.

FIG. 10.

FIG. 11.

FIG. 12.

FIG. 13.

FIG. 14.

FIG. 15.

THE MEASURES AND HOW TO TAKE THEM.

latter, then all the measures should be taken over the jacket.

Skirt Measures. — Figures 11 & 13.

The measures for a skirt are illustrated on Figure 13. First the waist measure taken closely as A G, next the hip measure about 7 inches below waist as at H, then the front length C D, the side length A B, the back length E F. These measures will vary according to fashion, but it is a very good plan to measure to the ground and deduct so much from it, always deducting an inch or so more from the front than the back.

Riding Trains

The measures required for riding trains are, waist, hips, and not length as for ordinary walking skirt: these are often enough, but it is advantageous, in these days of close-fitting skirts, to take a measure round the seat and knee, with the leg raised as Figure 11, as well as a measure from hollow of waist in front to top of knee when raised in the saddle, as this helps to locate the knee-cuts in their proper place.

Knickers. — Figure 15.

Tight waist A C. Hips, take same as at D. Side length A to B, which should be top of calf. If body length is desired, ask the lady to sit on a chair, and measure from waist to seat, which will give you the body rise, and this, deducted from side length, gives length of leg. The size of leg at E is the only measure necessary, and this is not important, for whether the knickers be finished with elastic and strap or buckle, a like latitude is allowed for.

The same style of measuring applies to pants and trousers.

Gaiter Measures. — Figure 15

Length of side, 1 to 2. Size of leg at top as at 3, the size of ankle as at 4, and the size round bottom of spat as at 5.

Ere we leave the subject of measuring, a few more words of advice may be useful. Avoid, as far as possible, nervousness, and, in every case, arrogance.

We strongly advocate the cutter making himself so conversant with the measures he takes that he is able to take them so readily that to the outsider he appears to be almost careless, and this proficiency can only be acquired by practice. Our readers will do well to avail themselves of every opportunity of taking measures they have, even if it be measuring for the sake of practice.

Take your measures in a business-like way, and it will be found no lady objects to any measure being taken that is necessary for the proper production of the garment she is ordering. It is not so much what is done, as how it is done, and if the cutter can only become possessed of that beginning, and middle, and end of all business qualifications, tact, he will find no difficulty in this respect.

With the view of supplying our readers with the average sectional measures of the various sizes, we append the following scale, compiled from measures actually taken in our own practice: —

Chest	Waist	Scye Depth	Natrl. Waist	Neck	Back	Full length Sleeve	Across Chest	Front Sholdr.	Over Sholdr.
24	24	$5\frac{1}{2}$	11	5	$4\frac{1}{2}$	20	5	$8\frac{1}{2}$	11
26	24	6	$12\frac{1}{2}$	$5\frac{1}{2}$	$4\frac{3}{4}$	23	$5\frac{1}{2}$	$9\frac{1}{4}$	12
28	23	$6\frac{1}{2}$	$13\frac{1}{2}$	6	5	25	6	10	13
30	23	7	14	$6\frac{1}{2}$	$5\frac{1}{4}$	26	$6\frac{1}{2}$	$10\frac{1}{2}$	$13\frac{3}{4}$
32	23	$7\frac{1}{2}$	$14\frac{1}{2}$	7	$5\frac{1}{2}$	$26\frac{3}{4}$	7	11	$14\frac{1}{2}$
34	24	8	15	$7\frac{1}{2}$	$5\frac{3}{4}$	$27\frac{1}{2}$	$7\frac{1}{2}$	$11\frac{1}{2}$	15
36	26	$8\frac{1}{4}$	$15\frac{1}{2}$	$7\frac{1}{2}$	6	28	8	12	$15\frac{3}{4}$
38	$27\frac{1}{2}$	$8\frac{1}{2}$	$15\frac{1}{2}$	8	$6\frac{1}{4}$	28	$8\frac{3}{8}$	$12\frac{1}{2}$	$16\frac{1}{2}$
40	29	$8\frac{3}{4}$	$15\frac{3}{4}$	$8\frac{1}{2}$	$6\frac{1}{2}$	$28\frac{1}{2}$	$8\frac{3}{4}$	13	$17\frac{1}{4}$
42	31	$8\frac{3}{4}$	$15\frac{3}{4}$	9	$6\frac{3}{4}$	$28\frac{1}{2}$	$9\frac{1}{2}$	$13\frac{1}{2}$	18
44	$32\frac{1}{2}$	9	$15\frac{3}{4}$	$9\frac{1}{2}$	7	29	$9\frac{1}{2}$	14	$18\frac{3}{4}$

SECTION FOUR.

The Draft to Measure.

We now come to one of the most important parts of the work, viz., the description of the system as worked out in harmony with measures taken direct on the customer.

For our purpose we take the following set of measures to work by, the order being the same as described in the foregoing section, which order we advise should be maintained: — Chest, 36 ; waist, 26; hips, 44; depth of scye, 8¼; natural waist, 15½; full length, 19; width of back, 5½; continue to elbow, 19; to wrist, 28; across chest (half measure), 7; across bust, 9 ; neck, 7½; front shoulder, 12 ; over shoulder, 16; nape to prominence, 13½; to waist, 19.

These measures we apply as follows: — Take your square, and draw lines at right angles to O, as in Diagram 1 For our own part, we prefer to draft towards us, so that line O 15½ would be some distance from the edge of the paper, in order to allow the cross line to be drawn forward. O is the starting point of our system, and from it we mark down O to 8¼ the depth of scye measure as taken on the figure, making no addition for seams, as that is not necessary.

Line 8¼ will require to be about 20 inches across, and line 15½ some two or three inches more.

Having done this, we proceed to mark off the quantities on the horizontal lines as indicated on Diagram 3.

From O to 2½* is one-third of the (half) neck; thus — neck, 7½; one-third equals 2½.

From 2½ to 6½ the width of back, plus 1 inch; this makes the necessary allowance for hollowing of the back, provision for seams, as well as curve of back scye.

On line 8¼ mark forward half an inch to ½ and the chest measure, plus 2½ inches from 8¼ or the chest measure plus 2 inches from ½.

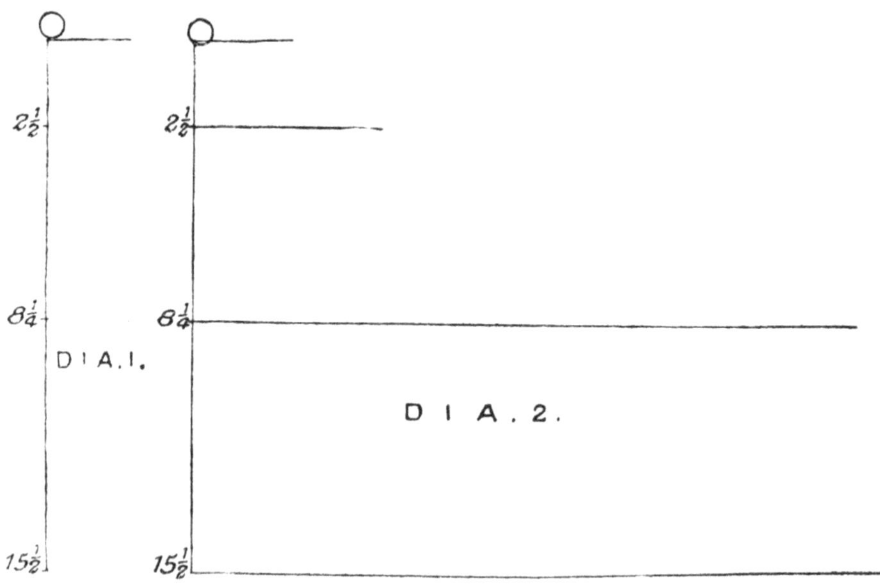

O to 15½ is the natural waist length, also applied exactly as taken on the customer. The position of these points relating to each other are most important; but, on the other hand, the location of point 2½ is quite a matter of taste; it makes no difference, as far as the actual fit is concerned, whether it is higher or lower, as any variation of this point would be compensated for in the ordinary working of the system. The guide we have for fixing point 2½ is one-sixth of the natural waist from O; but if it is desired to have a long sideseam, with the view of apparently increasing the waist length, then 0 to 2½ may be reduced to 1½ or 2, and *vice versâ*. This is just one of the points where free scope is allowed for the cutter's taste.

Having thus located the various points indicated on Dagram 1, we proceed to draw cross lines from points 2½, 8½, 15½, as illustrated on Diagram 2.

From this point mark back to 12½ the average of the across chest and across bust measure. This is obtained by adding the two together and halving the result. Thus, 7 and 9 make 16; half of that quantity, 8, would be used to mark back from 20½ to 12½.

From 12½ to 11½ may be made 1 inch, or to taste. Divide the space from ½ to 11½ into three equal parts, and so find 4¼ and 8, or these points may be fixed to taste. Thus all the points on line 8¼ which we designate the depth of scye line, are formed.

The points on the waist line are found as follows: —

15½ to 1 is one inch.

1 to 3 is rather more than half the width of ½, 44 on depth of scye line.

From 3 to 4 is one inch for all normal figures. If the blades are very prominent or the waist is abnormally small, then this may be increased, and *vice versâ.*

4 to 7¼ is half an inch less than 4¼, 8 on depth of scye line.

7¼ to 8¼ is also one inch.

8¼ to 11¼ is half an inch less than 8, 11½.

slightly hollowed between E and ¾. Curve the back scye from 6½ round to 11½. Draw back seam from O to 1 straight. Curve sideseam from 3 through 4¼ to back scye. Draw sideseam of sidebody from 4¼ to 4, suppressing it a little at top, say ¼ inch, and advancing top of sidepiece the same quantity.

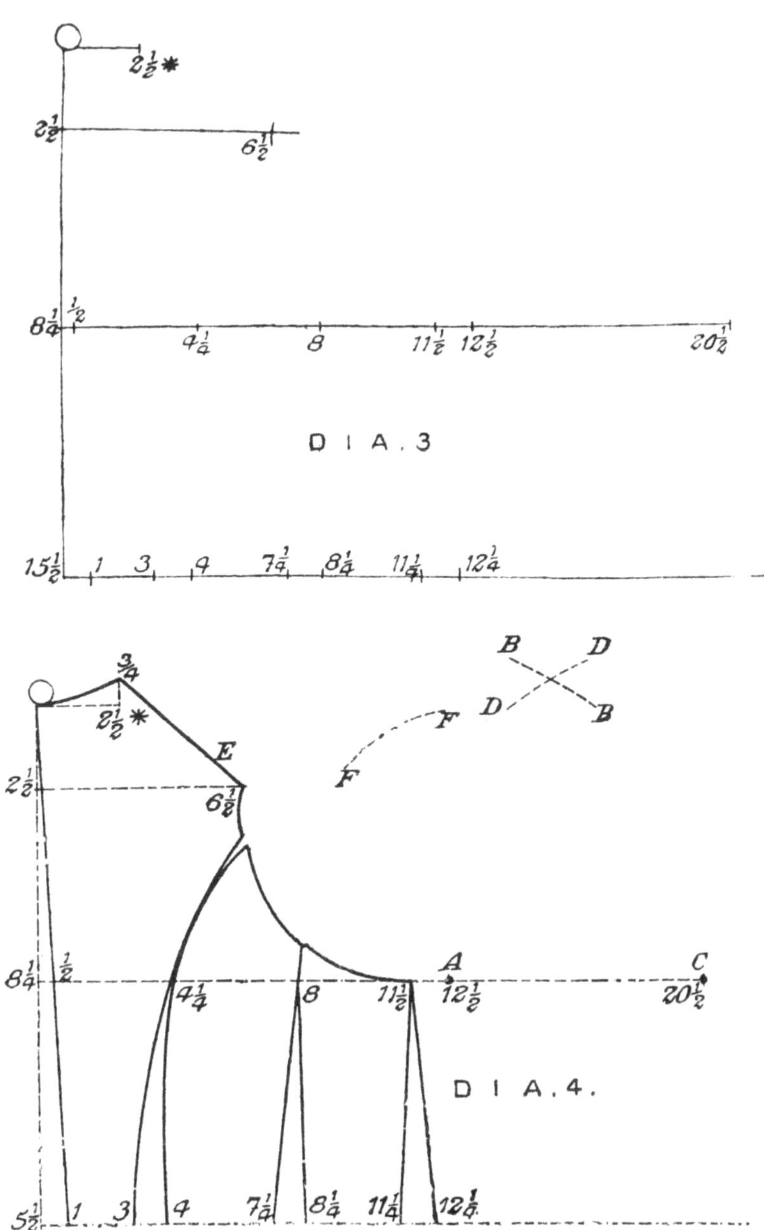

11¼ 12¼ is one inch.

Thus all the points indicated on this diagram are formed, and we proceed to connect them, as shown on

Diagram 4.

The back neck is formed by curving up from 2½, ¾ inch, and from ¾ to 6½ a line is drawn, and this is

Draw underarm seams from 8 to 7¼ and 8 to 8¼, and from 11½ to 11¼ and 11½ to 12¼, as shown.

Our next step is to locate the neck and shoulder points, and this is done by a series of sweeps or segments.

First deduct the width of back neck from O to ¾; from the front shoulder this will leave about 9½, and by this quantity sweep from A 12½ in the direction of B B. Having done this, add ¾ inch to the quantity previously used, making 10¼ in this case, and sweeping from C 20½, as indicated by DD.

Where these two segments cross each other, locates the neck point.

make all the provision that is necessary for extra prominence of figure, and *vice versâ*.

To find the shoulder point, measure from ½ to E deduct it from the over shoulder, and by the remainder sweep from A as indicated by F.

The distance from ½ to E would be 8; this

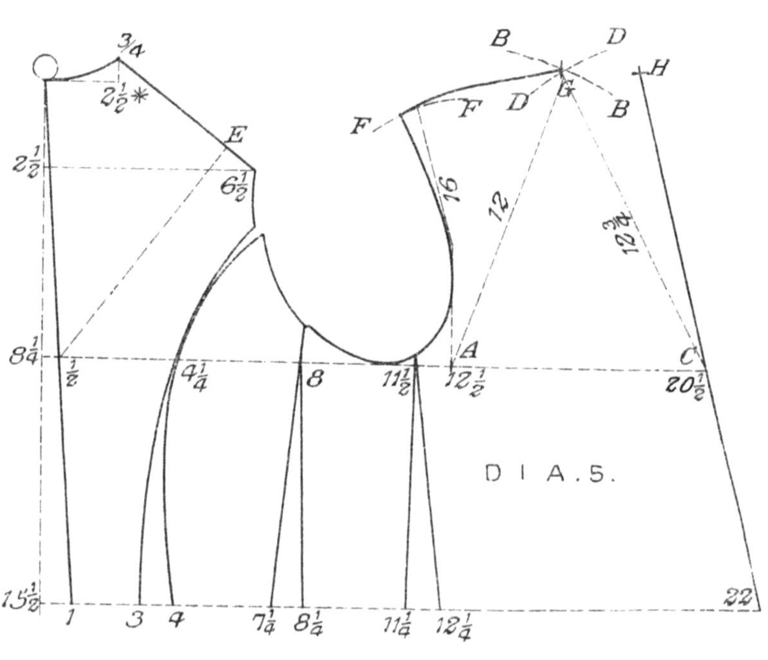

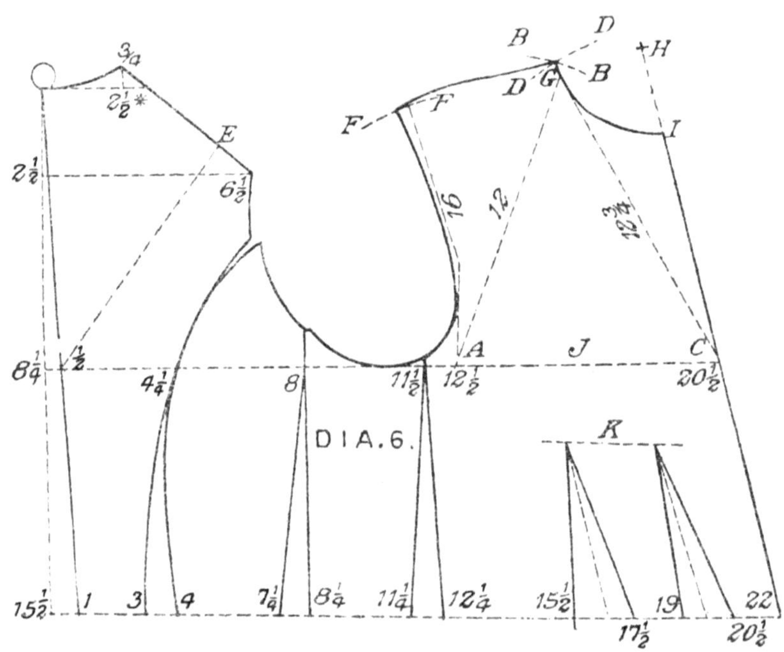

The three-quarter inch which is added is to make provision for the prominence of the chest, and may be taken as the standard quantity, as the extra suppressions of waists are generally sufficient to

deducted from the over shoulder (16) would leave 8, and by this quantity the sweep would be made, Diagram 5.

By these points draft the shoulder of forepart.

as from G to FF. Measure from G to find the width of shoulder, making all variations in width at Fend. The width of shoulder is made a quarter inch less than the back from ¾ to 6½

Now complete the scye, keeping it as hollow as possible just above A ; the curve should not be more than ¾ inch from 12½.

From G measure forward to H one-third neck 2½, making H the same distance from line 8¼, 20½, that G is.

Draw a line from H through C to 22; this forms the meeting edge to edge line, known as the breast line.

together measure 8¼; this placed at 12¼ and measured forward to 22, shows a total of 18½. Now the half-waist is 13, plus 2 inches, makes 15. leaving a surplus of 3½ inches; this is disposed of in one dart of 1½ inches, and a second dart of 2 inches. If preferred, the darts may be made the same size — *i e.*, both 1¾.

The front of the first dart should not be more than 1½ inches from the breast line, and the dotted line, giving the position of the top, should run from the centre of space 19, 20½ parallel to breast line. K may be fixed about 2½ or 3 inches below depth of scye line, or it may be fixed by actual measure,

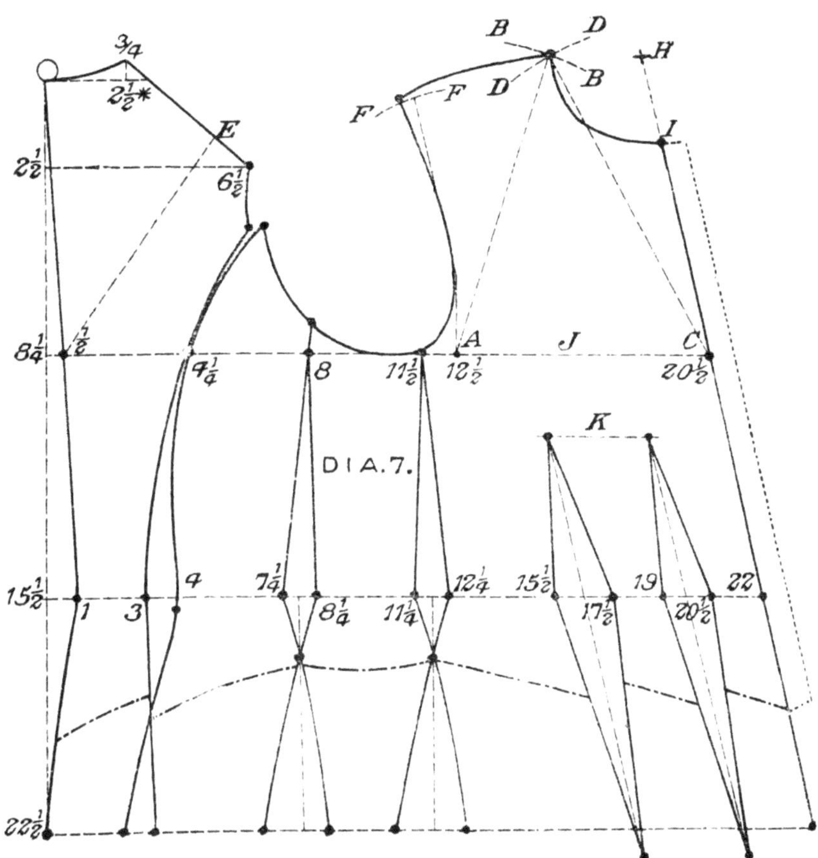

For our next step we refer to Diagram 6.

Measure from H to I one-third of the neck, and draft neck, or as it is more generally termed, the gorge.

Our next step is to reduce the waist to measure; this we do by adding 1, 3; 4, 7¼; 8¼, 11¼; to 12¼, 22; and whatever that measures, then the half-waist, plus 2 inches, is taken out in two darts. Thus the back, sidebody, and sidepiece added

allowing ¾ inch for making up. Thus, if the measure to prominence was 13¼ it would be applied from O of back neck past G to K.

Let the space between the darts be about 1½ inches, and follow the same course as with the first one, drafting dotted line parallel to breast line, and in the centre of the dart.

See that the top end is nicely graded off, so as to avoid all unsightly bubbles when the dart is sewn;

a little care in this matter will repay in the making up.

We now proceed to deal with the basque part. See Diagram 7.

The hip line, 22½ is fixed at 7 inches below the waist line; the darts are terminated 8 to 10 inches below waist, the connection between the various points being made by straight lines, afterwards modified.

It now remains to measure up the size of the hips from 22½ forward, and letting the various parts overlap.

To make up at least 3 inches more than half the hip measure, the easiest method for all plain-fitting garments is to let the sidebody overlap the back 1 inch, and let the sidepiece overlap the sidebody half the necessary amount less ½ inch, the remainder being made up by the forepart overlaping the sidepiece. As a general rule, it will be safe to let the sidepiece overlap the back 1 inch, and the forepart overlap the sidepiece 2 inches.

Let the overlap begin at two inches below the waist, and the spring commence immediately below the waist line.

The dot-and-dash line indicates the run of bottom for a plain bodice, and in this we would direct attention to the extra length of sidebody to the back, the slight round at bottom of sidepiece, and also the relative length of the bottom of the darts.

If it is desired to fasten the bodice with holes and buttons, it will be necessary to add on a button stand to the breast line, letting this be ¾ inch wide on the whole side and 1¼ or 1½ on the button side.

In all other points follow the diagram.

Thus we have the basis of this work, the "Cutter's Practical Guide", in its simplest form. We commend it to our readers as one that has stood the test of experience, and has enabled hundreds of cutters to achieve success. It treats each customer on her own requirements, and if sometimes the drafts do not bear much resemblance to the model here given, it must be borne in mind how very different the forms of customers are.

If the measures are taken accurately and applied to the draft as here laid down, we have no hesitation in saying the draft will produce a satisfactory fit for the body. The infusion of style is a matter that is beyond our control, as that it is the product of the cutter and not of the system. In the same way, the infusion of customers' ideas are to be provided for, and this will demand all the cutter's tact and ingenuity, more particularly in finding out what they are, for, once acquired, the system readily lends itself to the production of every desired effect.

The Sleeve System.

The "Cutter's Practical Guide" method of sleeve cutting is based on the requirements of the customer and the shape of the scye. First square lines up

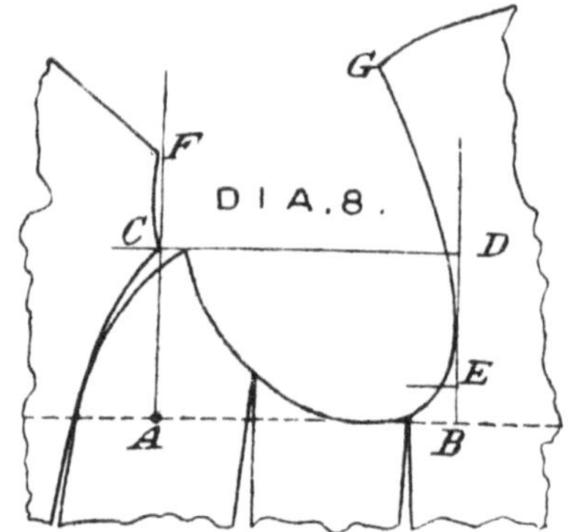

from A and B. Diagram 8 illustrates the most forward and most backward points of the scye. E is three-quarter inch above B. C is at top of sideseam. Draw lines at right angles from A and B to C D. Having done this, draw lines at right angles, as A B, Diagram 9. A E of Diagram 9 is the same distance as A B of Diagram 8. E D of Diagram 9 is the same distance as E D of scye, Diagram 8, plus ¾ to 1 inch for the ordinary figure, increasing the added amount for stooping figures and those requiring a forward hanging sleeve, and reducing it for erect figures and those requiring a backward hanging sleeve. The more the amount added, the greater the freedom in bringing the arm forward; the smaller the amount added, the cleaner the fit at the top of the hind arm.

Our next step is to measure up the scye from C to F and G to E straight (not following the round of scye).

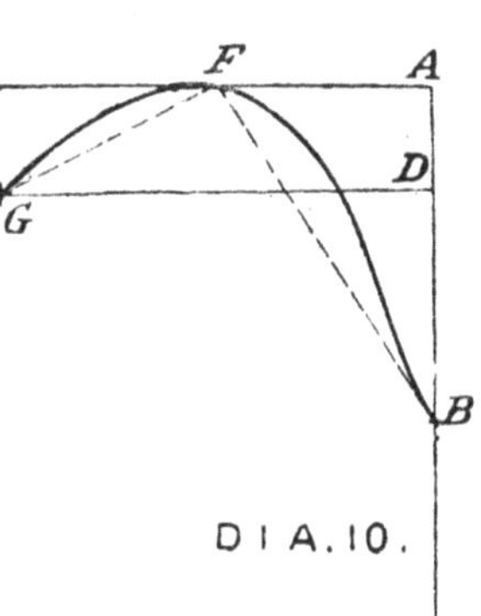

This quantity is applied to the sleeve, Diagram 10, from D to G.

The location of point F is formed by measuring across from A to F, half of the distance from D to G. mmDraw lines B F G. On line D round the sleeve head ⅝ to ¾ inch: more for a very hollow scye, less for a very flat one.

Continue the run of sleeve head with a graceful curve round to G.

Our next step is to measure off the length required; this is done by applying the tape with the width of back at, say 6, to G, measuring down to H, the length to elbow, and on to I the full length of sleeve.

Use G as a pivot, and sweep from I to J.

Hollow forearm at L 2 inches, and shape forearm, carefully avoiding any hollow between B and L and L and J. The better plan is to draw straight lines, and add on a little round, as shown on Diagram 11.

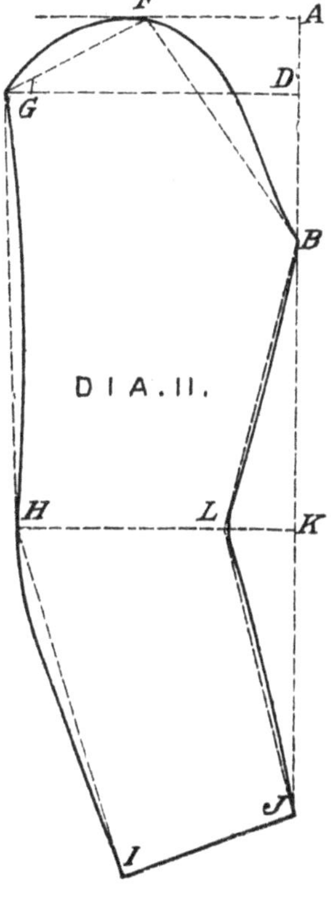

The width of cuff is generally made about 5 inches, and the elbow 6 inches; but this is quite a matter of taste, and may be varied at will.

If another guide is desired for run of bottom of cuff, square by J L.

It will be noticed the hind arm is rounded between I and H, and hollowed between H and G.

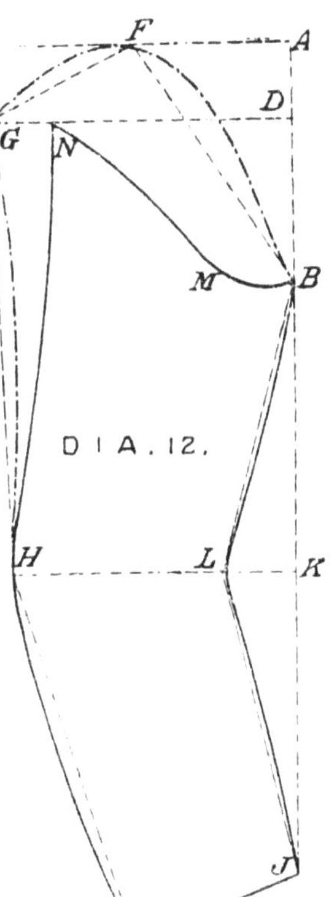

Diagram 12 shows the method of drafting the underside sleeve. The forearm is the same. The distance from B to N is found by measuring *round* the bottom of the scye from E to C, Diagram 8, and applying it across from B to line D G.

M is one-third the distance from B that N is from D. The undersleeve is hollowed between M and B, and moderately straight from M to N.

Connect N and H as shown, and complete undersleeve. The solid line of this diagram shows undersleeve, the dot-and-dash line at top indcating the relative shape of the topside.

Collars will be treated of later on.

SECTION FIVE.

Costume Bodice. Plate 7.

We now proceed to illustrate the application of the system to various styles of popular garments; and as the Costume Bodice is one that is in such constant demand, we take it as the basis of our first and in doing so we have kept it as plain and simple as possible. The addition of trimming can easily be made by our readers, should they so desire.

The System.

Draw lines at right angles to O.

O to 2, one-eighth of waist or to taste, higher for square-shouldered or short figures. Any variation here will not affect the fit, as the forearm is cut in harmony with the back.

O to 8 the depth of scye, as taken on the customer.

O to 15½ natural waist length.

O to 18½ full length of bodice desired.

Square lines at right angles to these points.

From 15½ mark in 1 inch, and draw back seam from O to 1, springing it out below waist, as per diagram.

From O to 2½ is one-third neck, mark up ¾ inch, and shape the back neck.

Mark off width of neck a little) below point 2, allowing for the seams; then connect points ¾ and 6.

½ to 20½ is the half-chest measure, plus 2 inches.

20½ to 12½ is the average between across chest and across bust measures; thus: across chest 7, across bust 9, average 8.

From points 12½ and 20½ proceed to sweep for

The Front Shoulder.

First sweep from 12½ by the front shoulder measure, minus back neck; thus, front shoulder 12, width of back neck 2½ quantity to sweep by 9½.

Now add ¾ inch to this quantity, and sweep from 20½.

Where these segments intersect each other, locates neck point F.

Sweep from 12½ by the over shoulder measure, minus back from ½ to W, and so find level of point D.

Make width of shoulder from F to D inch less than ¾, to 6 of the back, and shape shoulder seams as illustrated.

From these points the scye can be drawn, letting the front touch a point about 1½ inch above 12½, and keeping it as hollow in front as possible; and from A to C let it be as close up to the back of scye as possible.

We next draw the breast line by marking out from F to V one-third neck, and drawing line from V through 20½ to J.

Make V to I one-third neck. V and F are parallel to line 8 20½.

Position of the Seams.

We now turn our attention to the run of the seams, and here a good deal of taste can be displayed. It is always well to keep the underarm seam as far forward as possible, so we make 12½ to 11½ one inch; and then as a guide only we divide the space ½ to 11½ into four equal parts, making the back about ¼ inch wider and the under-arm piece ¼ inch narrower. This rule must only be looked upon as a guide, and may be varied to taste.

Make the width of back at waist 1½ inches.

Suppress waist ¾ inch between back and sidebody, sidebody and first sidepiece, first sidepiece and second sidepiece, and one inch between second sidepiece and forepart.

We now measure up the waist, and allow 2 inches for seams, and reduce by the aid of darts.

The front edge of the first dart should be 1½ inches from the breast line, and if there is any difference in the size of the two darts, let the front one be the smaller. Make the strap between the two 1½ inches. As a guide for the top of dart fix it about 2½ inches below depth of scye line, or if direct measures have been taken, apply them and allow about ¾ inches for seams, &c.

In like manner test level of waist at 22, and bottom of J, and complete draft, adding ¾ inch button stand beyond breast line for hole side, and 1½ inches for the button side.

As a general rule the bottom of front extends about 3½ inches below waist, and the side 2 inches, with the rest to taste.

The sleeves are usually pitched at the points indicated by B and >.

For any other details we must refer our readers to the diagrams, which, being drawn to the one-third scale, will enable them to follow it easily

A Few Hints on Making.

On no account sew the lining and the outside together at the same time, as the dressmakers do, because the linings require to be wider and longer in the hollow, and shorter over the curves, just as the inner edge of a circle is shorter than the outer, so must the outside be to the lining. In thin material an interlining is sewn in with all the seams, but any difficulty in getting extra length on the inside of this may be overcome by stripping or cutting it open. It is the tailor's aim to make the outside fit; the lining is merely an accessory; it is the dressmaker's aim to make the lining fit. Have your bone castings put in very long over the waist; let them be made from material on the bias; do not let them come higher than the top of the darts, or nearer the bottom than an ½ inch; let the bones be carefully prepared and firmly secured. In sewing the seams, full on the round ones a trifle,

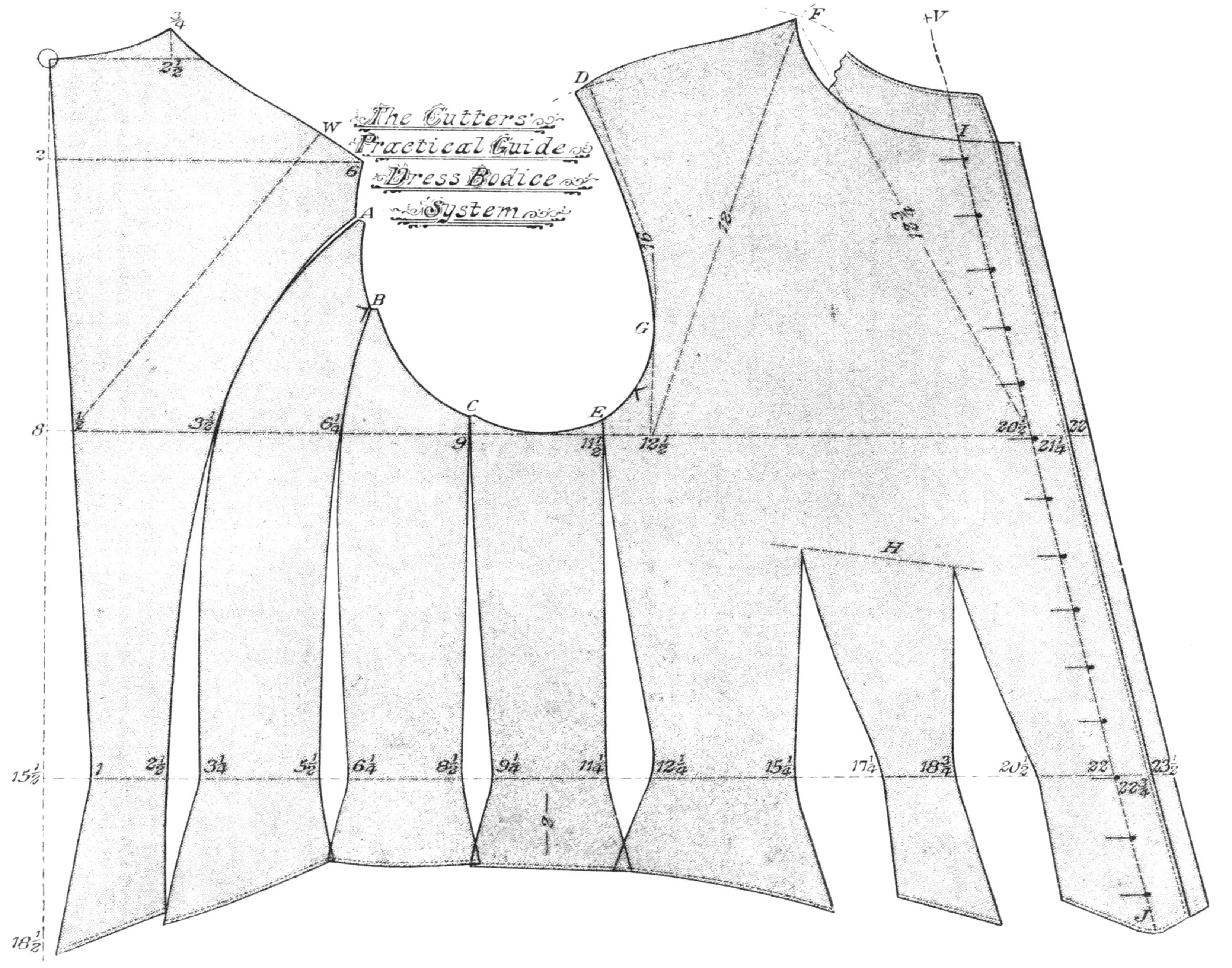

The Cutters'
Practical Guide
Dress Bodice
System

especially when they are joined to a hollow; put the collar on long in the gorge hollow, and keep the sleeve tight round the back scye. If wadding or padding is used, see that it is carefully graded off, as the height of art must always be to conceal art. Put a waistband at the waist, as it not only relieves any strain at that part, but it also holds the garment firm to the figure; have a hook to fasten the bodice to the skirt at the back, and so prevent the under-clothing being seen when the wearer bends or stoops. mmWe shall deal more fully with some of the special features of making in another chapter.

Ladies' Dress Bodice from Checked Material. No seams allowed. Plate 8

Many of the students who come to our office to study the art of cutting ladies' garments have been in the habit of allowing all the seams beyond their marks; this plan has many advantages, especially when cutting checked goods, or if the material is of a very ravelly nature, and when the usual ¼ inch seam would not be sufficient to stand the ordinary wear and tear. When cutting checked goods it greatly facilitates the matter of matching, and as the materials from which ladies' garments are now being made have a distinct tendency to large patterns, we deem it advisable to show the variations necessary to meet such cases in a work of this sort.

In garments from such materials, fit has occasionally to be sacrificed to some extent so that style may be allowed full scope; especially is this the case with the side-seam, where there is no suppression taken out, the usual inch being equally divided at the two nearest seams. The reason for this is: if any suppression were taken out, it would be found impracticable to match both the vertical and horizontal stripes; hence, in order that this may be accomplished, the fit is to some small extent sacrificed, and the possible defect that would show itself would be a horizontal fold running from 3¾ to 6¾, which would be more or less as the lady's blades were prominent or flat. With most ladies this would not show itself in a very marked degree, as the blades are generally flat as compared to those of men. Still, we wish it to be distinctly understood this method is arranged for a certain object, viz., to allow of check material being made up with all the cross-bars to match exactly, and not with the view of producing the most accurate fit. Some of our readers may desire to cut all their garments out

without any seams allowed; if so, they may use the ordinary 1 inch suppression from construction line at back, and take out the usual 1 inch suppression between back and sidebody and sidepiece, as elsewhere described. With these introductory or cautionary remarks, we will proceed to deal with the system applied for making bodices of check material, or, to be more correct, the adaptation of

The System. Plate 8. No seams allowed.

And for this purpose we proceed as follows: O 8¼ is the depth of scye, as taken on the customer, on to 16 the natural waist, and on to bottom the full length desired; O to 2½ one-sixth of the natural waist, or to taste, as any variation in this part is adjusted in the front shoulder; the width of back neck is fixed

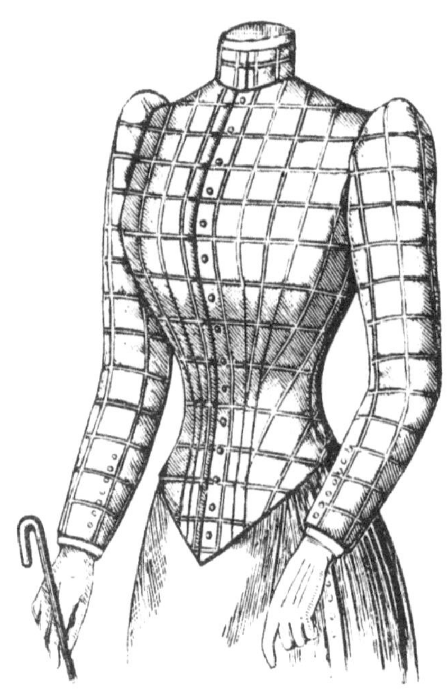

Bodice from Check Material.

by one-sixth of neck; from the centre of back measure across the width of back desired; from 16 come in 1½ and draw the backseam through from it to 1½, and arrange the spring in the usual way. Now measure forward from ¾ to 18¾, the half breast measure, and from this measure back to 10½ the average between the across chest and across bust measures less ½ an inch, and apply the front and over shoulder in the same way as we have previously described. Some surprise may be felt at this, thinking it would have been necessary to

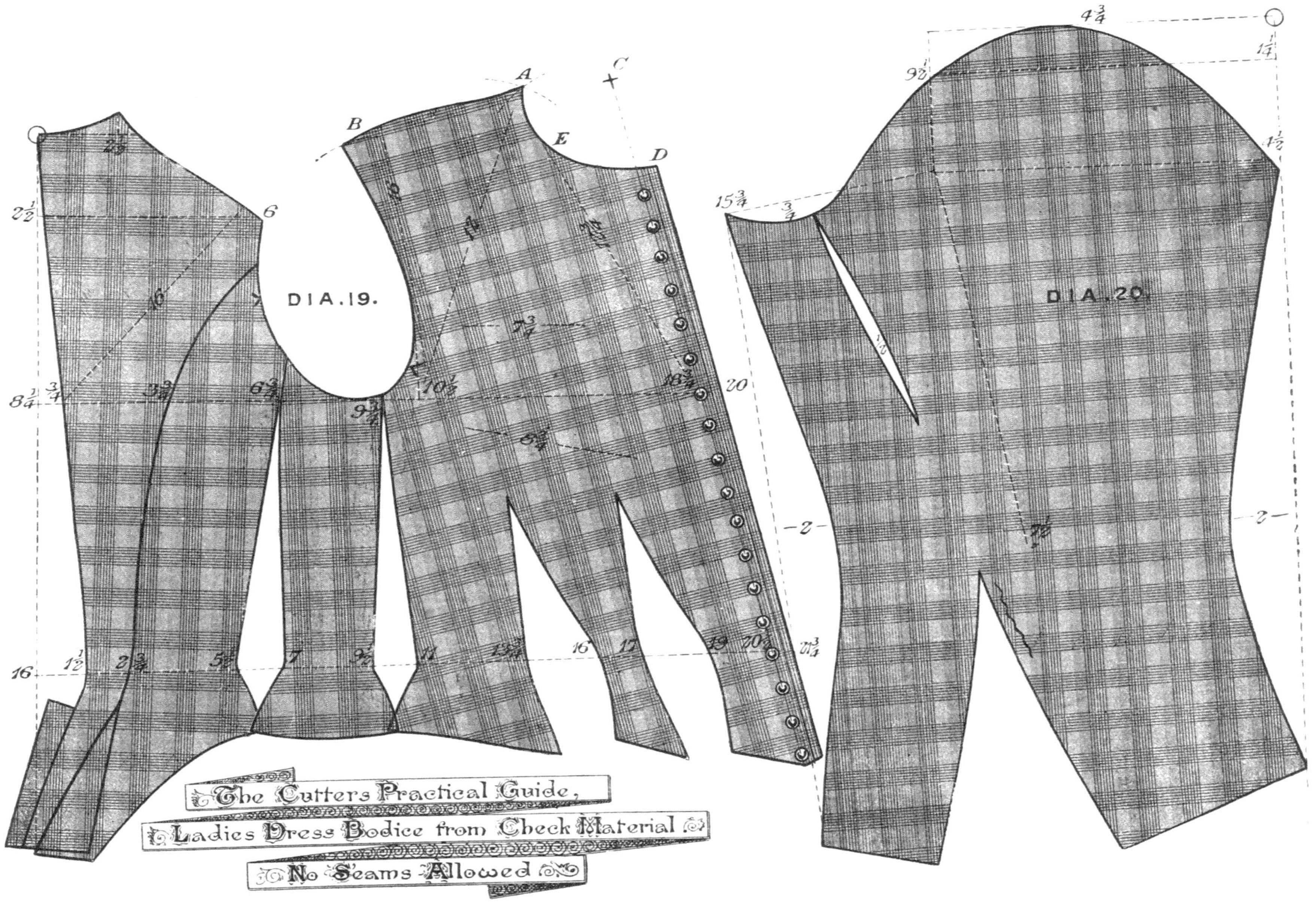

DIA. 19.
DIA. 20.
The Cutters Practical Guide,
Ladies Dress Bodice from Check Material
No Seams Allowed

deduct a certain amount from the measure owing to the seams being added afterwards. A little reflection, however, would soon show that though a seam is usually taken from the shoulder, as at A B, yet the scye is deepened the same amount, so that the depth of scye still retains the same relative position to the neck and shoulder points. No suppression is taken out between the back and sidebody at waist, but an extra ½ making 1½ altogether, is taken out between sidebody and sidepiece. In other respects the system is worked in quite the ordinary way arranging the seams in the style illustrated on this Plate, and in other details follow the same plan as previously described, so that it would be unnecessary repetition for us to go over all the points. We will only remark that the waist should be made up to 1 inch less than the nett size of the customer's waist measure, otherwise it will come out too large; even then it will do so in some very elastic materials, so that it will always be advisable to check the waist and make it up to measure by adjusting it at the underarm seam.

Hints on Making.

The leading feature to be studied in making up is, that the pattern shall match at all the various parts to a nicety; it will even be necessary to sacrifice fit to a certain extent for that purpose. It will, however, be impossible to get both the horizontal and perpendicular lines to match at all the seams, and to run satisfactorily with the front, and as the underarm seam is the one most out of sight, that would be the seam we should sacrifice in this way. There are several methods of getting the patterns to match in the sewing, but one of the best and surest we have seen is to turn in the back just to the mark, and then lay it on the top of the sidebody, and so get it to exactly match every bar and crossbar, and when in that position fell or baste it from the outside, which will then leave a row of straight stitches on the wrong side, and which will clearly indicate the place where the seam must be sewn. In cutting, it will be found impracticable to cut the goods on the double; each part must be carefully adjusted to the parts adjoining. We have indicated the most effectual lay of the pattern on the material, cutting through the perpendicular lines on the back seam, but arranging the front to run with it. The necessity of this latter arrangement will at once be apparent when we point out that it is the only way of getting the pattern to match down the centre of the front. A reference to Diagram 19 will fully illustrate this. It will be observed that the sleeve is cut without a seam up the hindarm above the elbow, a feature which very greatly facilitates the matching process, whilst in order to get the pattern of sleeve and forepart to harmonise, the pattern at top of forearm sleeve and the front pitch should be adjusted. As we treat of sleeves fully in a separate chapter, we refer our readers to it for a full explanation of the Sleeve System.

The Norfolk Jacket. Plate 9.

This garment, which is little affected by fashion, is always popular with a very large number of ladies, and is certainly a most becoming garment for holiday wear and sporting purposes. It is the ideal garment for fishing, and is one of the most frequently patronised style for pedestrian exercises. It seldom becomes the rage, while it is always to be seen in wear; hence our giving it a place in this work, and more especially so because it has many characteristics peculiarly its own. It matters not whether it is intended for fishing, walking, cycling, or equestrienne purposes, it is arranged in the same way. We will proceed to deal with

Diagram 21, Plate 9.

And explain the special features of cut. We shall not describe the system in minute detail, as our readers will readily gather how that is arranged by a reference to the description of Diagram 1. We would rather devote our remarks to the variations from Diagram 1. In the first place, the quantity allowed (2 inches) for making up may be excessive if the material is thin, so that it may be advisable in such a case to reduce the amount allowed to 1 inches. In the next place, it will be observed that the sideseam runs into the shoulder seam, and of course that involves an extra ½ inch, making 1 inch in all beyond the width of back measure taken. The location of the sideseam is fixed by the position desired for the pleats; in the Diagram we have retained our usual method of fixing point 4 at one-third the distance from ½ to 1½, but of course this may be varied to taste in accordance with

The Arrangement of the Pleats. Diagram 22. Plate 9.

These are strips of material cut double the width desired, as illustrated on Diagram 22, B C and E G

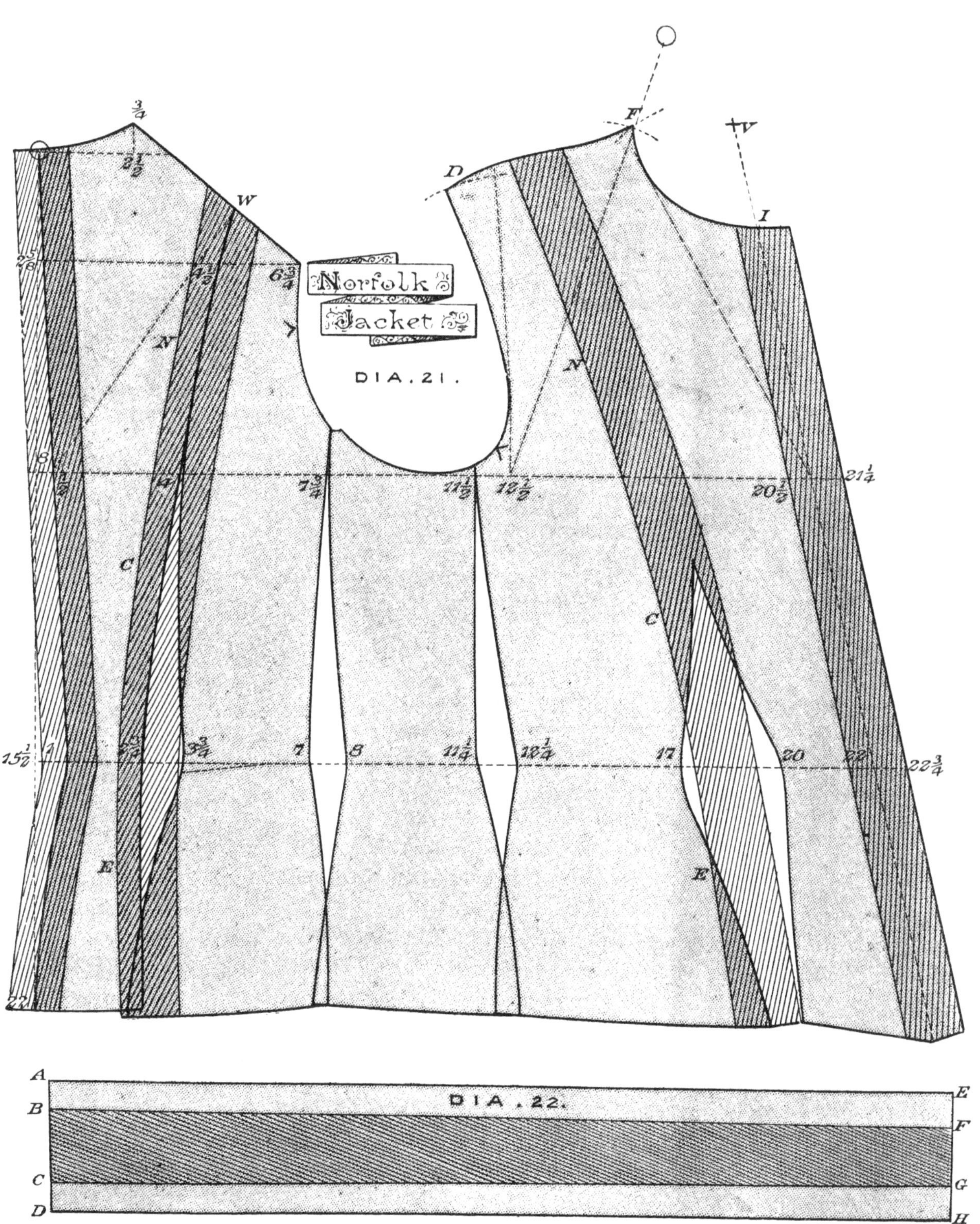
Norfolk Jacket
DIA. 21.
DIA. 22.

representing the width of pleat, and A E, D H the edges turned in; these edges are then serged together, and the pleat arranged in such a position as is most suitable to the wearer. Now, although these pleats are in reality separate pieces of material, the aim should be to make them appear as if they were all in one piece with the bodice, and with that end in view it will be advisable to keep them as straight as possible, and preferably the same width throughout, because if they are curved or made narrower at the waist — as they sometimes are — this idea is at once dispelled. There are usually three pleats behind, one down the centre seam of back, and one on either side, the side pleats meeting

ourselves to the special features of this jacket. In sewing on the pleats it will be necessary to remember that more length will be required over the prominences than for the waist, indeed, from N to C should be put on full, more or less so in accordance with the roundness of the figure, and kept tight in the hollow of waist from C to E; this latter is even more important than the former. The best plan will be to baste these pleats on over the knee, when due provision may be made for both prominences and hollows. The pleats are sewn to from the inside. Some firms stitch down the edge of the pleats, as illustrated on the Figure, to make them match the edges; it doubtless makes them

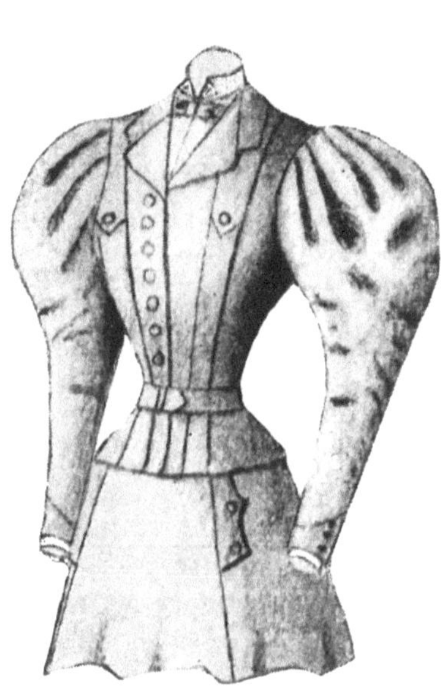

others on the forepart of the shoulder seam. The pleat down each forepart is generally arranged to go over the dart, and as will be seen, one dart only is taken out instead of two; this will necessitate its being taken higher than where there are two. A pleat is generally placed down the centre of front, and a very good style of finishing the cuff is illustrated on the Figure, consisting of two pleats somewhat narrower than those on the bodice placed on the bottom of the cuff. We will now give a few

Hints on Making,

But as we have dealt with this phase somewhat fully for the jacket and bodice, we must confine

firm, but at the same time it destroys much of the easy-going appearance of which this garment is so characteristic, so that we leave this for the cutter's individual decision, as it will be for him to decide whether it is an improvement or only time wasted; we know some tailors contend that it destroys the idea that the pleats are in one piece with the bodice, but whether this is so or not we will not stay to consider, but pass on to deal with

The Mode of Fastening the Front.

Some make them to fasten with hooks and eyes, and let the front pleat come half over the edge, but the more general mode is to fasten them with holes and buttons, arranging the front pleats to quite hide them, and so forming a kind of fly; of course there is no difficulty in doing this when the garment buttons up to the throat as our figure illustrates, but when a collar and turn is desired, a little judgment will be necessary, the forepart of either side will have to terminate at the breast line as low as the roll is intended to turn, and the pleat made V shape at top, so as to come up under the lapel; this will call in the aid of a hook and eye at the top of the centre pleat, where it goes over the button side. Sometimes when these jackets are made with collar and turn the front pleat is omitted. A belt is generally worn with this garment, and may either be made from the same material, or be a fancy belt made from leather or any fancy material; this may either fasten with holes and buttons when made from the material, or an ornamental buckle may be used. Small loops are occasionally left at the side through which the pleat is passed, and we have seen the belt passed under the pleats at waist; but this is unsatisfactory, as it not only destroys the sit of the pleats at waist, but explodes any idea that might have been previously entertained, that the pleats were in one piece with the bodice.

Large Size Dress Bodice. Plate 10.

It is sometimes argued that we only take the truly proportionate figure to illustrate the working of the various systems we publish, and doubtless this is to a certain extent true, as we look upon it as highly essential that the cutter should form an accurate idea of what is a truly proportionate pattern. But of course this is not enough; he must know how to provide for all ages and all kinds of disproportion; and our object at present is to help him in this treatment of at least one phase of this that is often met with.

Turning over the pages of our order book to select a set of measures by which to draw the diagram to illustrate this, we come across the following : 8½ scye depth, 15 natural waist, 22 full length, 7 across back, 19½ elbow, 28 sleeve, 8¾ across chest, 9¾ across bust, 12¼ front shoulder, 16½ over shoulder, 8½ neck, 13½ nape to nipple, 18½ nape to bottom of waist, 44 chest, 31 waist. The lady was one of those figures which, though past the prime of life, yet was by no means a badly made figure, and such as may be often met with in daily practice. The waist was clearly defined, and the bust well developed; she might fitly be described as plump, short, and rather stout. A glimpse at the measures would soon convince even the inexperienced cutter that some more reliable method of fixing the depth of scye than a division of the breast would be necessary; 44 breast and 15 natural waist would not at all meet that method; yet this is a very fair example of the measurement found in actual practice. It is a somewhat remarkable fact that the length of the natural waist varies very slightly: from 14 to 16 seems to embrace the entire range, and often when the figure gets stouter the waist gets shorter; hence, in ordinary figures, it will more often be found that the natural waist measures 14½ than 15½. It will also be noticed how small all the shoulder measures are in relation to the chest, as compared with the normal 34; at the same time they are very much more square, both features usually found in the large size male figure, but,not in so pronounced a degree as is here illustrated.

The Special Features

Of this diagram, apart from the points we have already noted, and which would be fully allowed for in the working of the system as previously described, are the number of darts and the arrangement of the seams of the sidepieces, &c. The sideseam, as outlined by 4, 2¾, and 3¾, is made as long as possible, so as to give the effect of length; whilst the sidepieces, being all cut narrow, also greatly facilitate this effect. One inch is taken out between all the parts at the waist, and so as to reduce the forepart to the size of waist without taking out very large darts, a third one is brought into play, which has a very much better effect; for, while adding length to the general appearance, it facilitates the fit over the hips, and enables a sufficient receptacle for the bust to be formed very much easier. It will be noticed that we still retain the straight front edge; indeed, we deem it of greater importance for figuies of this class than the normal; as any excess of length in the front edge would now show itself in a sort of frill at that part. It will be observed that we have added 1 inch to the front shoulder measure, instead of ¾ as laid down previously; our reason for doing so being to provide for the prominence, for the more that is added in this way the greater provision will be made for the busts. The length from nape to prominence is applied as per dotted line, always adding 1 inch to the actual length taken on the figure, to compensate the

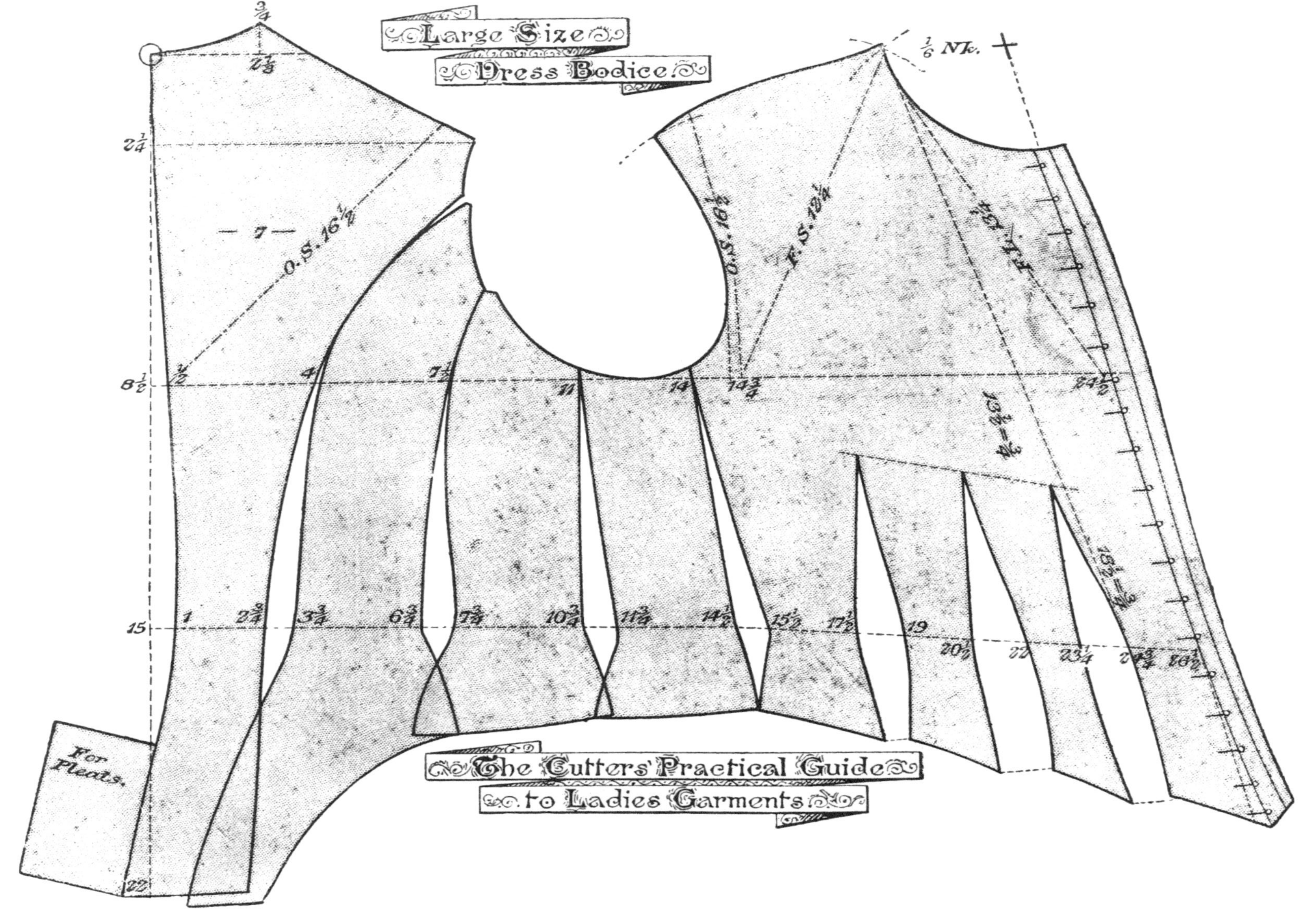
Large Size
Dress Bodice.
The Cutters' Practical Guide
to Ladies Garments
For Pleats.

seams on the shoulder. The same also applies to the waist line, which in this case drops a little in the front, and which drop commences from the side. We have found great difference to exist in the run of the waist line; some ladies are very "embonpoint", whilst others are very flat. With the former the waist generally runs up, whilst with the latter it runs down; hence a measure to exactly locate this will be found a great assistance. The lower termination of the darts must, of course, be arranged in accordance with the figure, but under any circumstances it will generally be found preferable to make it rather too tight than too loose, as the bones, &c., in the front keep it from riding up and round the waist.

Hints on Making.

Few remarks require to be made under this head after what we said for the normal Dress Bodice, as it nearly all applies with equal force to either large or small sizes, with the exception, perhaps, of wadding and padding, which we left as an open question. But in figures such as we are dealing with, it should be carefully avoided; indeed, any thing which has a tendency to make the figure — which is already too big — appear larger, should be avoided; and although many ladies of this class of figure make ease the first consideration, yet, as a general rule, it will be found they very much prefer a garment too small to one too large.

The stand of the collar should not be made too deep, neither should there be too much fulness in the sleeve heads, but we shall deal with the sleeves as we proceed, taking one of this size as an example. Although we are showing the working of the system by means of a Dress Bodice, yet as far as the principles of fit are concerned, they would be applied in the same manner to Jackets, Ulsters, and Dolmans, the variations in style being produced by altering the position of the seams, and increasing in a more or less degree the allowance for making.

Fancy Styles. Ladies' Zouave Jackets.
Diagrams 27 and 28. Plate 11.

Probably one of the most noticeable features in the garments of the last few seasons was the number of Zouave Jackets worn; and as they are mostly natty little garments, giving an amount of freedom for the various movements of the body without hiding the outline of the figure, there is every reason to believe they will be popular for some time to come, and especially during the summer months, as they are so very appropriate for wear over an ordinary indoor Costume for outdoor exercise, when the heat of the sun would make the heavier Jackets and longer Capes oppressive. They lend themselves so readily to ornamentation that they are often trimmed in the most elaborate style, making the principal feature in the Costume. Beads and gimp are the more general forms of ornamentation; but embroidery is also occasionally used on some of the more elaborate of these. The style we illustrate on the two Figures are of the plainer type, and shows the most decided tailor effects these little garments produce, though we do not wish to infer that all tailor-made garments are plain, for on the contrary, some of the richest designs in braiding, &c., have been the work of the ladies' tailor, giving a style and finish of an unmistakable character. Often, however, they are of the plain type, the lining and workmanship being the only features that give style. The lining is frequently brought to the edge, and the making is as perfect in matters of sewing and pressing as anyone could wish. Our illustrations show these garments worn over a Blouse of a loose-fitting character, the lower part going inside the skirt, and the band of the latter being hidden by a sash of some smart colour, the ends of which frequently hang down on the left side rather towards the front. Zouave Jackets are made both with and without sleeves, our illustrations showing them in the latter style, Figure 2 illustrating the large sleeve heads, whilst Figure 1 shows the plainer style. Let us now turn our attention to the cutting.

Diagram 27. Plate 11.

This is the same as previously explained, so we will only briefly recapitulate the points. Draw line O 14, and on it mark off O to 2½ one-sixth natural waist; O to 8 the depth of scye; O to 14 the full length desired; and from these points draw lines at right angles, and come in from 14 to 2 two inches. and draw the centre of back from O to 2. From O to 2½ is one-third neck, and 2½ to 6 is the width of back; from 8 to 20 is half chest plus 2, and from this point the front of scye is got by measuring back to 12 the across chest measure. The sweeps of the front and over shoulder are got in the usual way,

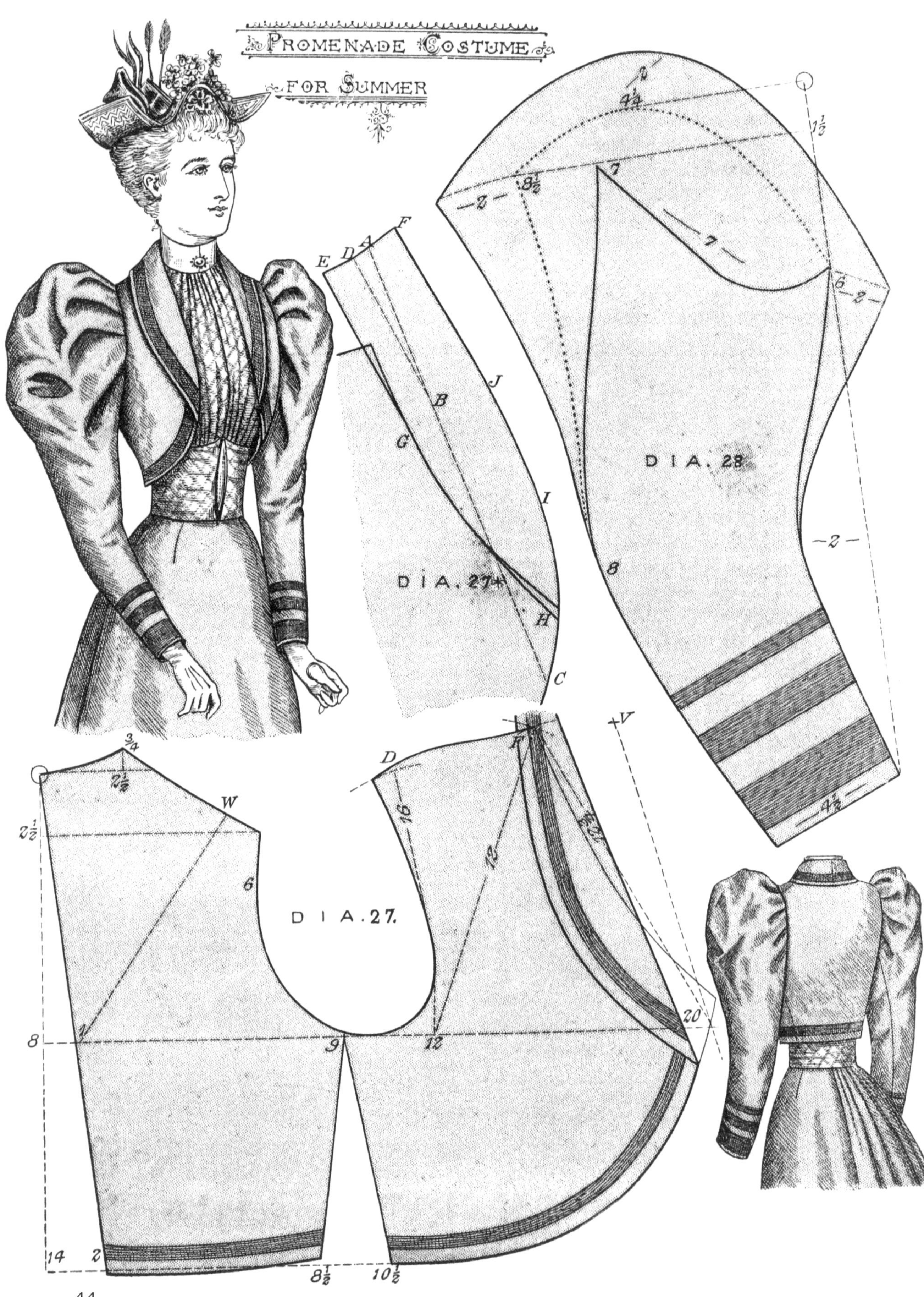

44

and the shoulder and scye produced in that way; point 9 is one-quarter breast from 8, and the width of back at waist from 2 to 8½ is one-fourth waist. The roll is cut in the style illustrated from F to 20, arranging the outline in accordance with taste, as also the run of the front. Sometimes a dart is taken out of the front to get the part below the breast to fit closely, but more generally an easy-fitting garment is desired, and this is produced in the way showm. That the turn and roll collar may be understood, we have drawn

Diagram 27*. Plate 11.

Which explains the collar system. G H C represents the forepart as cut in Diagram 1; C is the point at which it is desired to turn, and C H is the part of the turn that is left on the forepart. From G to B is ¼ inch less than the depth of stand, and a line is then drawn from C through B toA. Now decide what the fall or turnover part of the collar shall be, and deduct the stand from it; and come down from A to D the remainder; curve the crease row line from D to B, and continue to C. Now measure from D to E the stand, and from D to F the fall, and shape the centre of the collar F A D E by hollowing it at D. Complete the sewing-to edge of the collar from E to G and H, letting it overlap a bare ¼ of an inch at H. It only remains to draft the outer edge F J I, and the collar is complete. A good deal of taste can be shown in shaping the outline of the fall edge, and the diagram may be taken as a guide in this respect. So we will pass on to treat of

The Sleeve. Diagram 28. Plate 11.

The dotted line from 6 to 4¼ and 8½ illustrates the ordinary sleeve marked out in the usual way, as described in a latter section of this work, but as the style of sleeve worn now has very decided characteristics, we will deal principally of those. A reference to the figure will show a considerable amount of fulness at the top, and especially at front and back, the idea being to produce a wide sleeve at top rather than one with a puffed sleeve head, and the easiest way of producing this is shown by our diagram. Make a pivot of elbow at forearm; sweep from 6 2 or 3 inches, and shape the forearm as shown. Now repeat the process from the hind-arm, sweeping from point 8, and adding 2 inches as shown, complete by adding the same amount to the round at top, so that 2 inches is added at top of forearm, hindarm, and sleevehead.

Costume Jacket and Vest.
Plate 12.

This is a very popular style of costume for the Winter season, the extra length over the hips, the additional warmth of the vest front, together with the braiding, &c., make this a very suitable style for Winter wear.

The arrangement of the front to show a small portion of the vest affords plenty of scope for the introduction of a little brightness in the costume without it appearing in any way showy. The variety offered by the different modes of braiding as well as the contrasts that can be introduced by this means of ornamentation makes this at once a popular style of costume.

Draw lines at right angles to the various points.

O to 2½ one-sixth neck.

*2½ to 6 the across back plus ¾ inch.

15½ to 1 one inch, and hollow back seam from O to1.

½ to 20½ the half chest plus 2 inches.

20½ to 12½ the across chest measure.

Sweep from 12½ by the front shoulder measure minus width of back neck O to ¾.

Sweep from 20½ by ¾ inch more than first quantity.

Where these segments intersect locates neck point.

Sweep from 12½ by over shoulder measure minus ½ W of the back to find level of D.

Make width of shoulders F to D ¼ inch less than ¾ 6 of back.

Shape scye as illustrated, keeping it very hollow just above 12½.

F to V one-sixth entire neck measure.

Draw breast line from V through 20½.

V to I the same as F to V.

The Position of the Seams.

12½ to 11½ is 1 inch.

½ to 11½ is divided into three equal parts.

Width of the back at the waist 1 to 3 is half of ½, 4½.

Waist is suppressed 1 inch between 3, 4, 7¼, 8¼, 11¼, and 12¼.

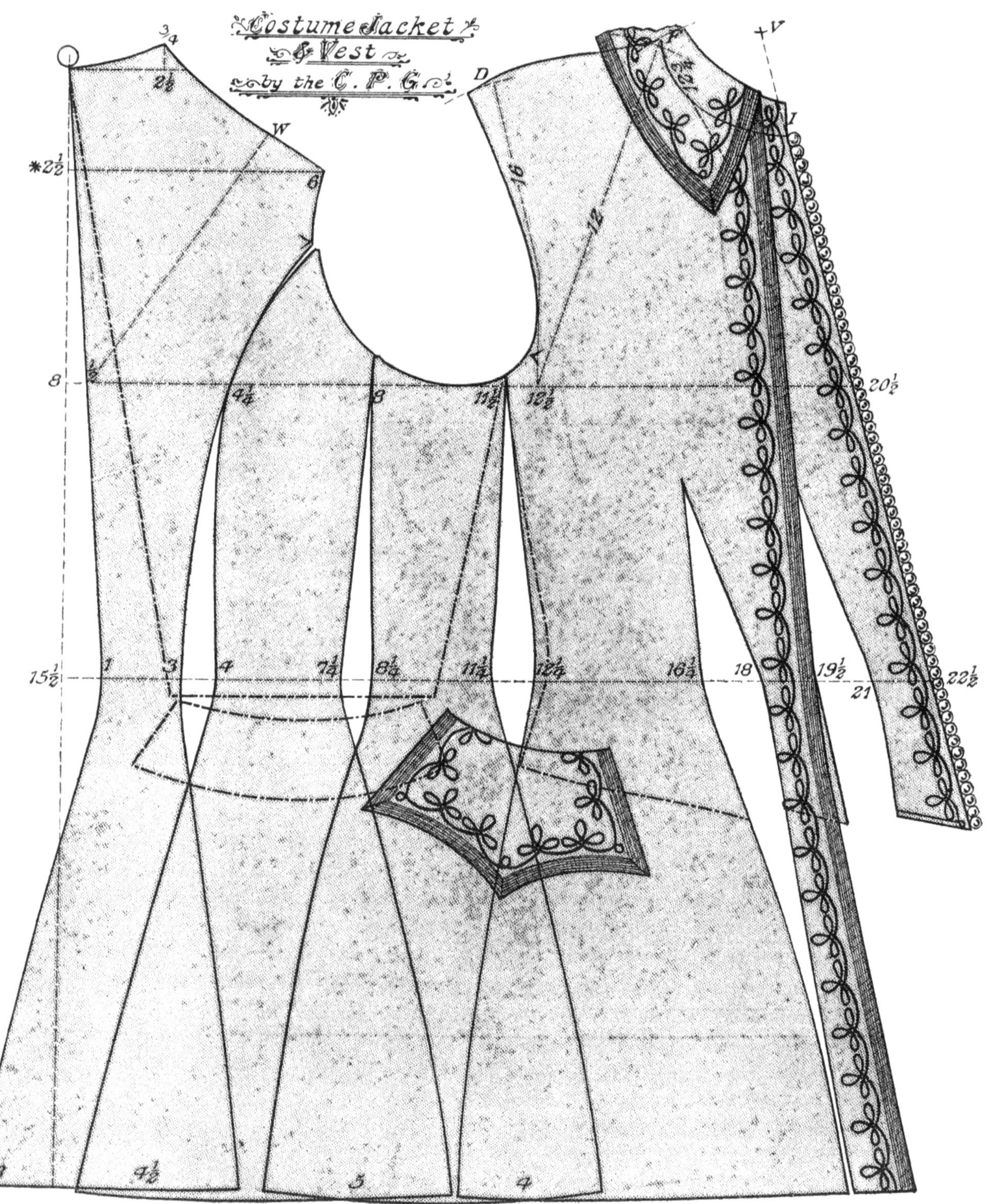

Costume Jacket
& Vest
by the C. P. G.

Reduce waist to measure, plus 3 inches, by the aid of darts, putting the front one 1½ inches from breast line, and leaving the same space between the two darts.

Width of sidebody and sidepiece at waist is ½ inch less than the same part is at the level of depth of scye.

Let the various parts overlap each other 4 to 5 inches, so that plenty of fulness may be located at the back.

The run of the various parts of the bottom may be arranged in the same style as the diagram, giving them a certain amount of round.

The Vest.

The front of the jacket would be cut away from about ½ inch at the top to run in a line with the back part of the front dart.

The vest forepart may either be cut to sew in with the scye, shoulder, and side-seams of the forepart, or what is generally considered more convenient, made with a separate back as per dotted lines; this is a matter of taste.

The diagram we think is sufficiently self-explanatory; a little extra waist suppression is made at the side of the forepart.

The back is hollowed 1½ at back and made up to one-fourth waist plus ½ inch.

A short skirt is put on sometimes below the waist, as indicated on the diagram, but this is quite optional.

The sleeve is arranged in harmony with the style of trimming, the gauntlet cuff agrees with the flaps on the hips, the same style of braiding being followed throughout.

The Vest generally terminates in front about 4 inches below the waist line.

SECTION SIX.

Ladies' Riding Habits. Plates 14. 15 and 16.

The Riding Habit has always been looked upon as a tailor-made garment, and there seems little doubt it will long continue to be so, for being made, as they frequently are, from heavy material, they are much better manipulated by the tailor's mode of treatment than the dressmaker's. In style, they change slowly. A few years ago the Habit Bodice was invariably made with Skirts sewn on from the waist downwards, or cut sharply over the hips, in the style illustrated on Figure 22. This is, however, now quite out of date, but we give it a place, as illustrating a style which may be required by some. The fashionable section are wearing scarcely anything else but the styles shown on Plates 15 and 16, and in the future it will doubtless substitute entirely the older style.

Old Style of Riding Habit.
Diagram 23. Plate 14.

The system is practically the same as described for the Bodice, the amount allowed for making up being fixed by judgment. We need not repeat the system in all its details, but rather treat of the special features of the Habit as distinguished from the Bodice. We will first notethe details of the back, and by a reference to the Diagram it will at once be gathered it is cut on thecrease; this was at one time looked upon as one of the special features of the Habit, but time has changed the fashion even of this, and it is by no means so universal as it once was. When it is cut on the crease it is only made ¾ of an inch wide at the waist, and of course this involves a readjustment of the seams, but we will deal with this presently. In order to give the waist as long an appearance as possible, the pleats are only commenced at 1½ inches below the natural waist, and the full length continued to 7 or 8 inches below waist. As will be gathered from the outline of Diagram, the skirts are cut sharply over the hips; the total width at bottom of Skirt when made would be 4 or 4½ inches. It is arranged with two side pleats at the bottom of side-seams with buttons placed, as previously noted, 1½ inches below the waist seam. The lengths below the waist line are about 2 inches at the side and 3½ in the front. The bottom edge of sidepiece, &c., should be slightly rounded, so as to form one continuous curve when made up, and avoid getting points at the seams. This is only a trifle, but it is a trifle often overlooked, the student occasionally drawing a freehand curve from front to back, in some cases even omitting to readjust the length of the dart seams to each other. We will now proceed to deal with

The Location of the Sideseams.

As these have a very decided effect on the artistic appearance, it is well to avoid extremes, at the same time bearing in mind what is considered beauty in the female form. Present-day ideals point to a flat back in the region of the blades, and a long waist; hence, with these points in our mind, we carry the sideseam as high as possible, and keep the sideseam flat, but not straight, a kind of

waist necessitates the sideseam being drawn free-hand, and having located it in that way to measure back from 12 to 11, 1 inch, and dividing the distance from 11 to 3½ into two equal or nearly equal parts, following the usual plan of making both sidebody and sidepiece each ½ an inch narrower at waistband than on the depth of scye line. The spring over the hips is not so pronounced as for Ladies' Costume Bodice, &c. We now give a few

Hints on Making.

A waistband is invariably placed at the waist,

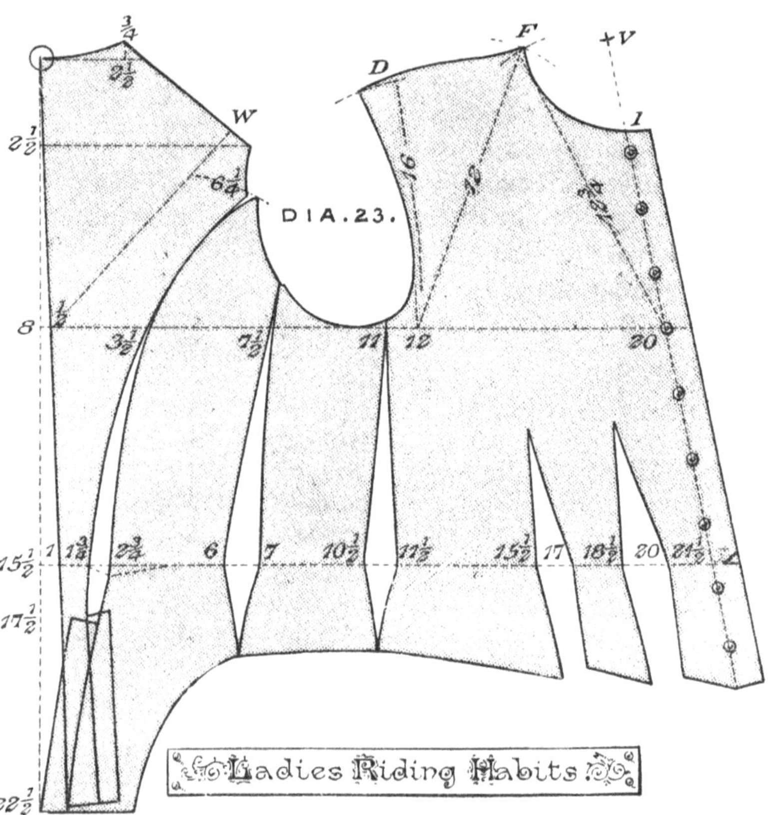

OLD STYLE OF RIDING HABIT.

deadened curve being best; a bare ¼ inch is taken out between the back and sidebody at the back scye, and the sidebody is lengthened a little at top to provide, in a certain degree, for the shortening tendency of seams 1 inch; is taken out at the waist between the back and sidebody, and 1 inch between the sidebody and sidepiece, and 1 inch between the sidepiece and forepart, when the remainder, necessary to reduce the waist to measure, is taken out in darts, allowing 1½ to 2 inches for seams at the waist. The narrowness of the back at

firmly secured to the seams at the back and side, below which tabs are placed, with either eyes or eyelets in them, at parts to agree with fastenings placed in the train; usually they are placed one at the centre of back, and one on either side at hips, the object of course being to secure the train. The bottom part of Bodice is faced with the same material as the outside, about two inches deep at front and sides, and continuing straight across the back skirts; and in putting the facing in the back skirts it should be put in rather short, so that the tails shall curl inwards. Whalebones are placed at all the seams (unless the customer objects), none of which should come higher than the top of breast darts, or lower than within an inch of the bottom; the bones should be put in as long as possible, curving the garment to the shape of the figure previously to fastening them, which should be done at top, middle, and bottom, the casings being made from Silesia on the bias, and care must be exercised in sewing them to the seams, and full them on over the waist.

If, as is usually the case, it is made to fasten with holes and buttons, it will be necessary to add on a button stand as illustrated on Diagram, and for this purpose add ½ an inch on the buttonhole side, and 1 inch or more on the button side. This allows of the holes coming exactly in the centre of the figure, and the extra button stand hides any possibility of the underclothing peeping through the ends of the holes. It will be advisable to put a V of silk in the button stand, as shown on the waist line, which allows it to go nicely to the figure at that part, and prevents any dragging tendency. The buttons are put closer together than was formerly done, which we think is an improvement. If made with stand collar, the collar has hooks and eyes placed at the top to keep it fastened. We recently had the opportunity of inspecting a Habit made for a very stylish young lady by the celebrated firm of Wolmerhausen & Co. It had an interlining over the back and forepart of horsehair, which kept it very firm above where the corsets reached; it was lined through with silk, pleats were placed in the forepart lining opposite the prominence of the bust, and another vertically, as is now generally done in Vests, running from shoulder downwards, and allowing ample scope for it to adjust itself, whilst of course it was put in very long at the waist section all round. Needless to remark, the sleeve linings were flash-basted to the seams, both forearm and hindarm, and two or three small pieces of Domett serged to the scye seams on the top of the shoulder, to facilitate the distribution of fulness in the sleeve head and at the same time produce as good form as possible.

New Style of Habit.

We now proceed to illustrate the new style of Habits, or, at any rate, one of them. In many cases the fronts are continued straight down the front, on the Diagram page they are cut away; this is, however, only variations of the same style.

These garments have a character and fashion of their own, so that they very rarely run into the extreme of style so often adopted for ordinary wear. Habits are more for use than ornament, and though we are fully aware of the importance most ladies attach to every detail of their outfit being correct, yet there is a consciousness that extravagant styles of sleeves and lapels are not helpful in a garment intended for riding cross-country in.

Our illustration shows the style of sleeve now mostly used in hunting Habits. There is even here a degree of fulness at the sleeve head that is superfluous, but it is only very small compared with the costume or jacket sleeves now worn. An addition of say 3 inches to the sleeve head would suffice for this style.

Materials

Necessarily vary with the fancies of different customers, though the dark grey Cheviot is undoubtedly the newest make for this style; it is of rather a heavy weight, and makes up a good substantial garment, and one especially suited for the demands of hunting. Many ladies, however, still adhere to the black Melton, which has been looked upon as the regulation material during the past few years.

Fancy vestings are largely used for hunting outfits, it being the custom with many hunts to have a special pattern vesting of their own, the pattern being in some cases registered, and consequently only procurable through certain firms.

The style of Habit here illustrated is very suitable for such, the front is made to roll fairly low, and so showing the fancy vest above the turn, and being cut away from the waist in front displays a fair amount of fancy vest below.

This affords opportunity for the display of a little colour in an otherwise quiet and plain outfit, but even with this, the beauty of a Riding Habit must ever remain in its excellence of fit, and its superiority of finish rather than upon the use of accessories in the way of trimmings, &c.

The Diagram

Needs very little description. The system used in its production is the same as we have previously described. We therefore merely direct attention to the special features only on this diagram, and first

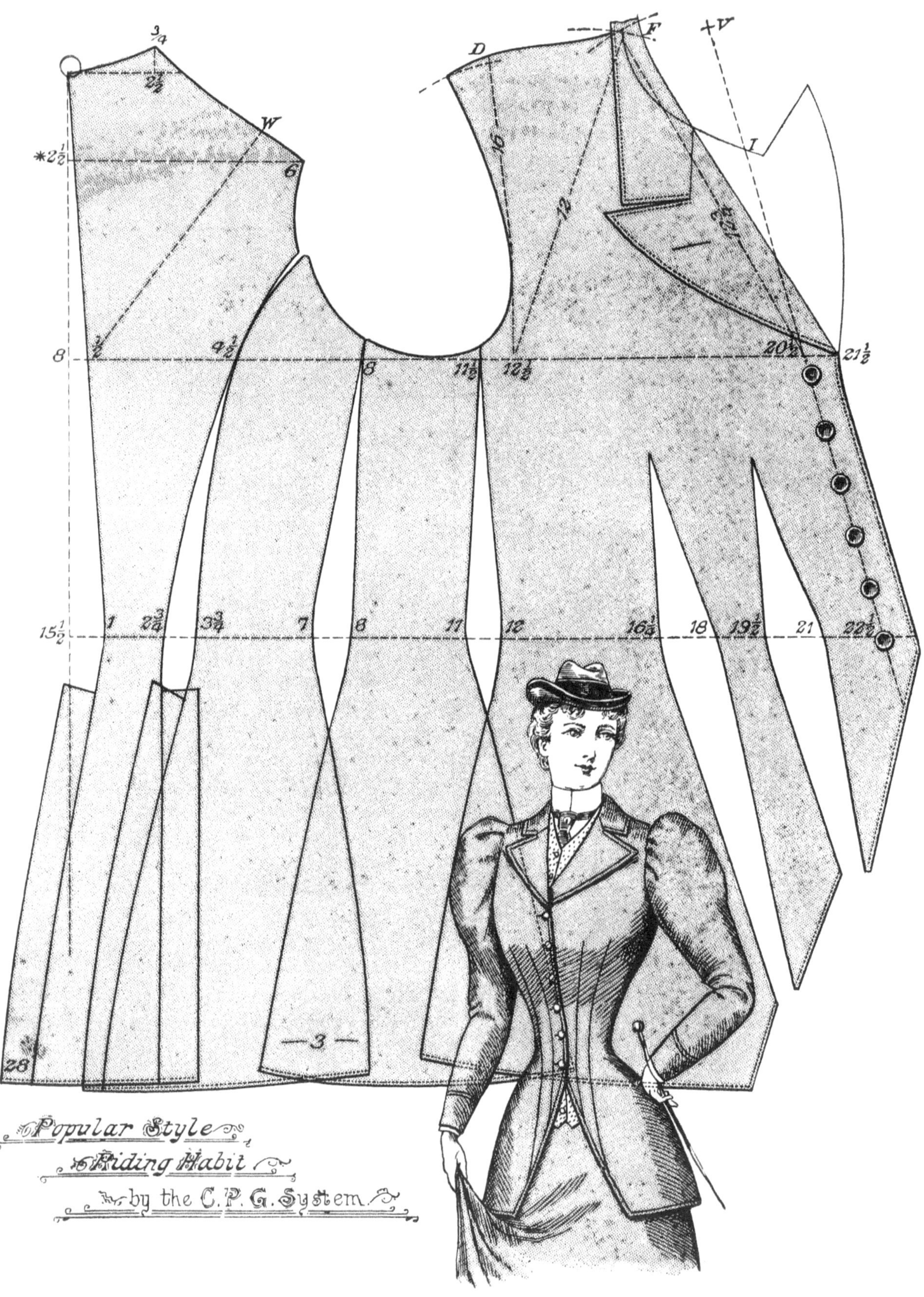
Popular Style
Riding Habit
by the C. P. G. System

of all we would notice the length. This is made from 12 to 14 inches below the natural waist, being made just to cover the horse's back, or just to cover the saddle at the back. An opening is left at the centre of back, starting about 2 inches below the natural waist, and it may be well here to warn our readers of the danger of getting the waist too short behind.

Side pleats are arranged at the bottom of either sideseam, and these are finished with a button at the top, level with back tack. The fronts are sometimes cut away from the waist, though, as previously noted, many of the very latest have the fronts cut to run straight, an alteration which can easily be introduced in the diagram, the bottom button is placed just in the waist. This style avoids any difficulty that might arise from dragging on the right side when the leg is lifted over the pommel.

In cutting the back it is best to keep it rather to the narrow side, as illustrated on diagram.

Trying On.

In trying on Riding Habits it is certainly desirable to fit them on in the saddle, most tailors who do any amount of trade in this way keep a dummy horse and saddle for this purpose. The importance of this is apparent when we direct attention to the fact that the body is somewhat shorter and wider than when standing. There is also a tendency to lean forward when riding, and unless this is provided for the front will appear too long across the breast, and the back will very probably be short in the waist.

In trying on the Train and Trousers or Breeches the same remarks apply, but here a little difficulty is found in the dummy horse, as the saddle may not agree with the one used by the wearer, and in fitting the Train the saddle plays a very important part, so that whenever possible it is desirable to fit the Train on the actual saddle generally used by the lady. It may be desirable in some cases to entrust this part of the business to the lady's maid, giving her instructions as to what to make a note of. But under any circumstances the cutter should retire whilst the lady puts on this part of equestrienne dress. Safety Trains continue in popularity, and the number of patents taken out for these increase. Some ladies' tailors find it advantageous to make these patented garments, and pay a considerable royalty to the patentee, who very often is a lady of influence in equestrienne circles, and it is worth something to be recommended by such, as when ladies order Riding Habits it is very unlikely their orders will be confined to such garments, and even if they were the tailor gets his ordinary profit on these garments, even though he may pay a heavy royalty.

We are giving diagrams of one of the most popular styles of Safety Trains in a later section of this work.

Newmarket Riding Habit. Plate 15.

Another style of Riding Habit has been growing very much in favour of late is illustrated on Plate 15. A glance at this will show that it partakes very much of the character of the Hunting Frock, now so largely worn by gentlemen.

They are worn much longer than the ordinary Habit, and this is doubtless an advantage, affording as it does an extra protection from the rain.

The system for the body part is the same as before described.

The outline of the lapel is a matter of taste, the form depending on customer's fancy quite as much as on fashion. Our diagram illustrates a medium style.

The Skirt.

This requires to be cut with plenty of fulness.

Draw lines at right angles to A.

From A to 6 is 6 inches.

Mark backwards from 6, 1½ inches, and draw line from A through 1½.

Add on ½ inch of round at the back of pleat.

Get the run of front from B to C at right angles from B 6 as per dotted line, and complete diagram as per illustration.

Fashionable Riding Coat, as made in the West-End.

We recently had the opportunity of examining a Riding Coat, made by a celebrated Habit Maker, who is well-known in the front rank of Habit Makers.

This coat was made from a somewhat heavy steel grey Angola, and as the style was somewhat out of the ordinary run, we have reproduced a miniature pattern of it. The diagram of this is drawn to the one-eighth scale, and if the various dimensions are

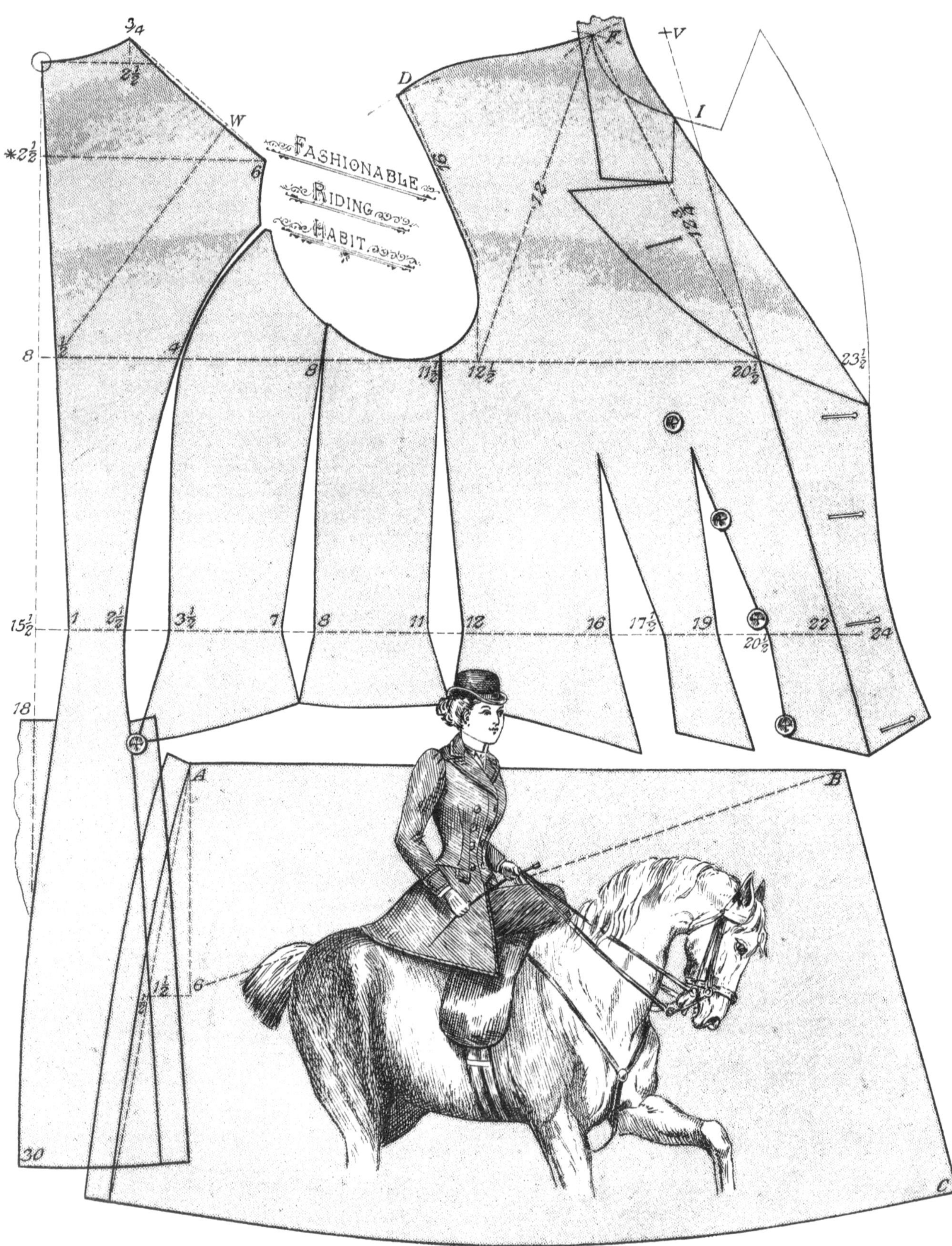
FASHIONABLE
RIDING
HABIT

reproduced by the ordinary inch tape, it will produce a pattern suited to 34 breast figure. Should a
larger or smaller size than that be required, a
graduated tape 2 inches larger than the breast
measure should be used, starting to mark in each
case from point O, and the straight dotted line.

The special character of this garment is the wide
lounge-like back, finishing at the bottom with a
deep (8 in.) slit, so that plenty of freedom is left at
the lower part for the lady when on horseback.

It will also be noticed there is extra spring on
the bottom of each forepart by quite 1 inch, starting
gradually directly below the waist. The foreparts
all in one piece in the style often followed in vests.
The fronts fastened with five buttons, the lowest
one being about 2½ inches below the waist line; a
hole was worked in the turn, and a button placed
under the other turn for use in wet weather. The
buttons were about 26 line, ivory two-hole, and
were placed on the left forepart. The edges were
double-stitched fairly wide by machine, but the
bottom was left plain; a good turn up was arranged
at the bottom, on to which the lining was felled in
the usual way. The body of the Jacket was
lined with a heavy silk serge — black. Pleats
were arranged in the lining from the top of

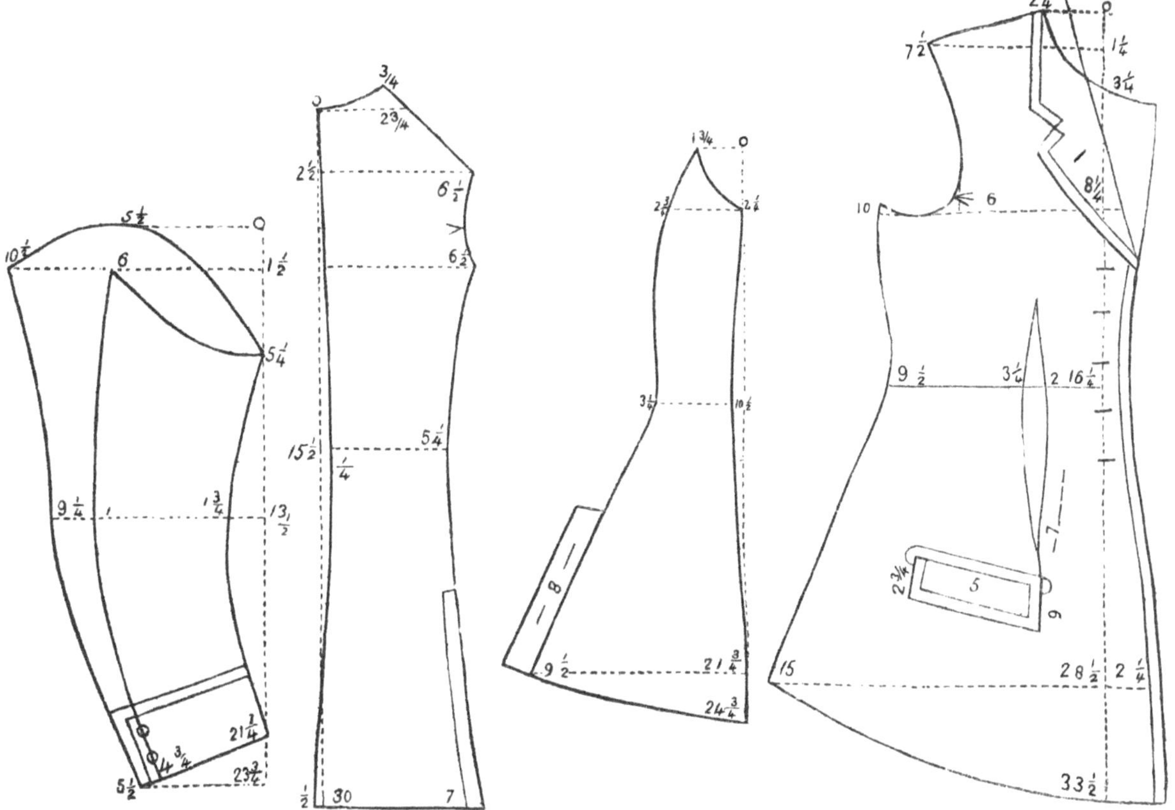

are made to define the figure, but not to fit closely,
there being a single dart taken out of the forepart
about 2 inches from the breast line.

The diagram will give a good idea of the style of
cut followed, so will direct our further remarks
more to the

Details of Finish.

It was made with a collar and turn rolling to 13,
and one feature of this was the absence of a
drawing seam to the collar, the facing being arranged
the breast dart to the shoulder, and another under
the arm to the hips. The front facings were
very narrow, being only just wide enough to take
the holes on that side, whereas on the button side the
lining came to within half an inch of the edge, and
made to cover the thread used in sewing on the
buttons. Below the waist the facing gradually
widened to about 3 inches at the bottom.

The forepart was interlined with French canvas,
but there was a total absence of everything else in
the way of horsehair or padding, as well as
whalebone, &c.

The Sleeves

Were cut with a fairly wide topside, as will be gathered from the diagram, and there was just the ordinary fulness at the sleeve head similar to a gent's coat. The cuffs were formed with a couple of rows of stitching to match the edges, and this was placed 3½ inches from the cuff. Two holes and buttons finished the sleeves at the hands.

The sleeves were lined with a bright drab and red striped satin lining. Pockets with flaps were placed on each forepart, as indicated by the diagram.

Of the noteworthy features of this coat we would direct attention to the length, the spring on the front, and the style of the back, whilst the low-rolling turn indicates its suitability for summer wear, or for the display of some of the fancy styles of hunting vests, now so largely worn by ladies in the hunting field.

Riding Habits for Girls. Plate 19.

The style of garment that is most favoured for girls is the Norfolk Jacket, the principal variations introduced being in the style of collar or turn.

In the style shown on accompanying Plate the front is made to fasten up to the neck, above which it is finished with a stand and fall collar.

The pleats are usually five in number — three up the back and one up each forepart. The back is cut wide, after the style of a lounge, care being exercised to provide plenty of spring over the seat and sides.

It is best to suppress the waist at sides and fronts unless the young lady is very stout at the waist, as is often the case with young girls.

The train is made after the same style as for the lady, though it is seldom made to fit as closely, ample provision being made for growing, both as regards length and width.

SECTION SEVEN.

Jackets of Various Kinds.

We now proceed to treat of one of the most popular sections of the Ladies' trade, viz., Jackets, and in the following illustrations we have endeavoured to give as much variety as possible, partly with the idea of showing the facility with which the system is adapted to the various styles, but also with the idea of posting the reader up to date in the newest styles. First of all, then, we take the close-fitting Jacket.

This is one of those standard styles that never seem to go out of fashion; true, the various details, such as the size of the sleeves and the spring over the skirts, have to be considerably modified from time to time; still, as a standard style, it is perhaps the best adapted to the explanation of the system, consequently we use it here for that purpose.

Diagram, Plate 16.

Draw lines at right angles to O.

From O to *2½ is one-sixth of the natural waist, or to taste.

From O to 8 is the depth of scye, as taken on the the customer.

O 10 is ½ the natural waist length.

22½ is 7 inches below the natural waist to find the level of the hips.

O to 27 is the full length desired.

From these points draw lines at right angles and mark off.

O to 2½ one-third of the half-neck measure, and form the back neck by curving up ¾ inch.

From *2½ to O is the width of the back, plus two seams.

Draw shoulder seam from ¾ to 6, as in diagram.

At 15½ mark in 1 inch, and draw the back seam, springing it out to 22½.

From 8 mark across to 22½ the half chest measure, plus 2½ inches.

From 22½ measure back to 12½ the across chest measure, as found by adding the across chest and the across bust measures together and dividing them by 2. From these points we proceed to find the shoulder points.

The Front Shoulder.

First sweep from 12½ by the front shoulder measure, less the width of the back neck, as from O to ¾.

Next cast another sweep, using 20½ as the pivot, and adding ¾ inch to the quantity used to sweep with in the first sweep; where these two segments cross each other locates point F.

Cast a third sweep, using point 12½ as the pivot,

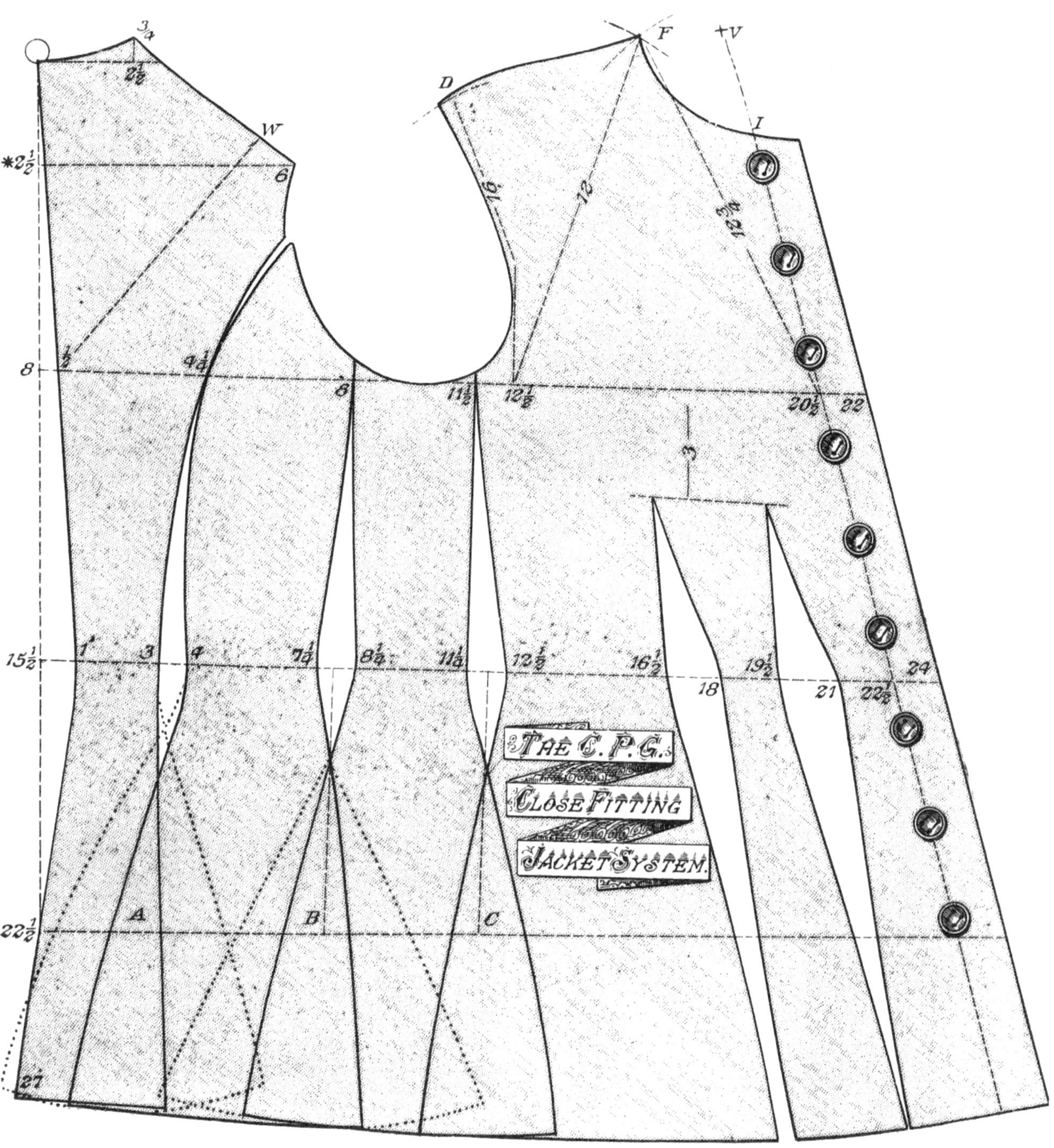

The C.P.G.
Close Fitting
Jacket System.

and finding the quantity from the over shoulder measure, less the distance on the back from ½ to W. mmMake the width of the shoulder from F to D a ¼ inch less than the back from ¾ to 6, and from these points shape the scye.

From F mark forward to V one-sixth of the neck, and draw line from V through 20½ and so find the breast line.

From V to I is the same distance as from F to V, and by these points shape the gorge.

Position of the Seams.

From 12½ mark back to 11½ one inch, and so find the position of the under arm seam.

Divide the distance from ½ to 11½ into three equal parts, as shown at 8 and 4¼.

The widths of the various parts at the waist are found as follows: —

From 1 to 3 is rather more than half the width of the back on the depth of scye line.

Between 3 and 4 one inch of suppression is taken out, and the sidebody is formed by making it ½ an inch less at the waist than it is on the depth of scye line; an inch is taken out between the sidebody and the sidepiece, and the width of the sidepiece is made half an inch less than it is on the depth of scye line; another inch is taken out between the sidepiece and the forepart, and thus the position of the various seams are found.

Measure the various parts at the waist, and allow two inches for making up, and take out the remainder in two darts as here shown. Let the front of the first dart be 1½ inches from the breast line, and take out half the quantity it is desired to reduce the waist. Leave 1½ inches for the strap, and take out the remainder. Always arrange for the darts to run towards the front at the bottom; in this respect the diagram may be taken as a guide.

The Spring over the Hips.

In the solid lines of the diagram we have arranged the spring over the hips in the usual close-fitting style, as that will best serve as a lasting basis, the guide being to take the hip measure rather lightly; and after measuring up the various parts, add on the necessary amount of overlap at A B and C.

The dotted lines on the diagram illustrate the amount it is necessary to add on when the present fashionable style is required.

It only now remains to add on the button stand, or whatever amount of overlap is desired in the front, and the jacket is complete.

Hints on Making.

Use especial care with the neck and waist sections to get them the right size. Let the shoulder be slightly stretched on all three sides, and be careful to avoid getting the collar on tight in the hollow below point F. See that the lining has plenty of surplus length to allow of the bend at the collar seam; indeed, it will be a good plan to always put a pleat in the lining of the shoulders, as is customary for vests. If the lady has prominent breasts, use every possible precaution to avoid getting the front of scye at 12½ full; keep your sleeve rather tight there, putting any fulness there may be in the underside at N, or taking it out with a fish. If thought advisable, put a little wadding at 12½ but it must always be borne in mind this will have the effect of reducing rather than emphasising the prominence.

If any padding or wadding is put in the breast, it should be carefully and skilfully done — nicely graded away, and for this purpose we have found horsehair the most useful, not the horsehair to be obtained by the yard at most trimming ware-houses, but the loose horsehair obtainable at the saddlers. Care must, of course, be taken to secure it firmly; if that is done, it will be found that it can be graded off very much nicer than can be done with wadding or cloth.

The waist section requires very considerable care in making. All the parts should be slightly stretched at the seams, and shrunk in the centre, as is usual with the sidebody of body coat for men. See that the waist does not make up too large, as some materials are very elastic, and it is difficult to exactly gauge the amount to be consumed in making. In some loose materials it will be found advantageous to baste strips of linen to all parts of the waist, and sew it in with all the seams to prevent stretching. It is a very good plan to measure up the size of the waist after all the seams are sewn, except the underarm seam, and then adjust the size at that seam.

Snip the button stand at waist and insert a V to enable it to lie smooth on the opposite side. Put all the linings in very long over the waist, as the sharp curve of the body at that part demands it. Always

remember that whenever there is a hollow on the body, the lining must be longer than the outside.

A waist band should be made up to the size of waist, and fastened to the centre and sideseams of back; it steadies the garment, and keeps it close in to the figure at the back, and also relieves the strain on the waist of jacket. If the garment is S.B. to button through, always arrange the eye of the hole to come on the breast line on the one forepart, and the button on the breast line of the other; otherwise the buttons will not come down the centre of the figure. We are frequently asked on which side to put the holes in a lady's jacket. To this we can only reply that there appears to be no universal custom amongst ladies' tailors. There can be no doubt, however, that ladies are more accustomed to have them on the right side, and by ladies' tailors this is most usually done; and as habit becomes second nature with many, it will be well to consider this matter carefully before putting them in the left side as is occasionally done by some ladies' tailors, and universal with all gent's garments. We shall now proceed to deal with some of the varieties of

Braided Jackets. Plate 17.

On this Plate we illustrate the various methods of braiding jackets; they are mostly of a military character. Before we deal with each style separately, we shall make a brief reference to the effect the different styles have on the body. Those having the braid running only in a horizontal manner give the effect of the width, which, although frequently very desirable, must not be done at the expence of the length, except in very tall, thin figures. To counteract the shortening tendency of these plain horizontal rows, drop loops, rows of eyes, and braid laid on in a vertical direction are introduced. Take for instance Diagram 13. The braid on the edges introduces one line, the eyes above and below each row of braid across the front introduce two more rows, and the drop loops introduce two more, so that there are five rows of ornaments running in a vertical, as well as five in a horizontal direction; and as the horizonal rows get narrower at the waist, several effects are produced. Length is added, width is added, and by the emphasis given to the width of the shoulders, the waist appears relatively small.

Diagram 5, Plate 17,

Illustrates a style of braiding very popular with ladies. A row of flat mohair braid is put all round the edge, and rows of tubular braid from ½ to ⅜ inch wide are laid across the front. In this diagram each rowisterminated with an Austrian knot, a plan which may be varied in the style illustrated by Diagram 6, which represents the drop loops for Rifle garments or Diagram 7, as used in the army for the Artillery and Engineers, when sometimes the eyes in the centre are ommitted; or the style illustrated on Diagram 13 may be used, which is the plan followed for Infantry regiments. The braid is always started from the loop end, the finish being arranged under one of the crossovers. Care must be used to prevent the ends of the braid from fraying, the best plan being to wind cotton or thread round the end several times, and so securely fasten it. Loops of braid are invariably left beyond the edge on the one side, to fasten over the olivets or buttons placed on the edge of the other. If this is not done, a very long neck will have to be put to the buttons. A master tailor of the army, stationed at Malta, recently spent a month at our Cutting Academy, and he kindly showed us the methods he adopted to arrange these drop loops and Austrian knots.

Diagram 8, Plate 17,

Is a piece of cardboard. It will be noticed there is a notch at the bottom of dotted line A; this is placed on the centre line, the point B being also arranged on this line, when the outline is to be marked round as per solid line 1,2, 3, 4, Diagram 10. Now turn the card over to the other side, still with notch A and point B on centre line, and mark as per dot-and-dash line 5, 6, 7; and small loop above 1 7 may then be formed by rock of eye, and to complete the bottom of the knot, turn the card upside down, fitting the circle in to the outline 3 4, and mark as from 5 to 6, and the Austrian knot is complete. Full instructions for tying these was given in Part I., so we will not again repeat them, merely remarking that throughout the entire knot the braid should run over and under the whole way.

Diagram 9, Plate 17,

Represents the piece of card the master tailor referred to used to mark the drop loops, the same as illustrated in Diagram 13; a line is drawn in

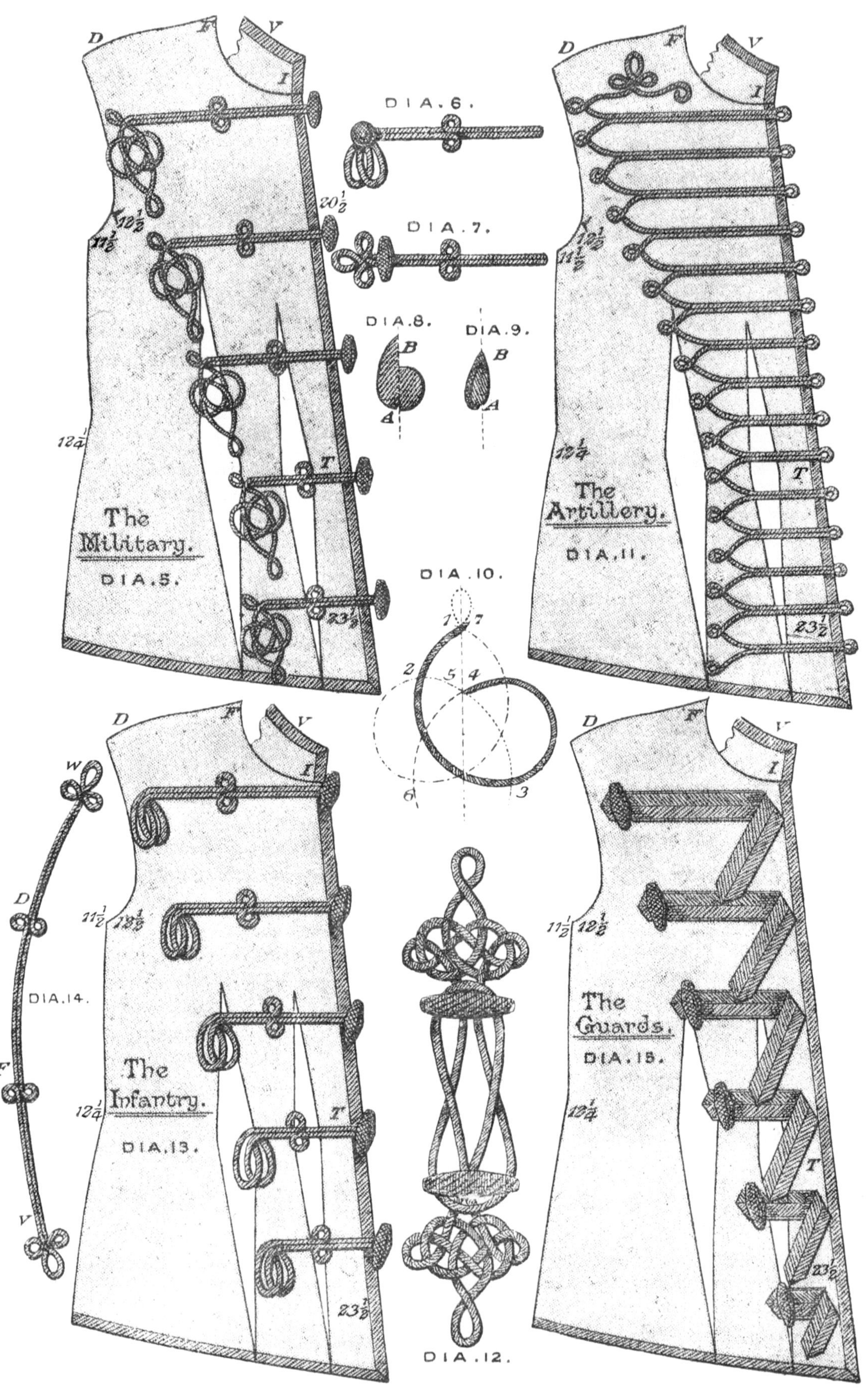
DIA.6.
DIA.7.
DIA.8.
DIA.9.
DIA.10.
DIA.11.
DIA.12.
DIA.5.
DIA.13.
DIA.14.
DIA.15.
The Military.
The Artillery.
The Infantry.
The Guards.
Braided Jackets.

the direction the loop should point, and the top B and the notch at A are both kept on this line, the larger part of this oval being on the outside. Now turn the pattern round so that A B still rests on the line, but with the larger part on the inside. If this course is followed, many of the difficulties of braiding will vanish, and what was looked upon as a difficult matter will be very simple.

Diagram 11, Plate 17,

Illustrates the Artillery style of braiding. This is frequently done with a round cord, but the cord is not so easy to manipulate as the braid; the rows of braid should go very narrow at the waist, and as broad as possible at the shoulders, often extending right to the shoulder seam. Ball buttons are the correct style of fastening down the front, though of course this is only the ornamental fastening, the real fastening being done by hooks and eyes. The edges are invariably braided with flat mohair braid. The back of the jacket should be trimmed in harmony.

Diagram 14, Plate 17,

Represents one very good style; strictly speaking, this is the style of back that goes with

The Infantry Forepart, Diagram 13, Plate 17,

But as there are no regulations for ladies' garments, this is often used, as it is very effective and very simple. The military regulation trimming for the Artillery jacket has a crow's toe at top, and an Austrian knot pointed towards the sideseam. mmThe braid across the forepart is generally of the tubular make and about ¼ inch wide, the top row reaching to the scye seam and sometimes overlapping it and graduating down narrower to the waist. Further details of this style of front will be found in the description of Diagram 5.

The Guards. Diagram 15, Plate 17.

This style of braiding is very effective; the braid is the same on the edges and across' the front, the ends are finished with a sprat's head, and olivets arranged up each front. The details of this are so clearly brought out in the diagram, that it is not necessary for us to give any elaborate description in the letterpress.

Jackets made in this style are often made with loose-fitting fronts, the braiding showing off rather more to advantage in that style than in close-fitting garments. The braid is generally mohair, from ¾ to 1 inch wide.

Diagram 12, Plate 17,

Is a little variation from the Austrian knot; an extra loop is introduced on either side, and, as the same instructions given for them will apply, we will not go into further detail, merely calling attention to this as a very popular style of braiding for loose-fitting fronts, the long loops being arranged to fasten over the olivets on either side, as the taste of the wearer may dictate.

Loose-fronted Jackets.

For several seasons past loose-fitting fronts have been very much patronised by ladies; indeed, at the present time, there are probably few more popular styles. They have a dash and go about them which recommend them to those who like something a little dressy and stylish. When these jackets were first introduced they were the source of much worry to even the most experienced ladies' cutters, and it was found that many patterns which produced most perfect-fitting tight jackets were anything but satisfactory when used for loose-fitting fronts; hence it was found that something more was necessary, besides omitting the darts, in order to produce these jackets to perfection. The great difficulty many had to contend with was tightness at the bottom of the front, below the waist, causing a nasty drag from under the bottom of the arm to stomach; this was soon traced to the front edge being too long, or perhaps, what a good many people would call too crooked. Needless for us to say, this defect was more apparent amongst those cutters who patronise a round front edge, and which we have so often pointed out as wrong in principle; and although it may, and undoubtedly does, produce passable fits, if not overdone, for tight-fitting garments, yet, when applied to loose-fitting fronts it is a failure; hence it is of the greatest importance that the line drawn from V through 20½ should be quite straight, that being the shortest possible distance between two points, and so producing that shortness of front edge absolutely necessary to balance the foreparts, and cause them to hang gracefully down the fronts.

But there are other changes also necessary; for this straightness of the front edge, combined with the darts being omitted, make it too large round the bottom, and especially over the hips; hence the necessity of taking out more between sidepiece and forepart at waist; from 1½ to 2 inches is the amount we have found to suit the majority of customers, and just letting the forepart and sidepiece meet at the bottom, or only slightly overlap. With these variations from the close-fitting jacket, previously explained, we have been able to turn out most successful garments for the majority of ladies; the exception being with those who are very prominent at the bust, when the shortness of the front caused a fulness to appear at the front of scye. With such figures, we found it advisable to take out a small dart from about 2 inches in front of the side at sleeve, and terminating just below the prominence; this has the effect of not only providing a receptacle for the bust, but also makes the waist to fit snug at the sides — always a desideratum in loose-fronted jackets. As far as the cutting of this class of jacket is concerned, we think we have said enough to point out the special features to be observed and the dangers to be avoided, so we will now pass on to give a few hints on the various styles in which these are being worn.

There is considerable variation in the style of back, some are made to fit closely, others to define the waist moderately, whilst others are made to hang decidedly loose and sacque-like. Thus some are cut with three seams, others have one, and others two sidebodies.

We therefore give illustrations of all these styles, and first of all describe the system as adapted to the close-fitting back, as cut with back sidebody-sidepiece, which is undoubtedly the most popular.

Ladies Covert Coat and D.B. Reefer.
Plate 18.

Square lines O, 2½ and O, 28.

O to 2½ one-third of neck.

O to 8, depth of scye.

O to 16½ natural waist.

Mark in at waist 1 inch, and out at bottom ¾. Draw line from O through 1 to full length.

O to 2½ one-third of neck (7½), raise ¾, and shape neck as diagram.

Measure width of back from centre seam, plus ½ inch for two seams.

Measure from ½ to 20½ half breast, plus 2 inches.

Mark back from 20½, 8 inches, the across chest measure. Raise from this point 1½.

Sweep from 12½/ and 20½ the front and over-shoulder measure, shaping the scye as shown.

F to V, one-third of neck.

V to I, the same.

From V, draw from 20½ to bottom.

Add 2 inches for fly and button-stand, which should terminate 5 inches below waist line.

Position of Seams.

12½ to 11½ is 1 inch.

½ to 11½ is divided into 3 equal parts.

Suppress waist 1 inch between each sidebody and back.

From 1½ to 2 inches may be taken out between sidebody and forepart.

Square down from the centre of this suppression.

Terminate sidebody and forepart at the hip line. Of course this will suit the normal figure, as this style of Jacket, at the present time, is worn close-fitting over the hips, but for a person with large hips and seat it would be increased to, say, about an inch, which should be divided equally on either side of perpendicular line.

The overlap of sidebodies should be about 1 inch each side on seat line (7 inches down from waist

Overlap side and back 1 inch. Add 1¼ on both sides of back, and also sidebody (about 2½ below the waist seam) for pleats. The length of turn is entirely a matter of taste, the diagram favours the long turn, rolling down to breast line.

For the D. B. Front, mark from 1 about ¾ to find step of lapel.

Add from 3 to 3½ from centre line (20½), and continue to bottom, as diagram.

Position of Pockets.

The ticket pocket is generally placed on the waist line. They may be either slanting (which at present is most popular) or horizontal.

It is about 1¾ wide and 3 inches long.

The top pocket is generally placed from 3 to 4 inches below, or 12 inches below the scye depth.

The length for a 36 breast is 5 to 5½ inches, and 2 inches wide.

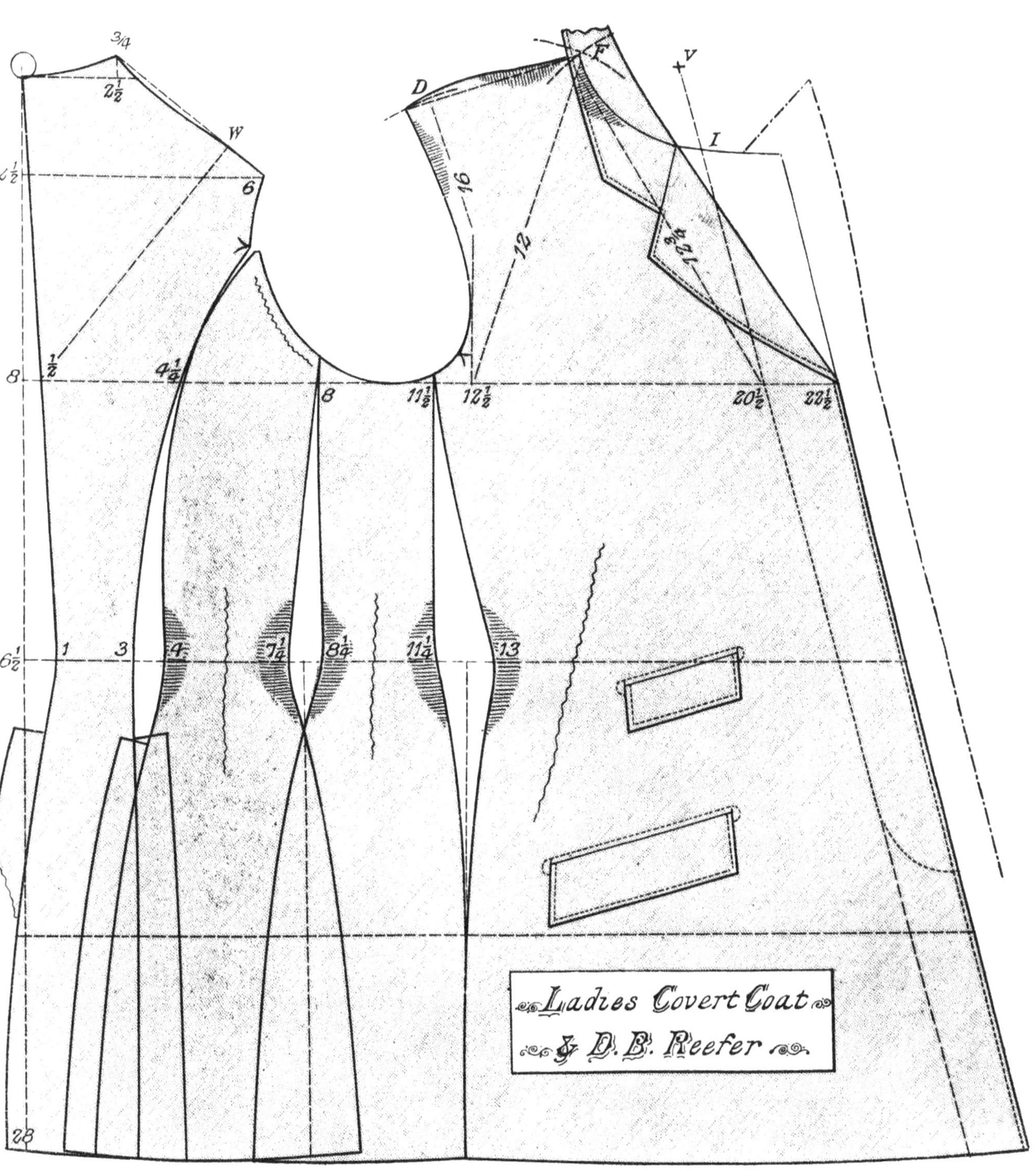
Ladies Covert Coat
& D.B. Reefer

Manipulation.

The shoulder should be carefully stretched on all three sides.

It is advisable to shrink at waist, as marked by wavy line.

A small dart may be taken out in the same direction for a prominent bust, terminating 2½ inches below the breast line.

The sidebodies should be stretched on the edges and shrunk in the centres, as shown on diagram.

Ladies' D.B. Reefer. Plate 19.

We now proceed to illustrate the cutting of the Reefer with one sidepiece.

Square lines O. Full length and O to 2.

O 2½ to taste (usually 2½ inches).

O to 8, depth of scye.

O to 15½ the natural waist measure.

22½ is generally located 7 inches below, as this fixes the hip line.

Mark in at waist 1 inch, and out at bottom 1 inch.

Connect O to 1 on to full length.

O to 2½ one-third of the half-neck.

Measure from back seam opposite sleeve pitch, the width across back plus half inch for two seams.

Shape back shoulder as diagram, springing out a little on end above sleeve pitch ½ to 20½ half of breast plus 2 inches.

Mark back 8 inches the across chest measure. From this point sweep the front and over shoulder measure.

Add ¾ to the second sweep to provide extra length of front for the prominence of the bust.

The width of front shoulder should measure a quarter inch less than that of the back.

Shape the scye as diagram, hollowing it at front and keeping it close to the figure at back.

From F to V one-third of the half-neck (2½), marking down the same.

Commence step of lapel within 1 inch of centre line, which should be drawn from V straight through 20½.

Add 3-inch overlap and shape lapel as diagram.

Position of Seams.

Mark back from 12½ to 10½ inches.

From ½ to 10½ should be divided into two equal parts.

1 to 4½ is half-inch less than ½ to 5½.

One and a-half is taken out between back and sidebody.

6 to 10 is 1 inch less than 5½ to 10½.

Take out 1½ between side and forepart.

From the centre of this suppression square down to seat or hip line. Overlap them about 2 inches (as a guide). In the case of a lady with large seat and hips it will be found advisable to measure up seat, and allow from 2 to 4 inches according to the amount of fulness (if any) required.

The back should be squared down from 4½.

Overlap the side and back on the hip line (4½) and 2½ inches at bottom.

The bottom may be rounded slightly, as diagram.

The pocket should be placed about 4½ inches below waist line and in a slanting position, its length being about 5 to 5½ inches and 1½ inches from buttons

A pleat is usually added to the centre of back, which should commence 2 to 2½ inches below waist line, increasing its width slightly at bottom.

Sac Covert Coat and D.B. Reefer. Plate 20.

Square lines O, 2½ and O, 30.

O to 2½ one-third of neck.

O to 8, scye depth.

O to 15½ natural waist.

O to 30, full length, plus ½ inch.

Mark in at waist ½ inch, and run out to 1½ at bottom.

O to 2½ one third of neck, raise ¾.

2½ to 6, the width of back, plus ½ inch for two seams.

8 to 20, half breast, plus 2 inches.

Mark back the across chest measure, 8.

From 12 and 20 sweep the front and over shoulder.

F to V, one third of half-neck.

V to I, the same.

Draw centre line from V through 20 to bottom.

Add 2 to 2½ for F F, or 3 to 3½ for D.B. and complete front, as diagram.

Position of Seams.

Mark back from 12, 2½ inches, and from centre seam to 6 one-sixth of breast.

Make width of back at waist half-inch smaller than at breast, and spring out slightly at bottom.

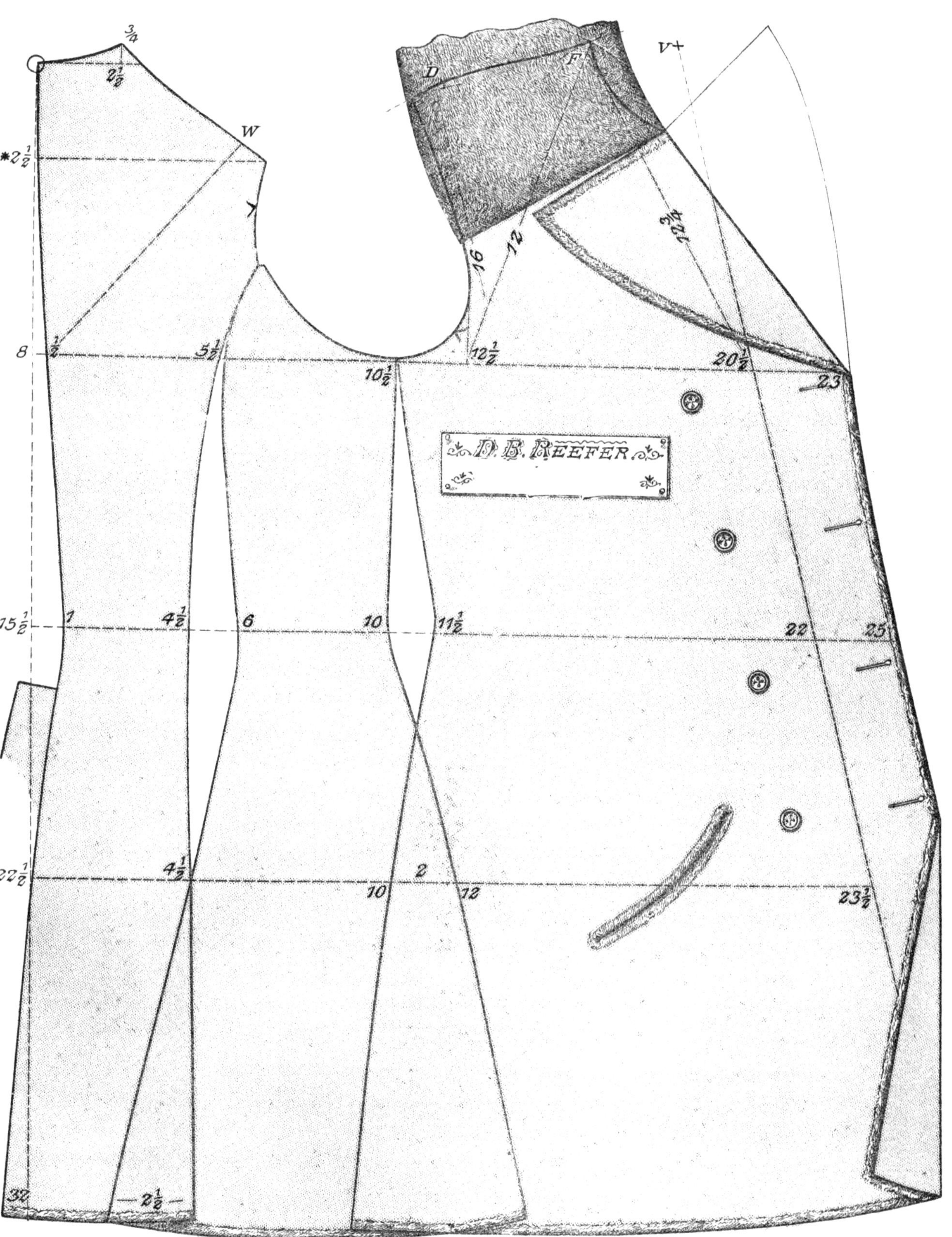

D. B. REEFER

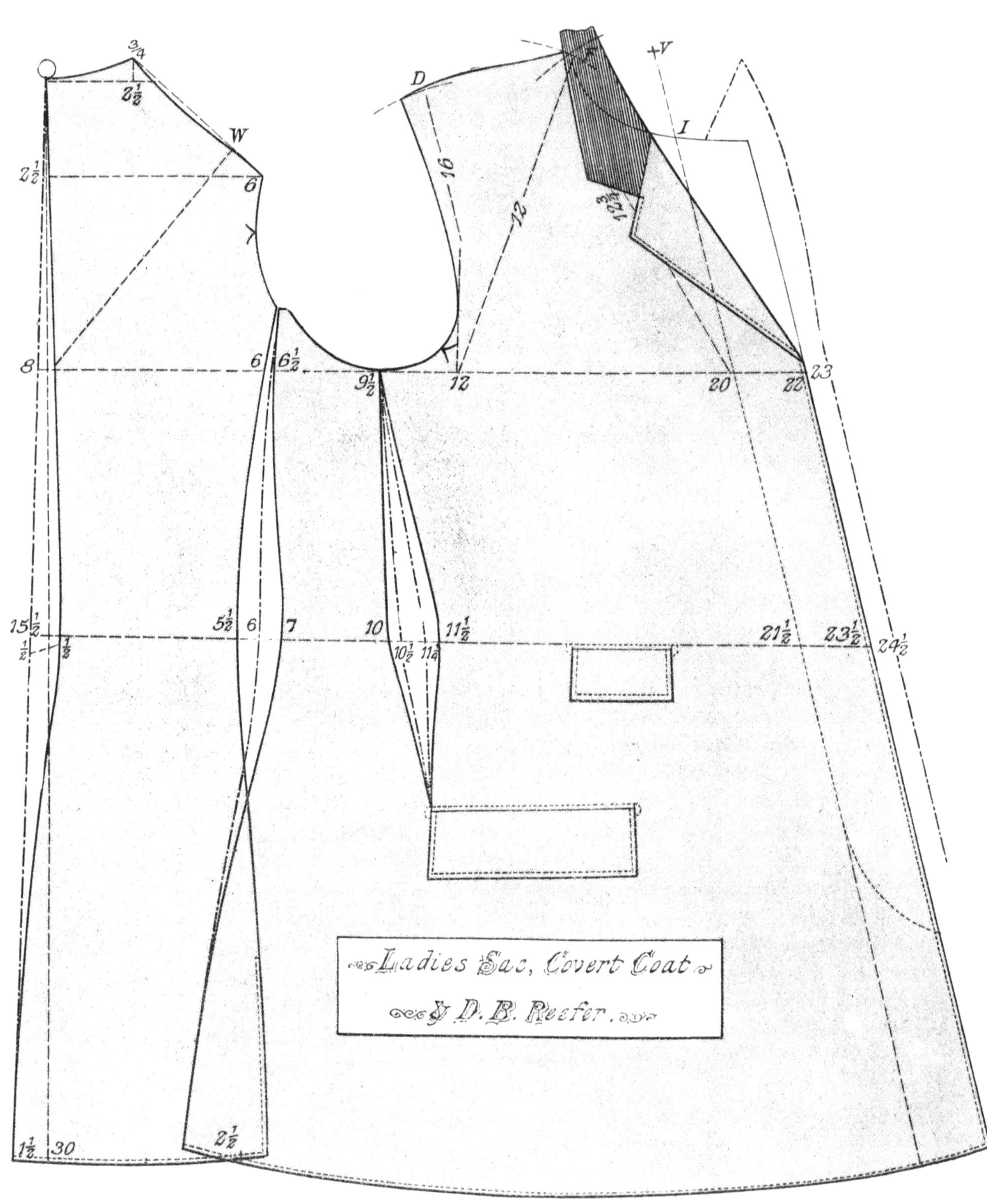

Measure up to hips and allow 3 to 4 inches.   A person with prominent hips give more overlap at 2½.

Take out 1½ inches between back and side, and the same at under-arm seam, which should be 3 inches from 7.

This suppression is for a semi-fitting back and sides, but if sack-back is required, then these would have to be filled up as dot-and-dash line. Mark out ½ inch at 15½ and draw straight down. Take out 1 inch between back and side, and ¾ under arm for whole back. The position of pockets may be easily calculated from diagram.

Spring over the Hips.

The diagram allows for a moderate amount of spring (2½). Of course, this would not be suitable for a person with large hips.

The best plan is as follows: Mark down from the waist at ½ and square out, on this line measure half the hip, plus from 3 to 4 inches. The extra amount should be added to the forepart.

If slits are required, leave on forepart 1 inch, about 5 inches up from 2½.

Shape bottom as diagram, adding ¾ of round on forepart.

Skirted Jackets. Ladies' Morning Coat. Plate 21.

This garment in its general characteristics very much resembles the Gent.'s S.B. Morning Coat. The back is made up with opening and two side pleats; there is a separate skirt, and often flaps are put on the hips. These features follow closely a gent.'s coat, adapted of course to the difference of the bust to be fitted. It is essentially a garment to be worn open, the run and character of the front being such as to show to advantage a fancy vest, which forms a feature in the dress. Though the skirts are smartly cut away, there is ample fulness falling over the hips. This accounts for the diagram skirt appearing more square in front than it does on the figure on the Plate. The revers, it will be noted, are of the ordinary S.B. type, and contrast somewhat from those frequently seen in wear. Those represented in this case are more in harmony with the garment on which they appear.

The system for the body part is just the same as previously described; one dart only is taken out of the front, and the run of the waist seam may be found by the quantities marked — viz., back of sidebody, 3 inches below waist line; sidepiece, 2 inches below waist line; and forepart, 3½ inches below waist line.

The Skirt.

Draw lines A B C at right angles.

Make A B of skirt the same distance as from bottom of sidebody and forepart; this will allow of two V's being taken out over the hips.

C to E is 2 inches; draw line from B through E, add on ½ inch of round opposite E, and make length up to agree with the back.

Leave 1 inch beyond this to form side pleat.

General Remarks.

The coat being generally worn open, and not being intended to fasten more than one button, the amount taken out at the dart is a,matter of taste, but for a garment that is intended to define the waist, we recommend from 2 to 2½ inches, and this is best located at about 2 inches back from the edge of forepart. If V's are taken out over the hips, it will be well to utilise the flaps to cover them, though this is by no means a necessity, inasmuch as it is quite common to take V's out over the hips, and if they be objected to, the amount can be put on in fulness and nicely pressed away.

This garment frequently forms part of a costume, in which case the skirt would be made from the same material, the vest being of some fancy make of silk or similar material.

S.B. Newmarket Jacket. Plate 22.

The popularity of the Newmarket jacket a few years ago was very great, so that it may fairly be looked upon as one of the standard styles that may at any time become popular again; and as there are many variations in the style, we select the most useful, and by describing the principles embodied in its production, lay a foundation from which our readers may be able to form any of the various styles which have, or may, become popular. The system for producing the body part is precisely the same as described for the Jacket, so we refer our readers to that for the upper part, and proceed to deal with the first special feature, viz., the run of the waist seam; and though this is largely a matter of taste, it may be as well for us to lay down some definite quantities as guides for the inexperienced.

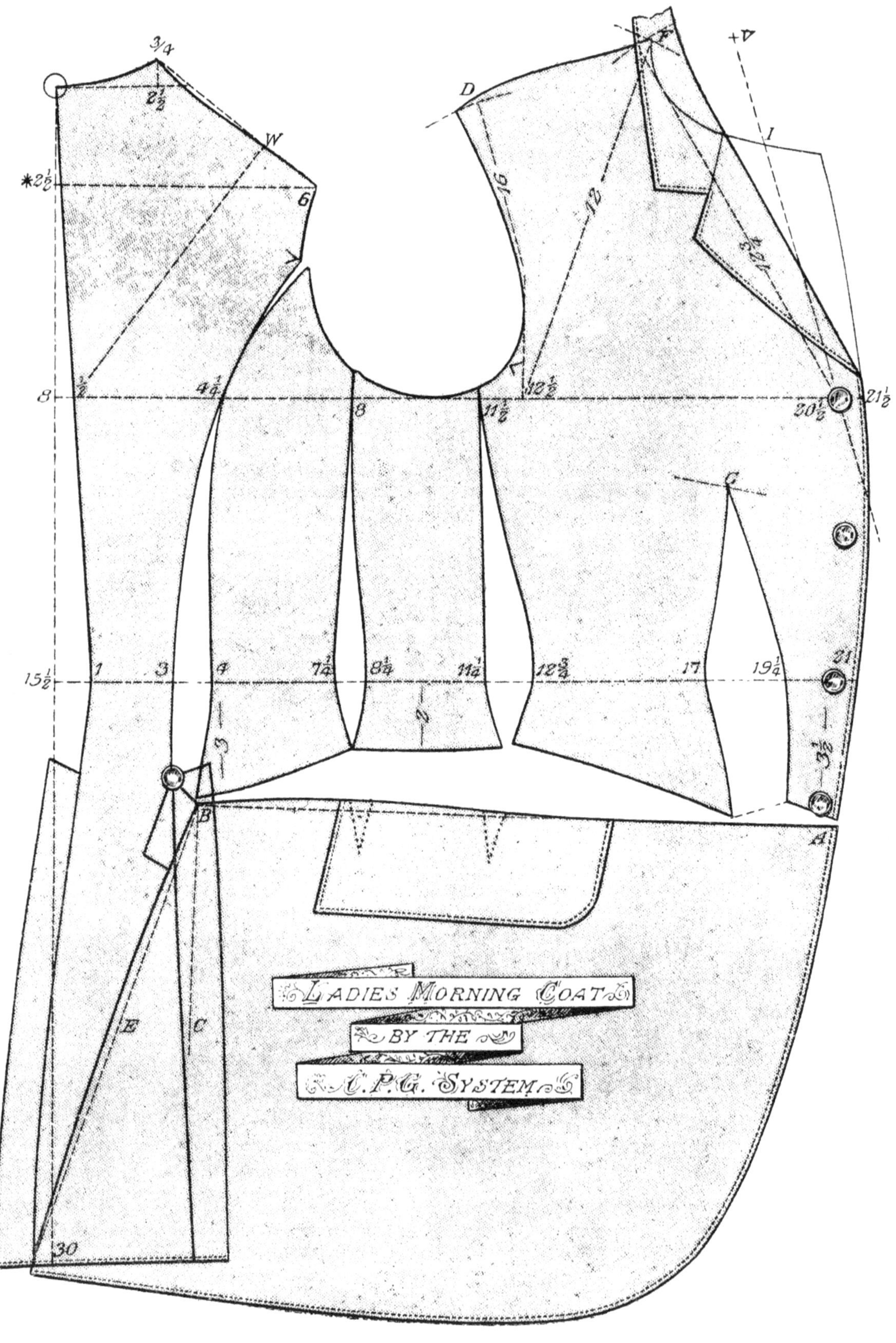
Ladies Morning Coat
by the
C.P.G. System

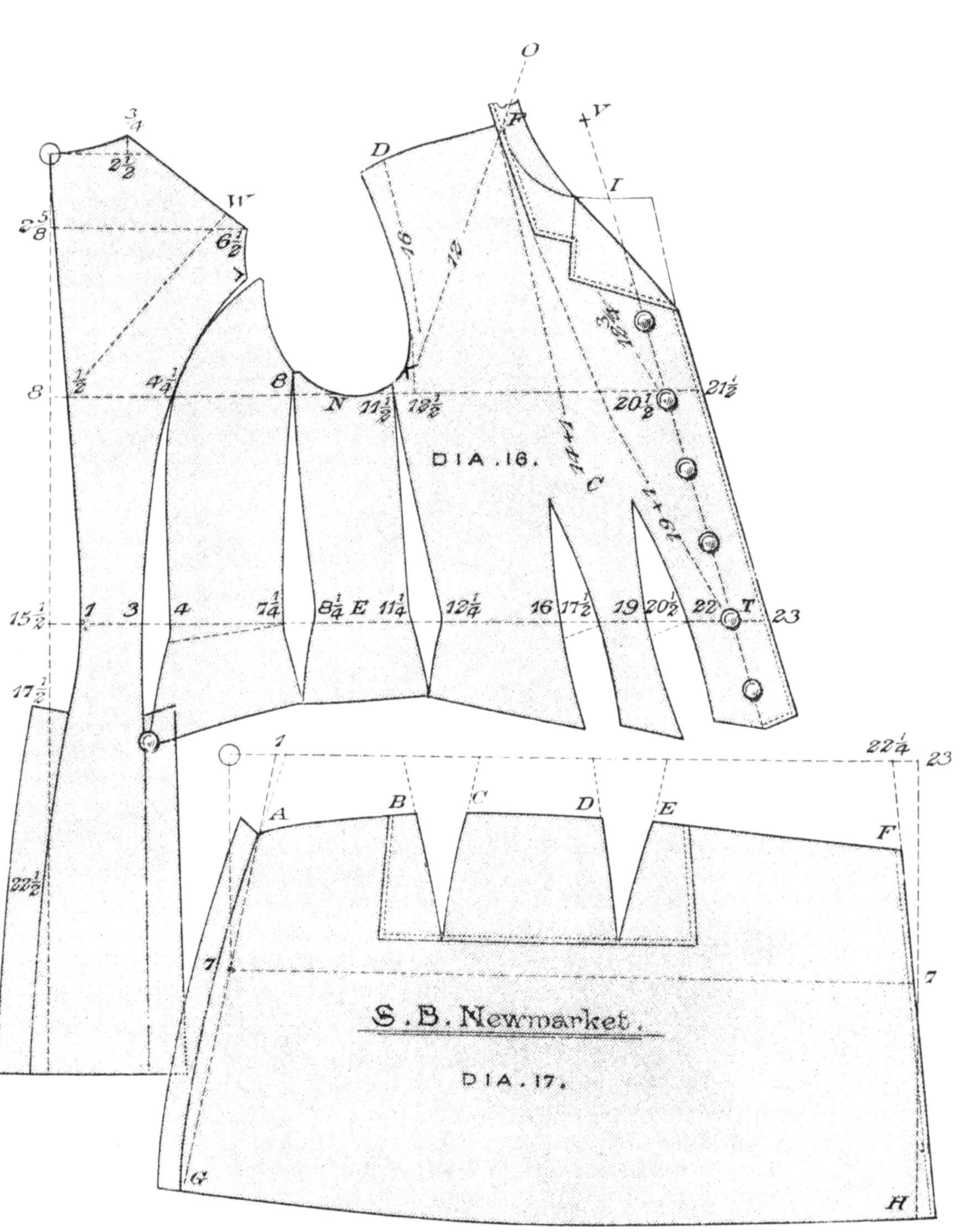

Skirted Jacket.

In doing so, it must be borne in mind that the quantities quoted are merely looked upon as guides.

Commencing at the back, then, we come down 2½ or 3 inches from the waist line, about 2 inches at the side, and 3 to 3½ at the front, taking care to adjust all the seams to agree with those to which they are intended to join, making all the parts slightly round at the bottom. As will be seen, the back is continued to the full length, about 1 inch being left on either side, as illustrated on diagram, for the formation of side pleats and opening in the back; the style of finish most usual for these being the same as for gent.'s body coats, though sometimes box pleats are placed at the centre of back when it will be necessary to allow 3½, 7, or 10½ inches according as single, double, or treble box pleats are desired; at present, however, these are the exception for this style of Jacket. We now pass on to deal with

The Skirt System. Diagram 17.
Plate 22.

Draw lines O G, 0 23 at right angles, making O 23 half the nett size of seat; measure down from O to 7, 7 inches always, and square line across to 7 in front. Now come in from O to 1, 1 inch, and draw line A, G from 1 through 7; come back from 23 to 22¼, ¾ of an inch, and draw line from 22¼ through F and 7 to get the run of the front. Next measure the depth of the body part below waist line at back, sides, and front, and whatever that is, come down from line O, 1, 23, to find the run of the waist seam of the skirt. Now measure the width of the sidebody at bottom, and make A to B of the skirt the same; take out 1 to 1½ inches in a V from B to C, and make C to D the same width as the bottom of the sidepiece. Now measure the width of the forepart after the seams are sewn, or allow for the seams in measuring, and make F to E what it measures. The distance from E to D is taken out in a V, when the skirt will only need plain sewing to the body part. Many ladies, however, prefer having the extra quantity fulled on over the hips, after the style usual for gent.'s body coats, only, of course, there is very much more fulness. If this latter method is desired, it will, of course, be necessary to omit the V's B C and D E. If it is desired to reduce the size of the V's or the amount of fulness, follow the plan illustrated on the new style of skirt.

Add half an inch of round at 7, and mark off the length from A to G in accordance with the customer's wishes, making due allowance for the seams. As fashion goes at present, it is customary to arrange the skirt so that it appears level all round, when 1 G and 22¼, H would be the same; but, of course, this may be varied at will, as also may the run of skirt in the front, many ladies having them cut away so as to show a much wider opening than our illustration shows.

Flaps are arranged to go on the hips about 3½ inches deep, and generally wide enough to cover the V's, the flap being cut without V's. When the skirt is closed at top, the hollow of the waist seam is taken as a guide for the top of the flaps, the loose part being arranged to taste.

NEW STYLE OF SKIRTED JACKET.

The illustration chosen for this style is the latest development of the Skirted jacket. The waist length is made as long as is consistent with the style of figure, whilst the skirt is finished with the usual pleats and buttons on the hips. This may be varied by the skirt being cut in one piece, without either opening or pleats. The fronts are made in the single-breasted style, finished at the neck with a stand collar. One of the special features of this jacket are the wings or revers, which for more wintry wear are generally trimmed with fur; but for lighter wear, they may be finished with "Florentine silk or Moiré Antique". With this addition, a character and finish is given, which considerably enhances the appearance of this garment.

The Cutting.

Draw line at right angles to O.

O to 2½* one-sixth of natural waist length.

O to 8¼ the depth of scye.

O to 15¾ natural waist, to 17¾ the fashion waist, and full length to taste.

From these points draw lines at right angles.

From back from 15¾, 1 inch, and draw back seam from 6 to 1, continuing on to 17¾.

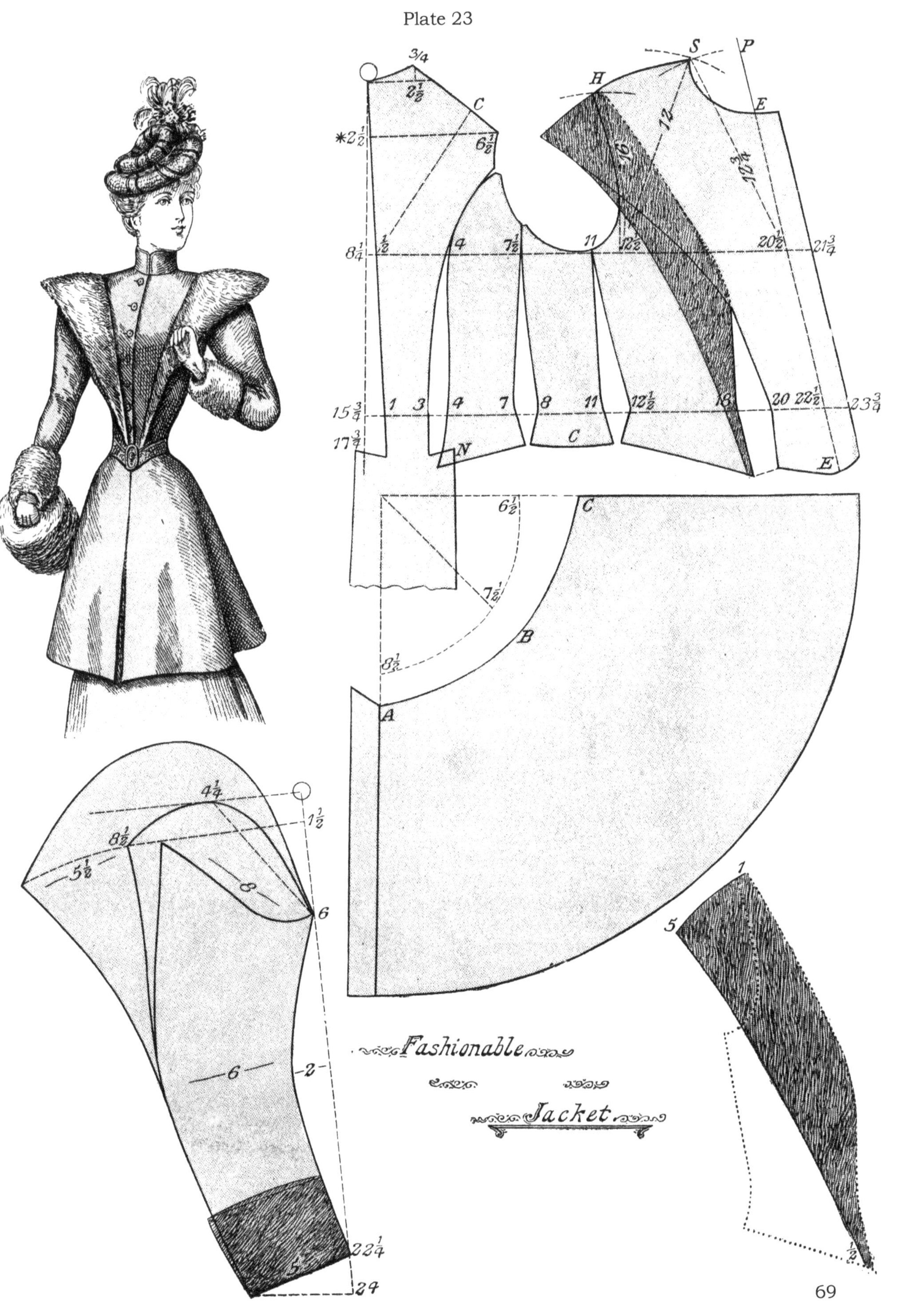
3/4
2½
C
2½
6½
8¼
½
4
7½
11
12½
15¾
1 3 4 7 8 11 12½ 18 20 22½ 23¾
17¾
N
C
H
S
P
E
12
16
10¾
20½ 21¾
12½
E
6½
7½
B
8½
A
4¼
1½
8½
5½
8
6
6
2
22¼
24
Fashionable
Jacket.
1
5
½

O to 2½ one-third of half-neck, and curve up ¾ of inch.

Mark off width of back, plus two seams, about 2 inches below shoulder slope, curve scye and draft shoulder.

½ to 20½ half the chest measure, plus 2 inches.

20½ to 12½ is the average between across chest and across bust measure.

Now sweep from 12½ by the front shoulder measure (12), minus width of back neck, 6 to ¾.

Add ¾ of an inch, and sweep from 20½; and where the segments intersect each other, locate neck point S.

Now sweep by the over-shoulder measure 15¾, less distance between ½ and C, and then form front shoulder, making the width ½ an inch less than back.

Shape the scye, hollowing it at the front above 12½ and close up round the back of scye.

To form the gorge and fix the breast line, mark out from S to P one-third of the half-neck measure, marking down to E the same amount.

Draw breast line from P through 20½ to 22½ on waist line.

We now come to the placement of seums, which to a great extent depends upon the cutter's taste and discretion.

Mark back from point 12½ at front of scye 1½ inches, and divide the distance from ½ to 11 into three equal parts, making the back from 1 to 3, half of ½, 4 on the breast line, and shape sideseam as illustrated on diagram.

Mark in from 3 to 4 one inch, and make the sidebody ½ an inch less 4; 7½ on breast line. Apply the same principle at points 11 and 12½ under the arm. mmMeasure up the waist, and allow 2 inches for making up, taking out the superfluous amount in a breast dart, placing the front edge of dart 2 inches from the breast line.

The position as well as the run of the waist seam is plainly depicted on the accompanying diagram. Point C being 1¾ inches from the waist seam, point E 3 inches. This will produce a fairly hollow waist seam slightly pointed at back and front. Care should be taken to preserve an unbroken line from the back to front, which can only be accomplished by re-marking the waist line when the body part is sewn ready for the skirt.

To draft the skirt draw lines at right angles, marking down from O to 6½ one-fourth of waist, O to 7½ one-fourth of waist, plus 1 inch, O to 8½ one-fourth of waist, plus 2 inches. From 8½ to A, the same as sidebody from 4 to N.

7 to B, the same as the sidepiece from 11 to C; 6½ to C, the same as forepart from 22 to E. Make up length to measure, and add on 14 for pleat down the back. If the skirt is required to fit all round without opening or pleats, cut points 8, A on the crease. Line 6½, C is the continuation of centre line of forepart.

The Sleeve.

Draw lines at right angles. Make O to 6 the width of scye, and O to 1½ one-and-a-half inches. Locate the sleeve pitches, the hindarm at top of sideseam, and the forearm ¾ of an inch above the depth of scye line at 12½ Measure the width of the upper part of the scye between the two pitches, which is 8½ inches; O to 4¼ half that amount. Now connect points 6, 4½ adding on 1 inch, and form sleevehead as shown. Measure off to length of elbow and cuff, and hollow the forearm at elbow 2 inches. The width of elbow and cuff is a matter of taste, the measures given on the diagram being about the average width. Measure round the under scye from pitch to pitch, making the under sleeve up to that measure, and complete draft, adding on the fulness at top in proportion to width desired: but of this we shall deal more fully in later pages.

We now come to the cutting of the wings or revers, which are sewn in with the breast dart at bottom of forepart to the scye end of shoulder, projecting beyond the latter point over the sleevehead from 5 to 6 inches. Care must be taken to give plenty of length to the sewing-on edge over the prominence of breast, otherwise a nasty dragging will be the inevitable result.

The Raglan.

This is certainly a very decided change from the ordinary jacket. Its leading feature is the sleeve, which runs right through to the gorge, thus doing away with a shoulder to the forepart, and producing a distinctive character. As now worn, it is made decidedly loose-fitting, with a whole back, and vents left at the bottom of sideseams. The pockets are pleated on the forepart, but the pocket mouth runs vertically, and the pocket is often patched on at the back of the forepart. The sleeve is cut easy, and usually finished with a narrow cuff, turned up,

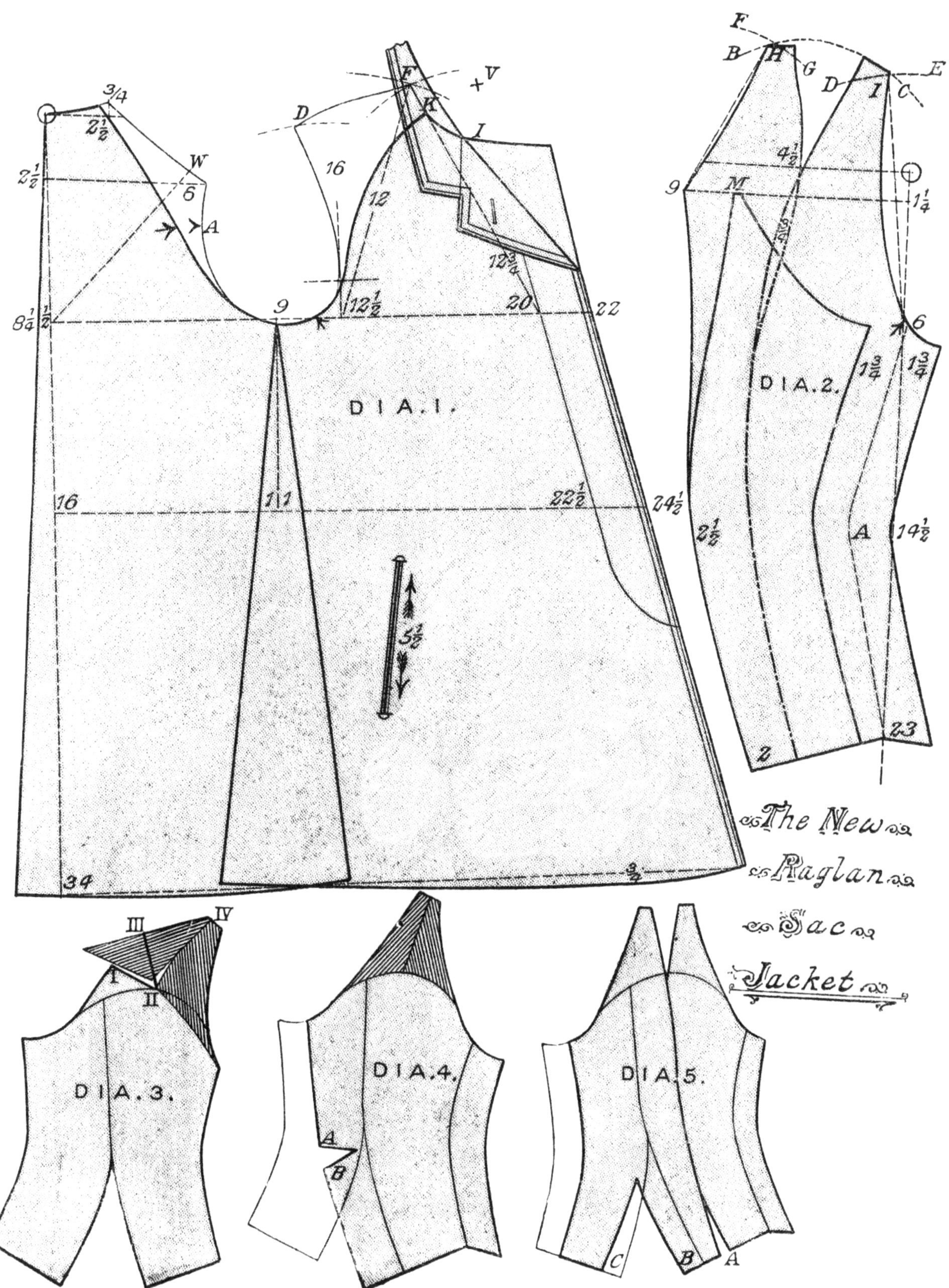
DIA.1.
DIA.2.
DIA.3.
DIA.4.
DIA.5.
The New Raglan Sac Jacket

which is so arranged that it may be turned down over the hands, if so desired. The coat itself is cut to reach just above the knees.

The popular material is a Drab Venetian, and it certainly is more suitable than the heavier makes of cloth, such as Meltons and Beavers, unless they were decidedly thin.

The System. Diagram 1.

Draw lines O 34 and O 2½.

O to 2½ to taste, say, one-third of scye depth.

O to 84 Depth of scye.

O to 16. Natural waist continue to full length, 34 inches. Mark out from 16, one inch, and connect O to full length.

O to 2½ one-third of neck, and raise ¾.

O to 6, the width of back, plus ¼ inch.

Mark out to 9, one-fourth of breast, and complete back scye, as diagram.

From 9 square down, and mark out each side 1 inch.

O to 20, half of breast measure, with 2 inches added for making up.

Mark back from this point to 12½, 28 inches the across chest measure.

Now use the front and over-shoulder as usual, and sink the scye a trifle below the line, say about ¼ inch.

F to V is one-twelfth of breast.

V to I to same.

Draw straight from V, through 20, which fixes the meeting edge of centre line. Beyond this, add 2 to 2¼ inches button stand or fly width.

The fly should terminate about 4 inches below the waist line.

Square out from 34, and drop forepart ¾ in front, gradually raising to line again, thus preventing the right forepart showing underneath the fly side when made up.

Draw beak of lapel from a point 1 inch out from centre of gorge and complete, as diagram.

Diagram 2. The Sleeve.

There is considerable diversity in the sleeve of this garment, but we select the most popular as the basis of this system.

Draw lines at right angles to O.

O to 6, the width of scye.

O to 1¼ is one and-a-quarter.

O to 1½ is half-distance from O to 9.

Deduct width of back from 9, and register the elbow and cuff, plus ½ inch.

Measure from A and 23, the width of elbow and cuff, plus ½ inch for seams.

Make a pivot of 4½ and sweep the width of shoulder from B to C.

Measure from forearm pitch to K; add 1 inch to this, and sweep from B to E.

Measure from 2½ to hindarm pitch, and bisect from F to G.

The other three styles may be easily followed out by laying top and undersleeve down hindarm together.

Diagram 3

Represents the two pieces of shoulder laid on the sleeve in their natural position.

Mark I, and make a pivot of II, sweep the back part until it touches IV.

The distance between it now and its former position will register the amount to be taken out from I to III.

Diagram 4

Shows the shoulder pieces closed at top, and the forearm as Diagram 2, but with 1¾ added to hindarm, and V taken out as A to B.

Diagram 5

Represents top and undersleeve with hindarm seam omitted, and neck seam continued to cuff of top side, as Diagram 2.

One and-a-half is added to B and taken off at C, reducing size of cuff slightly at A by opening the seam at bottom.

SECTION EIGHT.
Capes. Plates 25 and 26.

The continued popularity of Capes compels us to find a section for them. They may either be cut by the aid of Model Patterns or by System. We adopt the latter plan here.

The style we have chosen for this puipose is the one mostly used by tailors, leaving for the present the fuller and more fanciful types which are more frequently made by dressmakers and drapers. The

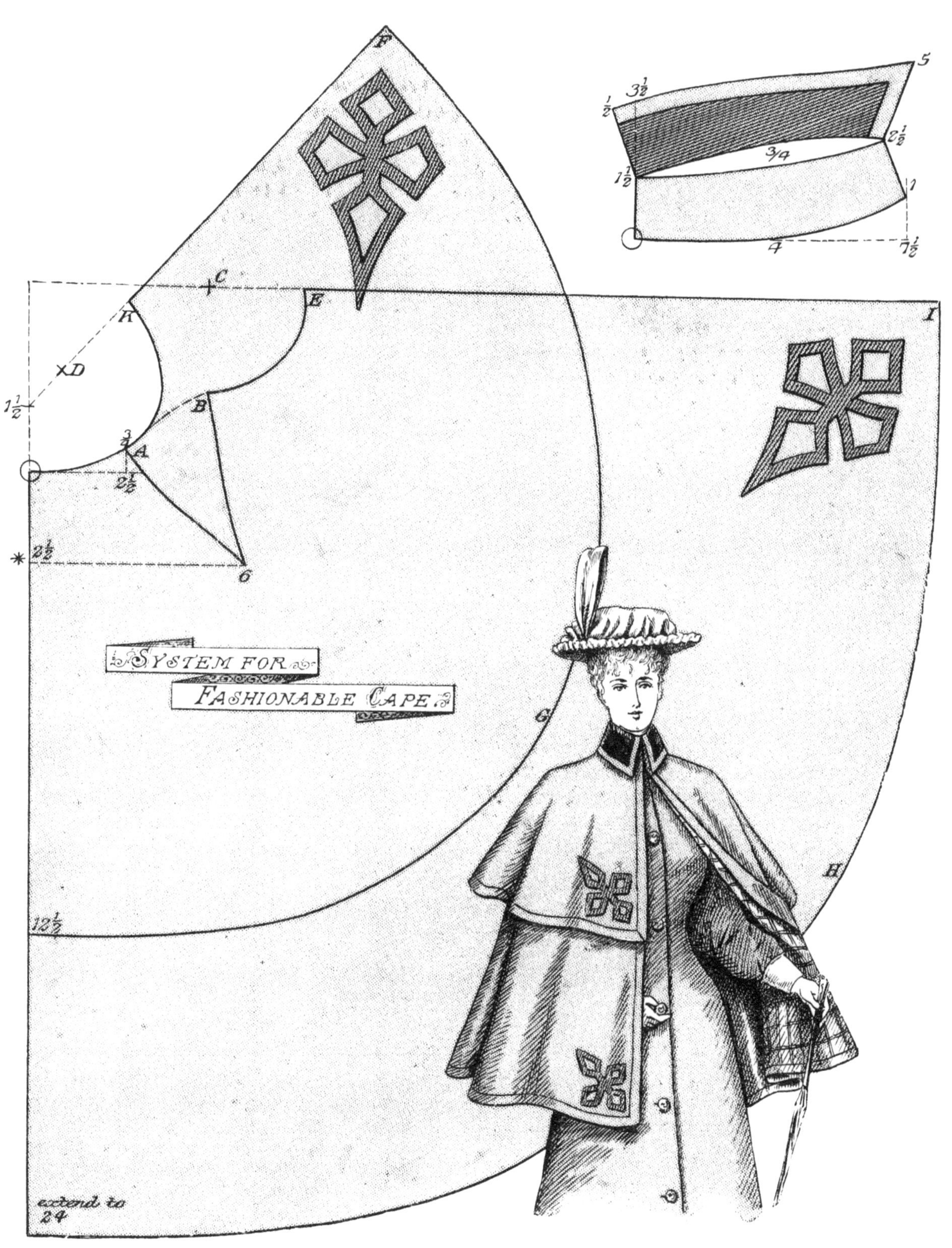
F
5
3½
½
2½
1½
¾
1
C
E
I
K
D
1½
B
¾
A
2½
2½
6
SYSTEM FOR
FASHIONABLE CAPE.
G
H
12½
4
7½
extend to
24

material used in the making of these garments must necessarily affect the style of cut, for in fairly substantial tweeds a fold of surplus material very quickly shows itself; whereas the same quantity in a thin cashmere or dress material would scarcely be noticed. We therefore preface our description of this system with a caution, so that the style of cut may be adapted to the material, otherwise disappointment will be experienced, and through no fault of the cut, but rather for the want of harmonising cut and material together.

The Half-Circle Cape System.

The measures necessary to cut a cape are few in number, viz., the length, the size of neck, and the size of chest. Let us suppose these stand in this case as follows: length 24, neck 15, chest 36. Draw line O 24, and mark off from O to *2½, 2½ inches for the average slope of shoulder, reducing it for square shoulders, and increasing it for sloping shoulders; O to 24, the full length desired, plus ½ inch ; square lines across from O to 2½.

O to 2½ one-sixth of neck; mark up ¾ inch, and shape back neck.

*2½ to 6, one-sixth of breast; connect ¾ and 6.

Make 6 a pivot, and sweep from A to B.

Take out V equal to one-twelfth of breast (3 inches).

B to C one-sixth of neck, and continue line O 24 up far enough to square line C E I at right angles.

C is the same distance from line O 24 that B is.

Make C a pivot, and sweep for gorge from B to E.

To find length of side, measure from 6 to H the same distance as from *2½ to 24, and of front from B to I 1 inch more than O 24, or if it is measured from E to I, make it the same as *2½, 24.

Three-quarters-Circle Cape System.

The shorter of the two Capes illustrated on the figure on the accompanying page of diagrams is cut much fuller than the lower one, and this necessarily involves a somewhat different arrangement. mmTo begin with, there is no V taken out on the shoulder, and there is really no necessity for any seam at any part of this except it be at the neck where the collar joins.

mmThe start is made from O in the same way as before, making O 2½ one-sixth neck, and coming up ¾.

From A to D is one-sixth neck.

From O to 1½ is 1½ inches.

Draw angle of front edge from 1½ through D K to F.

Let O K be equal to one-third of the neck, whilst it is also one-sixth of the neck from D.

The length can be found as for the half-circle cape, or measure off from 0 to 12½ length desired behind, and make A to G 1½ inches more than back length, and A to F 1 inch more than back length, and complete bottom edge with a good sweep all round.

In neither of these systems is provision made for buttoning, so that if it is desired to fasten them down the front a button stand must be added on.

The Collar.

Whilst many of these Capes are ornamented with strappings and fancy designs variously applied, the finish depends very largely upon the collar. These vary considerably; some are made with a very full upper edge, very much after the style of the Medici, that was so popular a few seasons ago; but the most popular is undoubtedly the style illustrated on our sketch, viz., the Panteen collar. The method of cutting this is as follows: O to 7½ is half the size of the neck; O to 4 midway between O 7½.

7½ to 1 from 1 to 1½ inches.

O to 1½ and 1 to 2½ regulates the depth of the stand of collar required, and from these points the upper edge of collar is drawn.

The fall of this collar is really a reproduction of the stand collar in reverse, with a little more spring and a slight variation in the lower edge. Our Diagram shows the upper or outer portion of the collar arranged above the stand, and when placed so, an opening of inch shows between them. In making up these the collar covering is arranged wide enough to just turn over the top edge, and the collar lining is felled on the top of this.

The remaining details of this garment do not call for any special comment, as the matter of lining, pockets, &c., are really matters on which customers' tastes have to be consulted.

Diagram 52. Plate 26.

Another way to cut Capes is to get a Jacket pattern such as will fit the customer, and then arrange the shoulder points of the back and front to

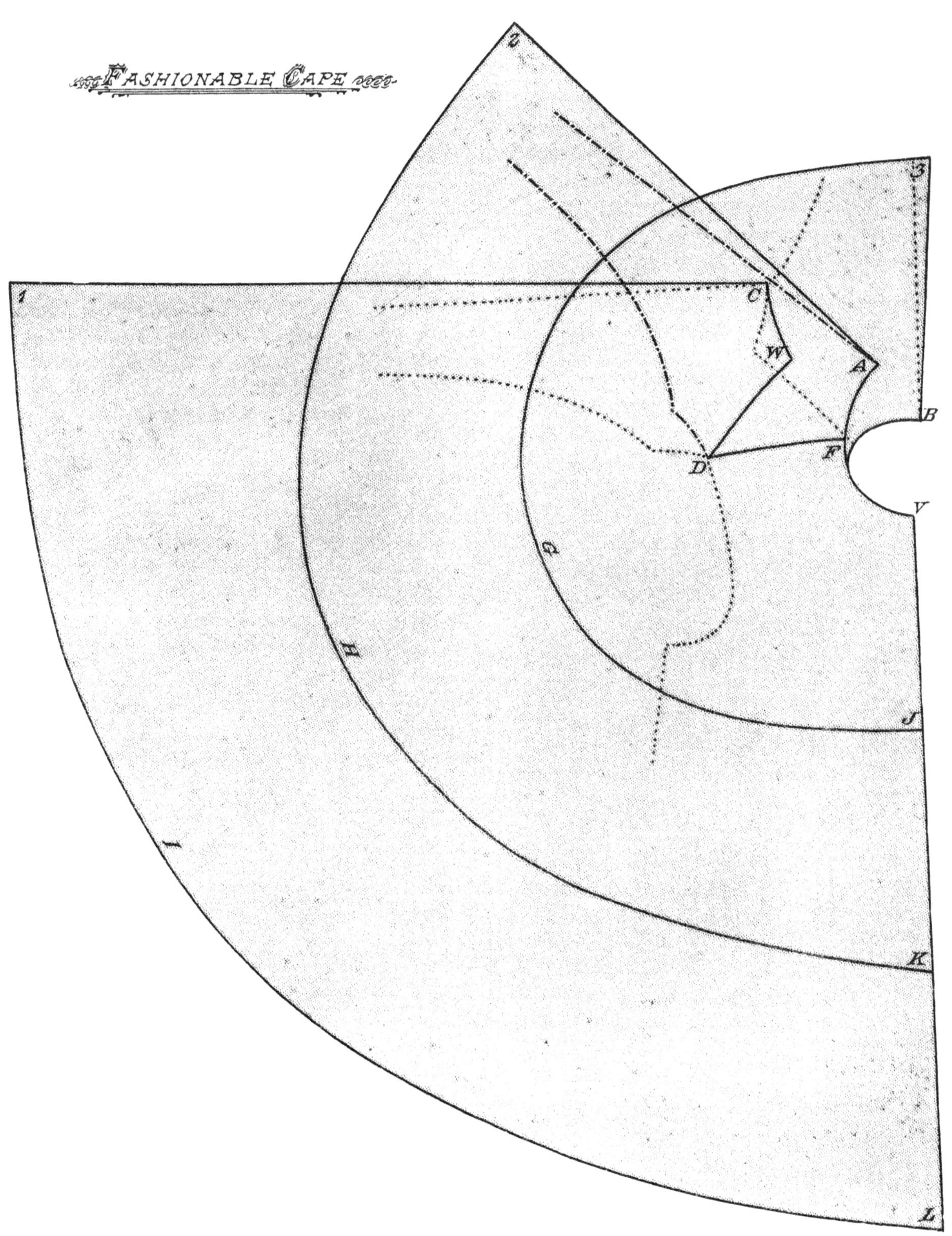

DIAGRAM 52.

touch each other with the centre of back and the middle of front running at right angles to each other. This will produce a V at the neck of about 4 or 5 inches, which must be taken out as shown in the diagram, the dotted lines indicating the back and forepart patterns. To get the length desired, measure off from C to 1 at back, and make from D to I the same length, minus 2½ inches, the length in front being got by measuring from F to L the back length, plus ¾ inch. This is the style known as the "Half Circle" Cape, and is moderately full; indeed, it is plenty full enough for any Cape, extending much below the waist. For shorter Capes they are usually cut fuller, so that the folds produced may be a more prominent feature. The way to do this is as illustrated by outline 2 on plate of diagrams. It will be seen that we have arranged the fronts the same for all, the variations being introduced at the back. The back in this diagram is arranged in a closing position at the shoulder seam, so that no V is taken out on the shoulder; this will be seen by the dot-and-dash outline of the back and forepart. The two sides of the Cape, when laid flat, usually form three-quarters of a circle, hence its title the "Three-quarter Circle Cape". The lengths of back, side, and front are all got in precisely the same way as for the half circle, so we need only remark that this Cape is decidedly full, and, when on, will fall in a plentiful supply of folds below the shoulder, and is especially suited for Capes of from 10 to 20 inches long. There is still a fuller style known as the "Circle Cape", which is very full, the folds starting almost from the neck, and consequently is the best suited for very short Capes of, say, 8, 10 or 12 inches deep. The method of cutting this is to arrange back seam of the block 3, B, to run in a straight line with the centre of front V L. This will necessitate a little adjustment of the outline of neck at F; but this can easily be done so as to retain harmony of outline at that part. The length of these latter is found just the same as the former.

These three styles of Capes will undoubtedly occupy an important place in the styles for the next season, as they will be worn in conjunction with Overgarments as well as separately.

Hints on Making.

The making of Capes of this class is exceedingly simple. There is no manipulation, no drawing in or shrinking; it is simply a matter of plain sewing. A piece of thin canvas is generally put down the front, and they are either lined through, or the lining extends far enough back to cover the canvas. They very seldom button through, it being the almost universal custom to arrange them with the edges to meet, and either fasten them together when so desired with hooks and eyes, or tabs and buttons. They are mostly made detachable, so that even when they form part of the Overgarment, the under-part may be left at home, and the Capes worn separately, so that they would be either sewn to a stand collar, or have the edges stitched together at the neck, and then either fastened with hooks and eyes, or holes and buttons, to that part of the undergarment. It is very often arranged for the undergarment to form a kind of skirt, and only to the waist, in which case a tab and button at centre of back would be the only means of connecting the upper and lower parts together. Pockets are often arranged in the front of these Capes, and it is also a good plan to put loops for the arms to pass through in front, so as to keep the Cape in position when the weather is cold and stormy, and for this same reason it will be well to put either hooks and loop, or tabs and button at front and back of the upper capes, otherwise in rough weather it will send them up round the wearer's head like an umbrella inside out.

In cutting these garments from the material a difficulty presents itself in the bias of the pattern, it being obvious that either the back or front will be unsightly, and so it becomes a question of choosing between the front and the back. We consider it best to study the front of the figure, and arrange the front first, and let the back take its natural lay from that. It will be seen from the diagram that back seams are not a necessity, though these Capes are mostly so arranged, as it simplifies both the arrangement of the pattern and the taking the garment from the cloth. These Capes cut into a lot of material, and in the three-quarter and circle styles the quantity is very large, especially if the Cape happens to be long, each inch that is added to the length increasing the amount very considerably.

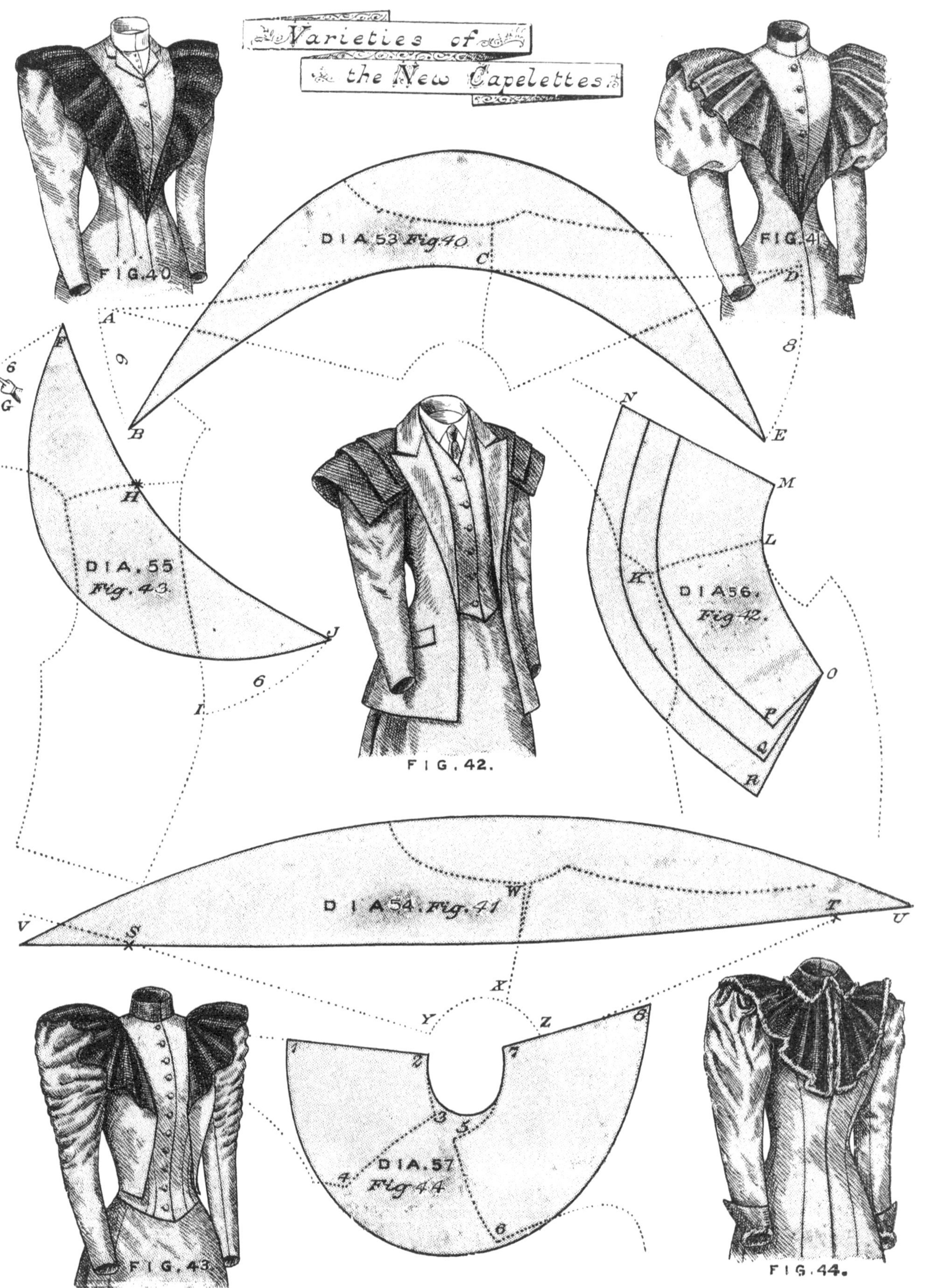
Varieties of
the New Capelettes
FIG. 40
DIA 53 Fig 40
C
A
9
B
D
8
E
F
6
G
H
N
M
L
K
DIA. 55
Fig. 43
DIA 56.
Fig. 42
O
J
P
6
Q
I
R
FIG. 42.
V
S
DIA 54. Fig. 41
W
T
U
X
Y
Z
6
2
7
3
5
4
DIA. 57
Fig 44
6
FIG. 43.
FIG. 44.

<h2 align="center">Varieties of Capelettes.</h2>
<h3 align="center">Figures 40 to 44, Diagrams 53 to 57, Plate 27.</h3>

The most noticeable feature in the fashions of the present time is the almost universal application of Capes to all kinds of garments. Jackets, Ulsters, Costume Bodices, all are finished in the same manner. The illustrations we give on this Plate of Figures and Diagrams will, therefore, be of special interest to those of our readers who are desirous of keeping up to date. These Capelettes are made not only from the same material as the body, but are frequently made of some contrasting material, such as a darker shade of cloth, or a light satin or velvet, and in this way a very stylish appearance is produced, the contrast proving very effective. They are generally lined through with an interlining, varying in thickness according to the material used. Those that are put on in pleats, &c., as illustrated on Figure 41, would only have the edges finished with a hem, the fulness of the material giving sufficient stiffness to the Capelette to hold it out.

On Figures 40, 41, and 43 we have illustrations of the most popular

Costume Capelettes.

Figures 40 and 41 start from the waist in front, go over the shoulder seam about 2½ inches from the neck, and finish with a point at the waist. The only difference between these two styles is that the latter is sewn on plain, and extra fulness arranged on the outer edge; whereas with the former the fulness is produced by a series of box pleats falling over the shoulder. Diagram 53 illustrates the mode of cutting Figure 40. Take the back and forepart, and put the shoulder together as illustrated by dotted lines at C; now mark the point on waist, back, and front, to which it is desired it shall come, and draw line from A to C, and C to D; this will sit plain if cut so, but in order to give extra fulness make C a pivot, and sweep from A to B and D to E say 6 inches, and draft the sewing to edge from B to C and C to E, completing the outline as illustrated.

Diagram 54 is produced in a similar way, only that instead of cutting a more hollow sewing to edge, more length is given. Each box pleat will require at least 2 inches, hence we allow for two box pleats in front of shoulder seam, and two behind it, adding 4 inches from T to U and S to V, com-

pleting the outline from U to V on the round edge, to taste.

Figure 43, Diagram 55, Plate 27.

Illustrates quite a different style, for in this the Capelette is put on a short loose front, and finishes round the back scye, just as if there had been a loose roll collar with a very full fall edge. Diagram 55 illustrates the forepart and back put in a closing position at shoulder seam; point H is that where it is put over the shoulder seam. Point I is the terminating point in front, and point G is at the back scye, where it is intended the Capelette shall finish. Now, in order to get the extra fulness as illustrated, make H a pivot, and sweep from I to J, 6, 8, or 10 inches, according to the amount of fulness desired; the more fulness desired, the more must be added from I to J. Repeat this process from G to F, and complete the round part to taste. This would be sewn on to the crease row of forepart from I to H, and sewn to the back from H to G, and turned over. When made from contrasting material, this gives a very stylish finish, and one which has been much patronised, though there is not the same demand for it now that there was for it a season or two ago.

Jacket Capelettes.
Figures 42 and 44, Diagrams 56 and 57, Plate 27.

Here we have two illustrations of the mode of applying these to Jackets, Figure 42 being a popular style, and produced by putting the shoulder seams together at K L, marking from M L to 6 along the crease row. M to N is the length desired; the outline is completed to taste, the three Capes, P Q R, being arranged also to taste. If it should be desired to produce more fulness on the outer edge, make L a pivot, and sweep outwards from 6 in the same manner as described for Diagram 53, making the neck, &c., more hollow. If the material is thin, this will be an improvement; but if it is heavy, it will probably be best to leave it as illustrated.

Diagram 57, Figure 44, shows a very full Cape sewn in with a collar seam of a garment fastening right up to the neck; this is produced by putting points 3 and 5 as nearly together as is consistent with getting a run to the neck, and opening points 4 to 6 according to the degree of fulness desired. This being very full, it is necessary to cut this

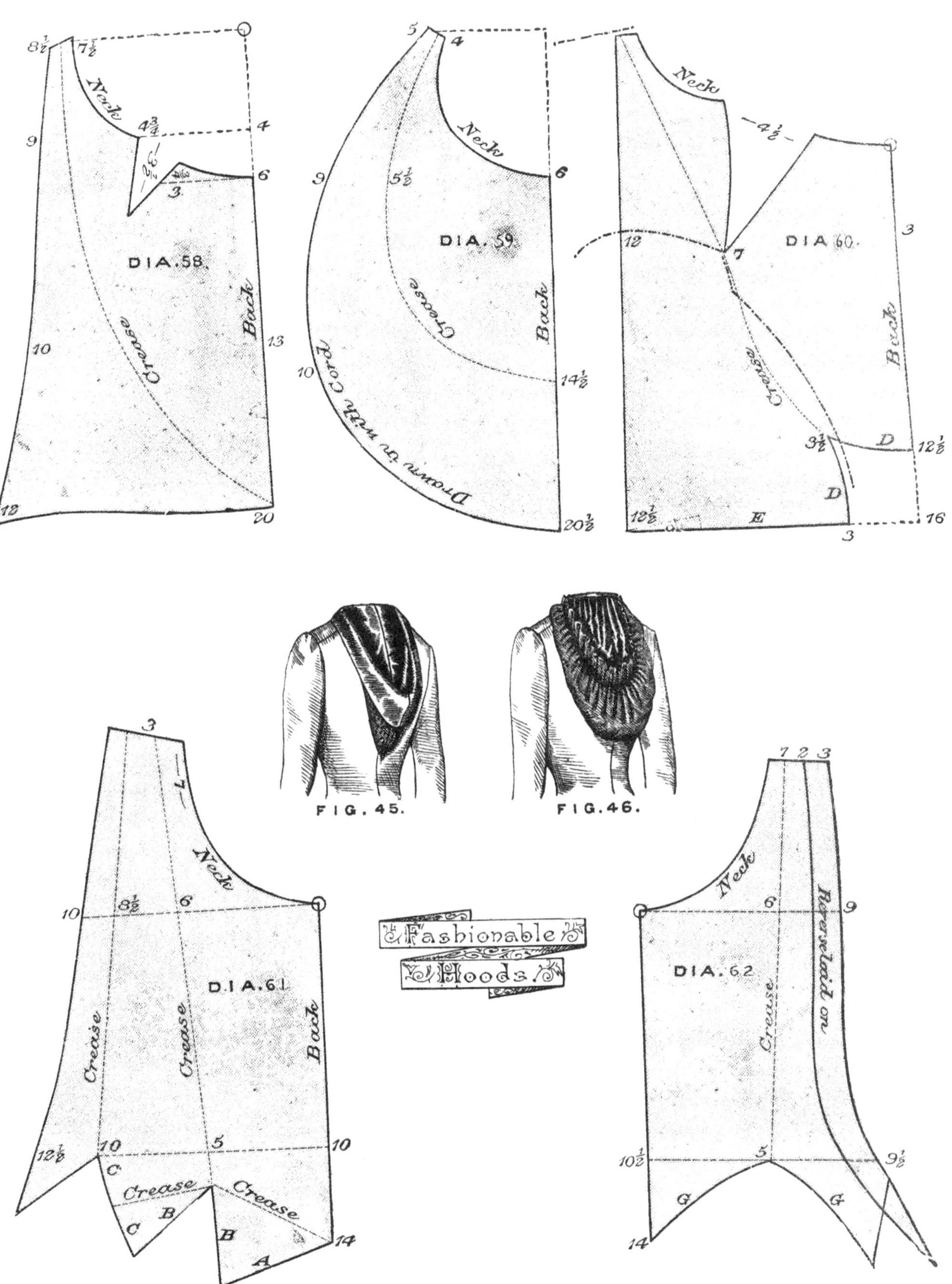
DIA. 58.
DIA. 59.
DIA. 60.
DIA. 61.
DIA. 62.
Neck
Back
Crease
FIG. 45.
FIG. 46.
Fashionable Hoods
Drawn in with Cord

rather fuller than the Circle Cape. 7 8 running forward from a line drawn straight through from 1 to 2, the outline of the bottom edge being completed to taste, a point being arranged in the front in the illustration, which might be repeated at the back, or that part might be left rounded.

HOODS.
Diagrams 58 to 62, Figures 45 and 46, Plate 28.

Now that these adjuncts to Overgarments are so very popular for both ladies and gentlemen, nothing could form a more appropriate conclusion to this section, especially as so few people really understand how to cut and make them. These we are now enabled to place before our readers, and embrace the leading styles which are now being worn. Full-size patterns of these can be obtained at our Office, as well as any other style our customers may require, provided sufficient instructions, or better still, an illustration is sent with the order. Anyone, however, possessed of ordinary intelligence can reproduce those illustrated by the use of the inch tape, square, &c.

Diagram 58, Figure 45, Plate 28,

Is decidedly the most popular type, and is pretty generally known under the name of the Jelly-Bag Hood. It falls open, as it were, and shows the lining to advantage, which is a feature worthy of notice when a stylish effect is desired; and as the materials used for lining vary so much, embracing silks, satins, plush, velvet, &c., there is no lack of material by which, in this way, to relieve and brighten a garment which would otherwise look very heavy and dull. Hoods are really an arrangement to cover the head, and this type is one of the most suitable for this purpose, being one of the roomy class. The diagram will readily explain how it may be produced. The back is cut on the crease or double edge of the cloth, and the bottom part, as from 20 to 12, is sewn together, the cut at neck from ¾ to 4¾ is sewn up, either to a band with holes to fasten to buttons placed round the neck, or it may be sewn in with the collar seam. The former plan is the one more generally adopted, as it allows for the Hood being detached if desired.

The Round Hood, Diagram 59, Figure 46, Plate 28,

Is a type of Hood not nearly so popular as it was formerly, when it formed part of the lady's Circular Cloak. It is cut on the crease down the back as the former one, and a cord is put into a hem run all round the outside and drawn in, forming a series of gathers, which gives it a rather graceful appearance. It is well to remark that this style should never be cut smaller than our diagram (except for a child), and in many cases a larger one would be. decidedly preferable. The neck of this may be sewn in the same way as that described for the last, and is, in fact, a method applicable to them all.

The Cape Hood, Diagram 60, Plate 28.

Is very stylish looking, and, when not in use, lies quite flat across the back from shoulder to shoulder, being double at that part. As will be seen, it is produced by the back and forepart being placed with their shoulder points touching, and a V taken out at neck, equal to ¼ of breast; the bottom part is at D, being rounded so as to give it a circular appearance at the bottom. It should be cut with the back on the double, and points D D and 3, 12½ sewn together, and the bottom, as at E, sewn to the corresponding part of the other half.

Fancy Pointed Hood, Diagram 61, Plate 28,

Is quite a distinct style from any of the foregoing, and is arranged more with the idea of producing effect than for use; still, it can be turned to practical use if desired. This style is a very favourite one with ladies, and allows full scope for the exhibition of any fancy lining desired. It lies quite flat with two points at bottom, and pointed revers which can be faced with any contrasting material. The back is cut on the double; B B is sewn together, and those parts as from 14, A C C to 10 are joined to the corresponding parts on the other side. Point 10, just above C, then lies on the top of 10 on the back. There is a point at 14, another just above it by the crease edge, between C C and the pointed revers 10, 12½ turning back and forming a most effective Hood.

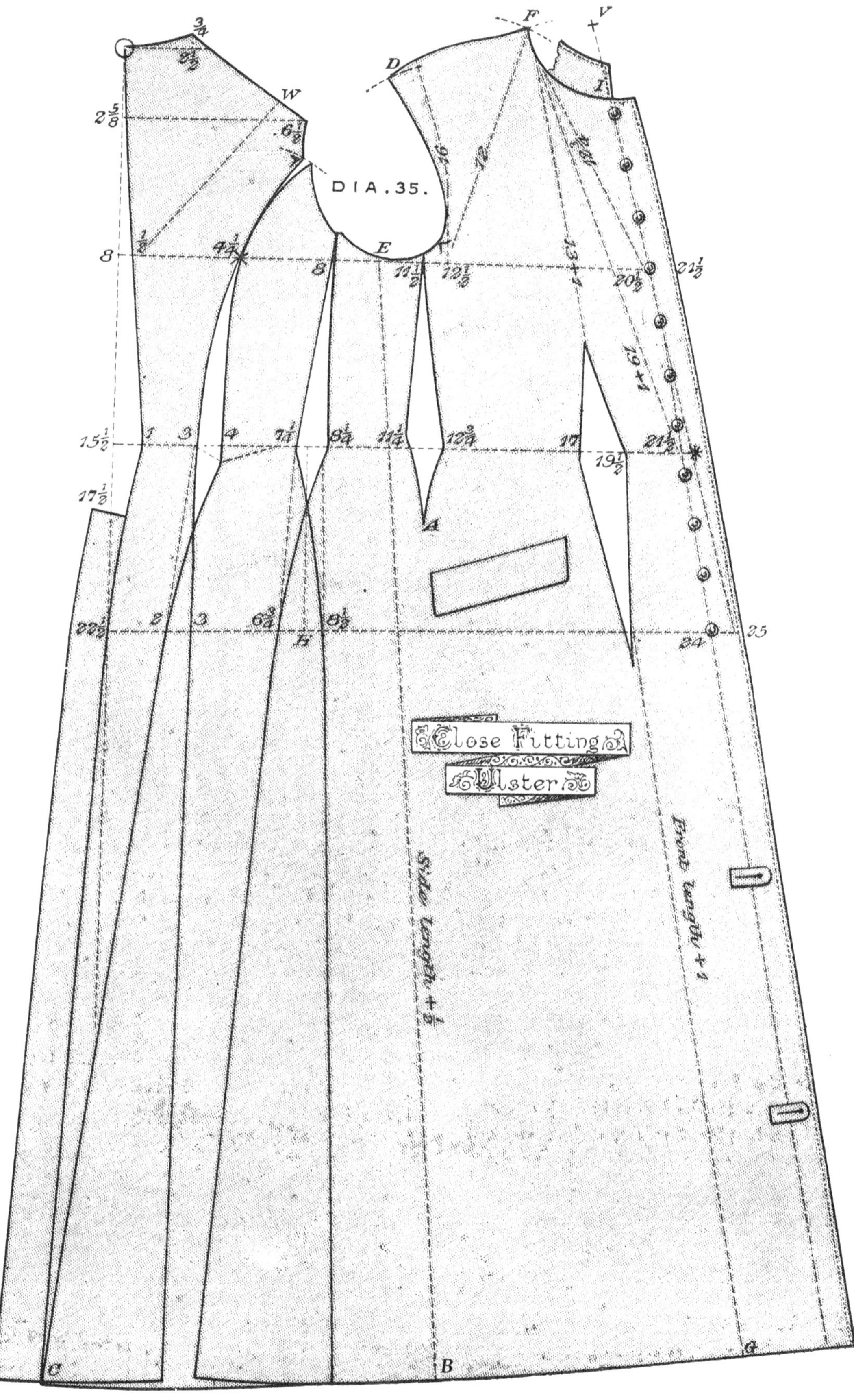

DIA. 35.
Close Fitting Ulster
Side length + ½
Front length + 1

Is another of the same type, having only one point at bottom, and revers sewn on to a hollow edge at 3, 9, 9½, going off to point, and overlapping each other at bottom. This forms a very pretty Hood, and is not quite so complicated as the last one.

Ladies' Ulsters. Diagram 35, Plate 29.

We will introduce this section with the single-breasted, buttoning-through Ulster, as that probably is the style more than any other patronised by the fair sex. This section is undoubtedly one of the most important in the book, and will probably be referred to more than any of the others, for, there must be few tailors, indeed, who do not get an occasional order for a Lady's Ulster, for the ladies have become so thoroughly charmed with the style in which tailors turn out overgarments in general, and Ulsters in particular, that even though they may prefer the flimsy finery of the dress-maker for their costumes, they come to us for their garments of this class. In measuring, it is an advantage to get the full length of side as well as the full length of front from nape, in addition to the measure we have previously explained, and which it will not be necessary for us to again recapitulate, so will at once proceed to deal with

The System. Diagram 35, Plate 29.

Draw line O, 2½ O C; O to 2½ below ¾ is one-third neck; from O to 2⅝ on back seam is one-sixth natural waist; to 8 the depth of scye; to 15½ the natural waist; to 22½ the prominence of hip; and to C the full length, plus seams; come in from 15½ one inch, and draw back seam from O to 1, springing it out below through point 22½, and running through gradually as shown; curve the back neck by coming up ¾ above 2½. About 2 inches below line 2½ measure the width of back, plus 2 seams, and curve back scye slightly out to find point 6½ and then draw shoulder seam from ¾ through W. Now measure across from ½ to 20½ the half-chest measure, plus 2½ inches for making; from 20½ measure back to 12½ the across chest measure, or the average between the across chest and across bust measures; deduct the width of back neck 2½ from front shoulder, 12, and by the remainder, 9½ sweep from 12½; having done this, add ¾ inch to this 9½ making 10¼ and

sweep by that from 20½; and wherever these arcs or sweeps intersect each other, locates the neck point F, and from which measure across to V 1/3 neck, and draw breast line from V through 20½. If, however, the lady is flat at the stomach, it will be found advisable to come back ½ inch at waist, as from * to 21½ and draw the remainder of breast line from 20½ through 21½. The effect of this will be to make the front slightly round at 20½, which round must be well worked back over the breast in making up.

Now measure from ¼ at 8 to W, deduct that from the over shoulder, and by the remainder sweep from 12½ to find point D, putting the finger on the tape 1½ inches up before sweeping, as previously described; get the width of shoulder by the back, making the front ¼ inch narrower, and shape the scye as shown, keeping it as hollow as possible above 12½ and well above 8. The + at V may be made a pivot to sweep the gorge from F to I. Having thus located the various points connected with the front shoulder, we are ready to proceed with

The Location of the Seams,

And here we apply much the same method as we adopted with the Jacket; indeed, an Ulster is very little different from a long Jacket. Come back from 12½ 1 inch, and divide the distance between ½ and 11½ into 3 parts, equally or nearly so; make the back from 1 to 3 half what it is from ½ to 4¼ and shape the sideseam as shown, continuing below the waist at right angles; come in from 3 to 4 1 inch; make 4 7¼ half an inch less than 4¼, 8; take out 1 inch between 7¼ 8¼, make 8¼ 11¼ half an inch less than 8, 11¼ and take out 1¼ inches; now measure up the waist, and take out the surplus in a dart after allowing 1¼ or 2 inches for making up; the dart should be placed to run parallel with breast line, running rather towards the front at the bottom, and at the waist it should be about 2 inches from the breast line.

The Spring over the Hips.

Measure across from 22½ to 24, and see how that corresponds with the hip measure, and say 3 inches, most probably it will be small; if it is, add on two-thirds at 6¾ 8½ and one-third at 2 3. The mode of extending the various seams is to draw a line from 3 through 2 for the sidebody; square down from mid-way between 7¼ and 8¼ and put half the spring to be located there on either side of H, and then draw a line straight from 7¼ through 6¾, and from 8¼ through 8½ on either side, care should be taken at the present time to allow plenty of spring round the bottom edge. Now, if you have the length of side and front, use them to get the run of the bottom of skirt; if you have not got these measures, measure down from the waist line at side 1 inch shorter, and at front 2 inches shorter than the back. Add on a button stand all down the front of 1¼ inches. The finish of the back varies so much that it is difficult to say which is the most popular; the diagram illustrates the necessary allowance (1½ inches) for a plain pleat or opening.

Hints on Making.

A facing is generally put down the front right to the bottom, but it is not often taken through the shoulder; the body lining extends usually to line 22½ 24 at the hips, and in putting this in, care must be taken to give plenty of length over the waist. The buttons down the front are usually terminated about 24; but tabs and small buttons are often put to fasten the garment below. Carefully press any fulness there may be at the bottom termination of dart well towards the side, and any excess of room or fulness here is to be carefully avoided. The sleeve is generally pitched at the sideseam, and of course the usual care used in putting it in. If any wadding is used at any part, see that it is carefully graded away, so that its existence cannot be detected. The usual precaution of keeping the collar long in the hollow of gorge must not be forgotten, as it applies universally. We will not dwell further on the points to be observed in making, but proceed to deal with

D.B. Ulster, Plate 30,

Which illustrates a double-breasted Ulster with lapels sewn on, and foreparts cut across from the bottom of the back dart; it is really more with the view of illustrating this latter phase than any other we have drawn this diagram, for one of the worst difficulties experienced by all ladies' tailors in these garments is to get rid of the superfluous material below the waist in front, which invariably locates itself if the front edge has been kept straight, and proper provision made for the breast by means of darts. We know in practice that suppression at one

part causes fulness at another, and if that suppression is done in the form of a fish, it throws fulness both above and below, and as the breasts are usually much more prominent than the stomach, it follows as a natural consequence that there is too much material below the waist in front. There are two ways of avoiding this difficulty. The first is illustrated on Diagram 35, and is the one mostly used in this country, and consists of coming back from the straight breast line ½ an inch at the waist, and drawing it through to bottom. This method

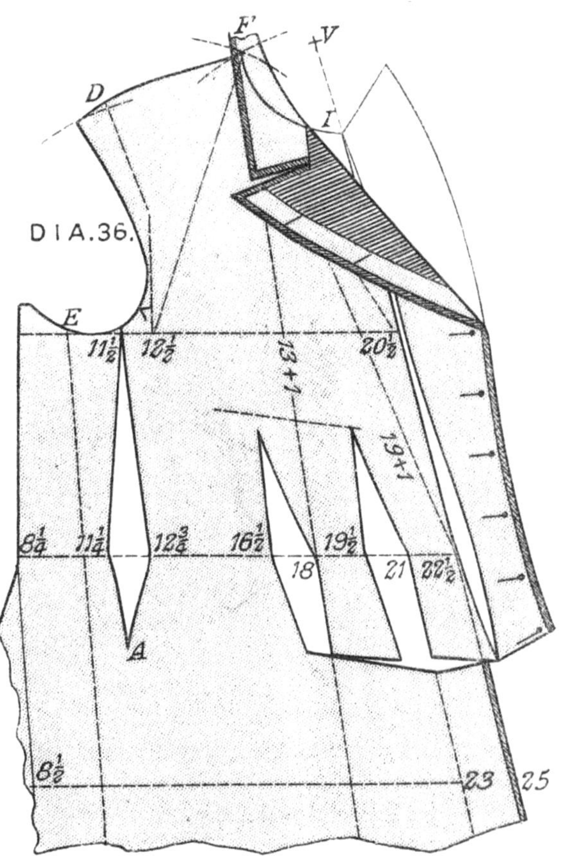

PLATE 30.

produces a slightly round front edge; but if the round is only properly drawn in and worked back, and the front edge brought to a straight line, and the fulness pressed back over the breast, it answers satisfactorily. The second method is undoubtedly the best, and is the one most used by the ladies' tailors in the West-End, and is illustrated on

Diagram 36, Plate 30.

The body part is got on exactly the same lines as

described for Diagram 35, with the exception that the front line is drawn straight through from V to 22½ and the waist then suppressed to the necessary size by means of darts. These are terminated about 2½ or 3 inches below the waist line by the foreparts being cut across in a nearly horizontal direction from the front, when the surplus material may then be passed away in the front. It is best to arrange this cut to slant slightly downwards, as it produces a better effect. The lengths on either side of the darts must be adjusted to each other, and this will produce sufficient space for pointing up the overlap beyond the centre line to meet and form a continuation of the lapel as illustrated on diagram. It will be found advisable when cutting D.B. garments of this class to spring the forepart out from the waist line downwards a trifle, taking off at the dart below 21 whatever has been added below 22½; and in cutting

The Lapel

Use the front edge as the guide for shaping the sewing-to edge, and finish to taste. There is no doubt a good deal of style may be introduced by means of the lapel, so it will be well to give it careful attention; it is the almost invariable rule to make it narrow at the waist and wide at chest. We illustrate on the diagram one of the most popular modes of finishing these. Silk facings are put on the lapels; and, as with gentlemen's coats, sometimes the binding is put on the top of the silk, and at others the silk is sewn on the top of the braid and coming to the top of the lapels. We prefer to see the facing put over the braid, but there are many of our best cutters who prefer the other way, so our readers will be able to take their choice.

In all other respects Diagram 36 is produced on the same lines as described for Diagram 35, so that it will be unnecessary for us to dwell on them here, but at once proceed to deal with some of the

D.B. Loose-fronted Ulsters.
Diagram 37, Plate 31.

Loose-fronted Ulsters of the D.B. type are very popular, and during the past season there has been considerable variation in the general style, not only as regards the style of the hips, but also in the position of the seams, and this is illustrated on the Diagram on Plate 31.

The vital points of the shoulders, scye, and breast line are all formed in the same way as we have previously described, so that we need not again repeat them, but will at once proceed to direct attention to

The Position of the Seams.

As this is always a matter of taste, it follows that any directions we may lay down regarding these must be taken as a guide, which may be varied from at pleasure. The width of back at waist is here fixed at 4 inches. This is not a proportion of anything, but merely a quantity fixed by taste, and from this point the sideseam is draughted up to the scye, and continued below the waist at right angles to 1, 5; between this and the sidebody 1½ inches are taken out, and then it becomes necessary to fix the under-arm seam; from 12½ to 10½ measure back 2 inches, and from this point square down and take out ¾ inch on either side, and complete the draught by making up the hips to measure and three inches, applying the measure about 7 inches below the waist, and letting two-thirds of the overlap required go at the underarm seam.

One other point about the seams: Give plenty of spring to the bottom; an extra inch will be on the right side, as present fashion goes. The usual width will be about 2¾ yards at the bottom of the skirt. An opening is generally left up the centre of back, and side pleats are very often arranged at the sideseams, but this is a matter for the tailor to decide in each case. The position of the pockets, as well as of the buttons, are clearly defined on the diagram, so that we can now leave the Ulster, and direct attention to

The Capes. Diagram 38. Plate 31.

These form an important feature in the ladies' garments of to-day, and impart a decided character. They are cut very full, and vary in length considerably. The method of cutting them is to take the back and the forepart, and place them with the shoulder seams in a closed position; then mark round the neck down the backseam, and down the front, arranging the front in accordance with the style desired. The Capes terminate behind the buttons, so that in our diagram about 2 inches has been cut off the front from 3 to 13. Measure off the length from 1 to 8, 10, 12, and make the front ¾ of an inch longer,

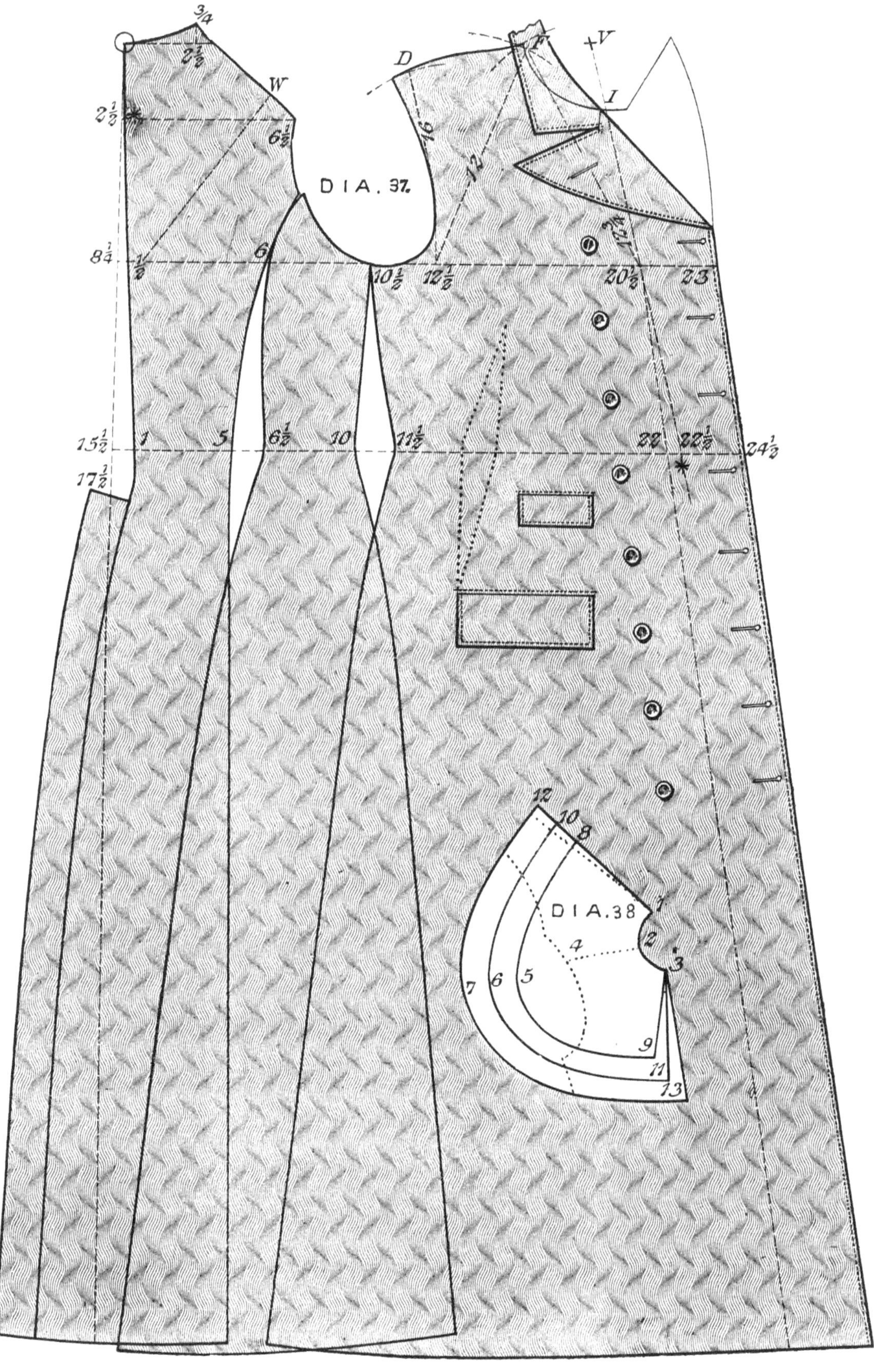

3/4
2½
W
2½
6½
DIA. 37.
D
+V
I
16
12
8¼
½
6
10½
12½
20½
23
15½
1
5
6½
10
11½
22
22½
24½
17½
12
10
8
DIA. 38
1
4
2
3
7 6 5
9
11
13

applying the measure from 2 to 9, 11, and 13. The length of the side is made 2 to 2½ inches longer than the back, measuring from 2 to 5, 6, 7. These are made up detachable, being arranged to fasten on the neck with either hooks and eyes or holes and buttons. We treat of these more fully in a later part of this work, so that we would refer our readers to that section for further details.

New Style of Driving Cape.
Plate 32.

The style of illustration here given is a new Driving Cape, the special feature of which is the combination of cape and sleeve, permitting it being worn over any garment, at the same time warm and comfortable, and also a protection from the biting winds and sleet. For driving this is doubtless an ideal garment, and is usually made from a heavy material, and frequently lined with woollen plaid. It is cut in the D.B. style, and finished at the neck either with a step and roll or panteen collar. The back is cut in the three seam style, fitting close enough to define the figure slightly at the waist. The pockets are of the half-moon shape, being a more convenient form for this style of garment. The diagrams are cut by the "C.P.G." System, with which our readers are thoroughly conversant, so we will at once proceed with the system.

Draw line at right angles to O.

O to 2½* is one-sixth of natural waist length.

O to 8¼ is the depth of scye.

O to 15½ the natural waist length, then on to the full length required.

From 15½ measure in half an inch, and draw back seam from O to ½.

Draw lines at right angles to O 2½, 8½ and 15½.

From O to 2½ is one sixth of neck 15.

Measure across width of back, plus half an inch.

Draw back neck from O to ¾, and shoulder seam from ¾ to 6½ Measure across from 8¼ to 21 the half chest, plus 2½ inches. From 21 to 13 measure back the average between the across chest and the across bust.

Sweep from 13 by the front shoulder measure minus width of back neck O to ¾.

Now add three-quarters of an inch, and sweep from 21, and where the segments intersect each other locate neck point S.

To find over-shoulder, sweep from 13 by the over-shoulder measure, minus back from 8¼ to C; and

then form front shoulder, making the width by an inch less than back shoulder. Now shape the scye as illustrated, keeping it as hollow as possible above 13, and close up at back of scye. Now draw the breast line from P through 21, but in order to avoid excessive fulness at the bottom come back from this line at waist about half an inch; and from 21 draw the breast line through 22 to the bottom. Beyond this add on amount necessary to form the double breast, varying from 2½ to 4 inches, according to the style of garment; the amount on diagram being 3 inches, then forming the lapel to taste. The width of back at the waist is made one-sixth of the breast measure; the spring over the hips is got by marking down from 15½ 14 inches, and squaring at right angles to those points, applying the same principle to the sideseam of forepart. For

The Sleevelet or Cape,

Take a sleeve pattern corresponding to the breast measurement of garment, and mark out at forearm and hindarm 4 inches, more or less according to the quantity of fulness required. Now add the round on at sleeve top, marking down from the pitches of sleeve the width of cape desired round the bottom, the quantity marked on pattern producing an average width.

To produce the collar, which is of the panteen shape, O to 6½ half the size of neck; 3½ midway between O 7½; O to 1½ and 1 to 2½ the depth of stand and fall required; and complete in all other respects as diagram.

Varieties of Ladies' Ulsters.
Plate 33.

We must first thoroughly understand how to infuse the principles of fitting the figure; and having done this, to vary according to the fashion desired. It is now a generally acknowledged truth that the ladies' tailor must do something more than fit the body. The seams must be located with due regard to harmony and proportion, and, whenever possible, going over the prominences and hollows of the body; for then plain sewing noly is necessary, whereas as soon as the seams are placed on either side of a prominence, then that part which goes beyond the prominence must be fulled on in order to get the receptacle for it in the proper place, but this we have dealt with in the letterpress referring to Diagram 35.

The New
Driving Coat
with
Bell Sleeves
DIA. 2.
N
30
DIA. 3.
2½
1½
1
7½
3¾
34
2½
2½
C
6½
H
P
E
8½
15½
6 7
13
21 24
22 25
DIA. 1.

Then we have to consider our customers' tastes and wishes, for we must remember we are making the garment for them, and as it must always be our aim to please them, we should lay ourselves out to understand what *they* wish; and though customers will sometimes ask for garments quite unsuitable to their form, still, if they have fully made up their minds, the best course for us to adopt will be to modify the style in such a way as to make it as far as possible in harmony with the figure. It is in this way the tailor with taste and artistic talent shows his skill, in sending forth his customers in becoming garments. When they come to him with their minds fixed on a certain style, if it is unsuitable, they can modify it by the material and trimming; or, if they have decided on material, he can reduce the unbecoming nature of the pattern by the infusion of a style having an opposite tendency. The styles we have selected to illustrate the varieties of Ladies' Ulsters are the Loose-fronted D.B. and the Cross-over Front. The former is very popular just at present, as we have previously noted in describing Diagram 37. It will be noticed the fish is omitted in this diagram from the forepart at waist. But when it is desired to have the garment very close-fitting at the side, a fish is taken out as per dotted lines; and when dealing with a figure with prominent breasts, it will be very advantageous in providing extra room at that part. We should, however, advise this to be left till the trying-on, as it does not suit all types alike. Then the one side can be pinned up on the figure, and the judgment brought to bear as to which produces the effect desired in the best way and arrange accordingly.

The Cross-over Front. Diagram 40.
Plate 33.

Is a style which seems more than likely to become a prominent feature in fashionable Ulsters. When trimmed with fur, as shown on our illustration, it is very effective. The diagram is self-explanatory in this case, and shows how the overlapping part is added on; and though these garments are generally made close-fitting, still a moderate looseness at the waist rather adds to than detracts from their beauty. The under forepart is generally cut to the breast line only, and a series of hooks and eyes put down to fasten it at that part, so than an ornamental clasp or button at the side will be quite sufficient to fasten it. This will be readily understood by a reference to the figure and diagram. We will now direct attention to the

Variations in the Back, Diagram 39, Plate 33,

Necessary for Dolmans and Winged Cloaks. As they will form the subject of another section, a reference to Diagram 37 will show the plan adopted, viz., continuing the sideseam right through to the scye point of shoulder of back, which part is added to the sidebody when sleeves are worn under the wing, but more frequently the forepart and sidebody are cut away at the scye, when all that is necessary will be to make a mark on the back where the sidebody is to begin, in order to retain the balance. This, however, is a feature which more correctly comes within the scope of the section on Dolmans, though, of course, that is no reason why, if customers so desired it, the sideseam should not terminate at the point of, or half way across, the shoulder seam; indeed, this feature was very prominently brought out in the fashions of a few years ago, and may be revived at any time. mmThere are doubtless many other variations we might dwell on in reference to Ladies' Ulsters, but we will conclude this section by a few remarks on

Newmarket Ulsters,

In their various styles of S.B. and D.B., as they are so very popular at present. These are cut on exactly the same lines as laid down for Newmarket Jackets, and which our readers will find fully described in the section treating of Jackets. All that requires to be done is to extend the skirt to the length desired. It will always be well for the cutter to bear in mind that the ladies' Ulster does not bear the same relation to the ladies' Jacket that the Chesterfield does to the Lounge for gentlemen; on the contrary, the ladies' Ulster is in reality nothing more than a very long Jacket, preferably cut a trifle easier on account of it being often made from thicker material, and being more used in winter, when thicker underclothing is being worn.

The Russian Circular Cloak. Diagram 41, Plate 33.

The popularity of these garments during the past few years has raised them to a position of importance

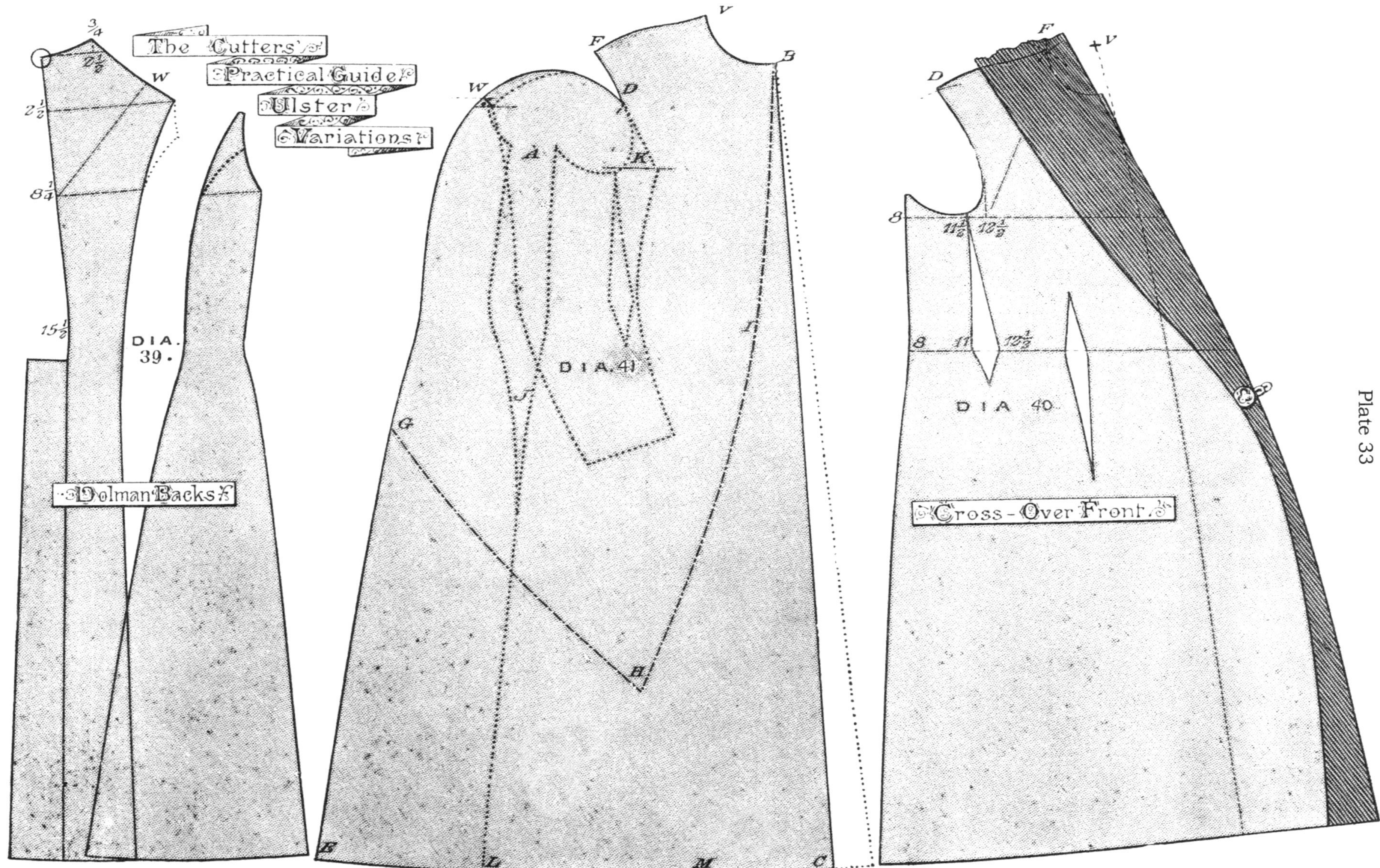
The Cutters' Practical Guide Ulster Variations
DIA. 39.
Dolman Backs
D I A. 41
D I A 40
Cross-Over Front.

in Ladies' Garments; and as they combine both warmth and comfort, it is more than likely they will continue popular for some time to come; hence we regard them as one of the most important of the various styles of Dolmans we shall deal with. They embody almost all the principles of cutting for all the various styles, but this will be easily understood as we proceed. The body part would be cut as Diagram 42, as we have previously noted, the means of drafting the Ulster, and as this diagram explains the necessary variations, all that is necessary is to describe the wing or outer forepart.

Lay the cut-out forepart and sidebody in the position shown on Diagram 41 — touching each other at bottom L, and with a space of not less than 3 inches at A; and in laying them together in this way, notice that the balance is not disturbed, or, in other words, see that the sidebody is not passed up ordown. Now take the sleeve. Having arranged the sleeve head in the style it is desired the sleeve head of wing shall be, that is, plain or puffed, lay it with the forearm overlapping the forearm pitch about 1 inch as at K, and then bring the hindarm to the back pitch W, and the outline of wing may then be drawn, starting from B to V to F and D by the forepart, from D to W by the sleeve, and adding on whatever amount was lost to the back at the hindarm pitch, in continuing it up to the shoulder seam; now come down from W to G, and it will be found preferable to fill up the hollow above G a trifle, say half an inch; then continue on to E and across the bottom from L to C. The forepart may be completed from C to B to taste, the dotted outline representing the meeting edge-to-edge line, cutting it away more or less from the front of forepart as fancy or customer's wishes may dictate, but it is well to remember there is a tendency for them to appear more cut away than they really are, owing to the movements of the arms.

Hints on Making Russian Cloaks.

The one great feature in these garments is to get them to fit nicely over the shoulders, with sufficient room, and yet to fit snug in at the hollow of waist. To secure this, the balance must be carefully preserved, sewing point W to the hindarm pitch of back, and carefully distributing any fulness there may be from W to D in the same way as for a sleeve; the shoulder and gorge, F V B, are sewn to the back and collar at the same time as the fore-part, and in like manner the sideseam from W to E is sewn to the back with the sidebody. Tabs should be placed about 14 or 15 inches up from C, by which to secure the wing to the forepart, or otherwise, in boisterous weather, these have a very "fly-away" tendency. As we have previously stated, the under or body part is usually the same as an Ulster with sleeves, or with the armhole cut away to the waist, but sometimes a strip is cut off the forepart, as from V to M, Diagram 41, and this is secured to the wing, an opening being left about I for the hands to come through; but this is only one of

The Variations of Style

That may be introduced. The dot-and-dash line, G H I, shows another style which has found much favour, especially with ladies who objected to the weight of the Russian Cloak, whilst it also has a fanciful appearance which readily lends itself to various styles of ornamentation.

SECTION NINE.

Dolmans and Cloaks.

To the inexperienced ladies' cutter, Dolman Capes, and the like garments, are probably a greater source of anxiety than any other styles; and yet, if the principles on which they are cut are but once grasped, they are as easy to cut as the simplest garment worn. We find young men can better grasp these by cutting one out, basting it together, and trying it on a figure of the same breast measure as the pattern is cut for. We seldom cut them out by system, that is, by drawing lines and angles, for they are generally worn as part of a garment, and as such must necessarily be made to harmonise with the parts it has to be worn with; hence, we invariably use the parts of the pattern they will be worn in connection with, such as the forepart, sidebody, and sleeve, to draft them out by. This will be best understood by following the arrangement we will describe.

The body part of these may be cut exactly the same as the Ulster, with one exception, viz., the sideseam running into the scye point of shoulder, instead of about two inches below; the scye may be

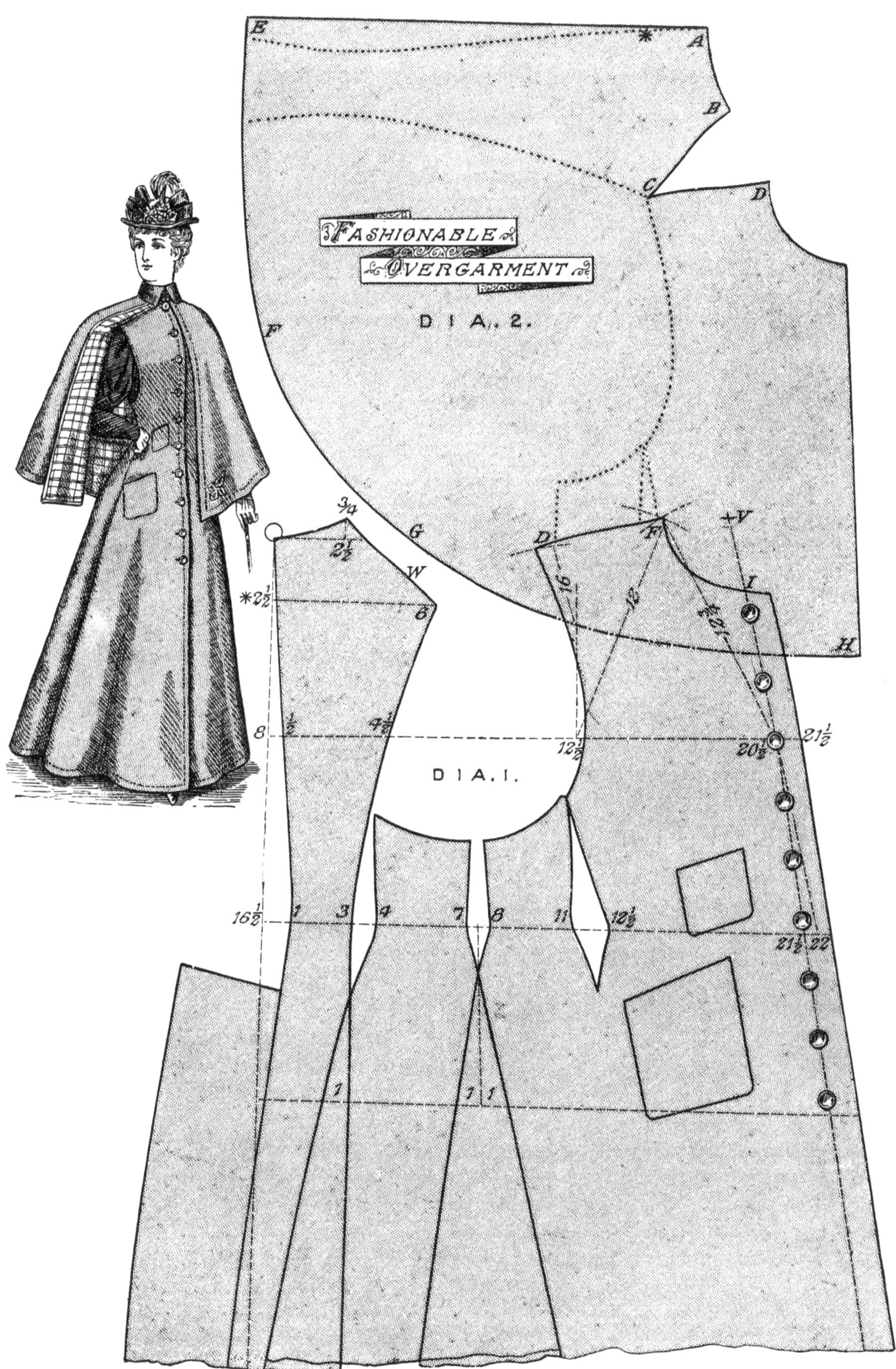
FASHIONABLE
OVERGARMENT
DIA. 2.
DIA. I.

made in close-fitting, and sleeves added in the usual way, if so desired.

We will now briefly describe the cutting of one of these without sleeves.

Diagram 1, Plate 34.

Illustrates the cutting of the bodypart of figure on Plate 34, and in its general features it is arranged on the same lines as we describe elsewhere, so we will merely note the points of difference.

It may be desirable to allow an extra half inch for making up, though this by no means necessarily follows; indeed, it would only be necessary when the garment was desired to fit easily.

The shoulder of both back and forepart is cut the usual width in the diagram, though in actual practice they are sometimes made fully 1 inch narrower. This, of course, is not important, as there are no sleeves.

The scye is deepened from 4 to 5 inches. The method of doing this is extremely simple, and a reference to the diagram will fully explain it. It will be well when cutting out the back to put a mark where the sidebody joins it, or the balance may be affected to the spoiling of the fit.

The spring over the hips is found in the draft by letting the sidebody overlap the forepart 2 inches on the level of hip, the sidebody also overlaps the back 1 inch. From these points the spring of the skirt is obtained.

The position of the patch pockets are shown on the diagram, as well as on the figure. A good guide for the top of these is about 4 inches below the waist line for the lower ones, whilst the ticket pocket may be placed as much above.

The pleats at the bottom of the back usually start about 2 inches below the level of the waist. Fully 3½ inches should be allowed for these, and if more than one is required it will be necessary to allow the same quantity on the side of back and the back of the sidebody.

The full length of these garments generally extend to within an inch of the bottom of skirt; indeed, some customers have them to cover their dress skirts. Our diagram does not extend to the full length, but it will be an easy matter to continue the run of the various seams to any length desired.

Capes. Diagram 2, Plate 34.

The bulk of the Capes which go with these garments are cut on the half-circle plan, which means that the entire Cape when laid flat takes the form of a half circle.

The method of arranging them is to take the cut out of back and lay it down in the way illustrated by dotted lines, the back of Cape at neck agreeing with the neck of pattern, and at waist being 1 inch away from the hollow of waist.

Take the forepart pattern and let the shoulder points touch at C, and arranging the opening at B D about 3 or 4 inches or so, that the front of Cape is at right angles to the back.

The length of the Cape is found by measuring from A to E by length desired, plus ½ inch; at C to F and C to G by 2½ inches less than A E of back. At front D H is made 1 inch more than A E, unless it is desired to point downwards in the front, in which case it becomes a matter of style.

The front of Cape is frequently made up with buttons and tabs, and sometimes they button through. Our diagram does not allow for this latter method.

Pockets are occasionally inserted in the lining of the Capes, which serve the double purpose of being receptacles for gloves, &c., and also of enabling the wearer to keep the Cape in position in boisterous weather.

The front of the body part does not usually button through to the bottom, but in order to keep the garment from blowing open, a couple of tabs and buttons are placed inside so that they may be used if so desired

The fronts are not intended to fit the figure closely in the front, though they define the form closely at the back and sides.

Diagrams 43 and 44. Plate 35.

The Yoked Cape was for a considerable time very popular. In cutting these it is far more a question of the infusion of style and ease than fit, consequently a reliable Block Pattern forms the best basis of operation.

Diagram 44, Plate 35,

Shows how the yoke is cut; the back and forepart are placed with the shoulder seams together, and when in that position mark those parts outlined by W, O, 1, 2, V, comprising the back, gorge and front. And now comes the part where all the taste

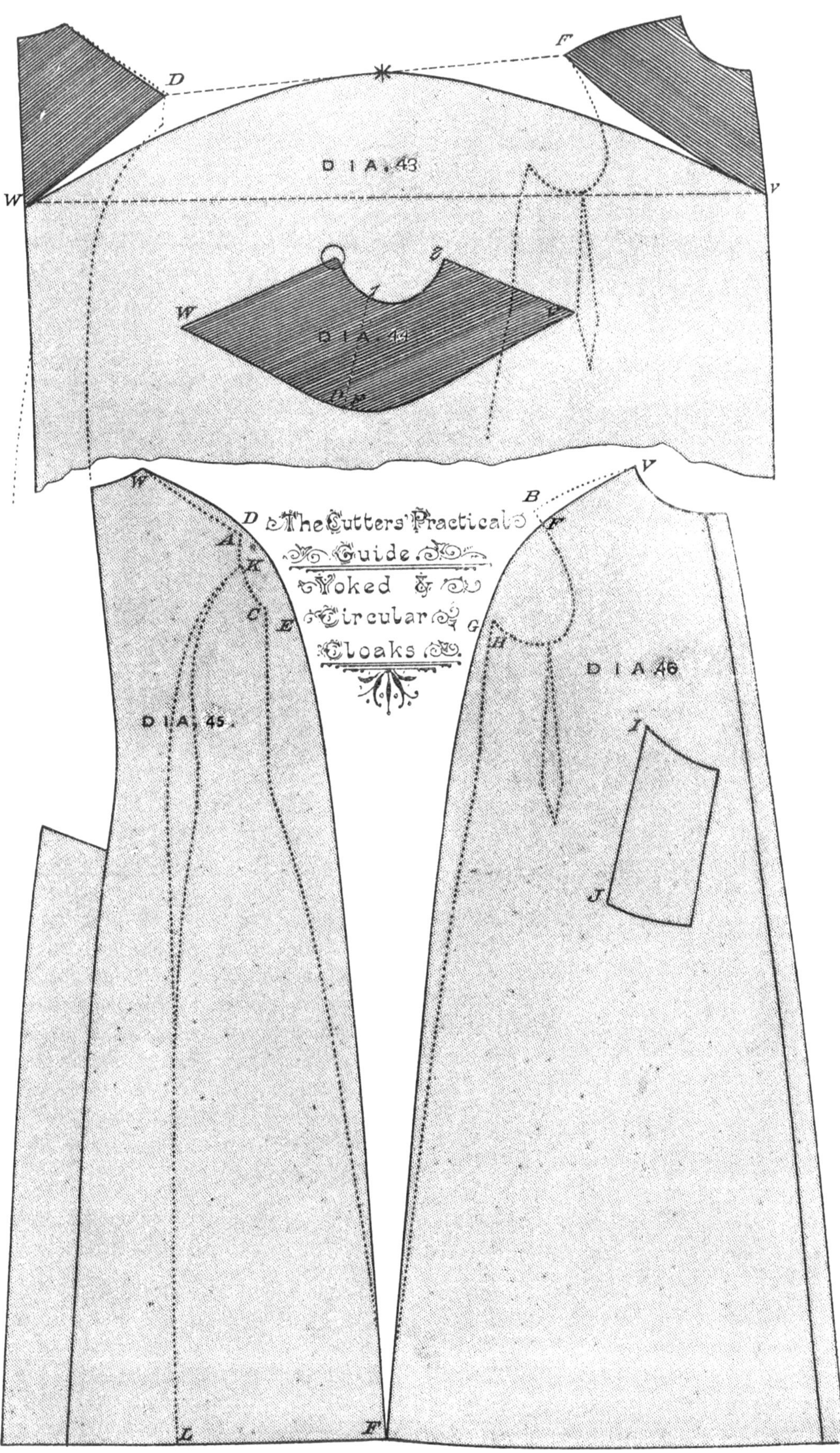

D I A. 43
D I A. 44
The Cutters' Practical Guide
Yoked & Circular Cloaks
D I A. 45.
D I A. 46

may be displayed, for certainly the outline of the bottom part and the length allows ample scope for the designer's skill. Some make them very pointed, and to reach down to the waist; others keep them short and round both back and front, whilst others give extra length to the front, consequently we cannot lay down any definite rule in this direction. In the style illustrated on Diagram 44 the yoke is made pointed back and front, starting at the depth of scye on the back at W to shoulder point D of back, and then from the corresponding point of front shoulder and to the depth of scye line of forepart V. These are generally cut without a shoulder seam, but if any improvement can be made in the run of the pattern or for any other purpose, we see no reason why a shoulder seam should not be introduced. These yokes are very frequently made either of velvet or else ornamented very richly with braid, and there can be no doubt they make a very stylish feature in these garments, which combine a taking style with all the comforts of the more "grandmotherly" sort.

The Bodypart, Diagram 43, Plate 35,

Is merely a straight piece of material with the top part rounded off so as to adjust it to the yokes. The width from W to V depends to a large extent on the substance of the material; to infuse the same appearance of fulness in a garment made of thin material, these must be cut much wider than would be necessary for a cloth, for which we should advise W to V to be about 36 to 40 inches. The same width is generally retained to the bottom, though in the event of a very thick material being used, it would be as well to slope both back and front a little, in which case the distance from W to V may be considerably reduced.

The adjustment of length (Diagram 43) is often a puzzling detail in these garments, but it is really a very simple matter. Draw line W V, and place the back on this line with the depth of scye line resting on it; then take the forepart and repeat the same operation. Now draw a line from the two shoulder points D and F, and at * (which is midway between D and F) make the top of the round; but if a large amount of puff is desired to the shoulder, extra round must be added above *; the full length may then be adjusted by measuring down from top of back in the usual way, allowing for seams where consumed. It will, of course, be understood our

diagram does not extend to the full length, that varying from 40 to 50.

Most of our readers will doubtless understand the details of making these garments — that the body part is fulled on to the yoke all the way round, the back gathered in very much at the waist, and tied in with a waistband usually made of ribbon, and that the yolks are usually the only part lined, except where the front edge is faced with silk. The body part is omitted when these are worn very long.

The Circular Cloak or Plain Cape

Now claims our attention. It is a garment largely used by nurses, elderly ladies, and others; and from the demand for patterns of this kind coming at regular intervals, we are disposed to regard it as a garment that is never out of fashion; and it will doubtless be in the recollection of many of our readers, that some four or five years ago they were the most popular of ladies' overgarments, indeed, the Russian Circular Cloak is only an adaptation of this garment. There are many degrees of fulness to which these may be cut, but the style we illustrate on our diagram is as close as we should ever advise, and from this it will be easy to deviate in the matter of extra room.

Diagram 45, Plate 35,

Shows how the back is cut. Take the Block Pattern of the back and sidebody of an Ulster, letting them just touch at the top of sideseam K, and the bottom L. The back seam and neck may be drawn exactly the same as the back, but in order to get the seam to come on to the top of the shoulder, it will be advisable to come up from A to D about 1 inch; C to E is from 2 to 3 inches, and draw sideseam by W D E F; mark off the length to agree with the customer's measures, and arrange the finish of the pleats in accordance with the ladies' own ideas, and the back is complete.

The Forepart. Diagram 46, Plate 35,

Is produced on similar lines; what was added to the back from A to D is taken off from B to F, whilst another 1 inch is added to the sidearm at H, thus making an excess of 3 to 4 inches beyond the Ulster size in the body, that being the minimum amount necessary in a garment to be worn over the arms; the difference between the measure of chest and over

arms and chest being from 6 to 8 inches; the side-seam may then be drawn from V P, G to F. If it is desired to fasten down the fronts with holes and buttons, the usual button-stand must be left on; but when, as is often the case, these garments are lined with fur, they are made to hook and eye. Sleevelets are often placed on the forepart in some-thing of the style shown, the seam from I to J being generally hidden by some mode of ornamentation. If fur lining is required for this, a pattern of the garment is sent to the furriers, who will send you the fur all made up to size, just ready for the outside, so that the making of a garment of this class is a very simple matter. The same principle employed here will also produce a very pretty shoulder cape, if cut off about 14 or 15 inches from the neck, but this will doubtless suggest itself. mmWe will now proceed with illustration of

Inverness for Ladies.
Diagrams 1 and 2. Plate 36.

Capes have been popular so long that the diffi-culty has been to invent new styles in order to keep them fresh, and amongst the many attempts that have been made to combine the advantages of the Jacket with the ease of the Cape, none have been more successful than the style which forms the subject of our present article.

It is not a novelty in design, though in its adapta-tion of Ladies' wear there is a decided freshness; and when made from some of the light fancy materials now used for Ladies' overgarments, they have a dashing style about them which is sure to make them popular.

The System. Diagram 1. Plate 36.

The body part is cut as follows: —

Draw lines at right angles, and let O be the top corner.

O to 2½ is one-sixth natural waist.

O to 8 is the depth of scye.

O to 15 is the natural waist length.

Continuing on to full length, from 30 to 34 inches.

Draw lines at right angles to these points.

O to* 2½ is one-third of the half neck, 7½.

Draw curve of back neck by coming up three-quarters inch.

From 2½ to 6½ the width of back, plus seams.

8 to 20½ the half chest, plus 2½ inches.

Mark outwards from 15½ two inches, or more if it is required very full, and draw centre of back from O through 2 to bottom, and is usually placed on the crease.

The Forepart.

From 20½ mark back to 12½ the across chest measure.

Sweep by the front shoulder measure minus the back neck, from 12½ to find point F.

Sweep again by three-quarters inch more than the latter quantity from 21½.

Where the segments cross locate point F.

Sweep by the over shoulder measure (minus distance from 8 W of back) from 12½ as indicated by D.

Make width of shoulder about 3 inches.

Mark forward from F to V one-sixth neck, and draw breast line from V through 20½.

Draw sideseam of forepart by letting it overlap back two inches or more at waist line, and draw line from shoulder point of back through 4½.

Complete forepart by drawing scye as illustrated, and, if desired, to keep it a little closer over the hips, take out a fish of from 1½ to 2 inches as illustrated from 9 to 10½.

The Wing. Diagram 2. Plate 36.

Place the body part down, as illustrated by dotted lines, Diagram 2.

Mark down the front, round the gorge, and across the shoulder.

Make F D quarter inch less than ¾, 6½.

Draw line across back from hind arm pitch, and mark in three inches, and draw line from that point through 8.

Form sleeve head as illustrated at A, and complete shoulder.

Use * as a pivot, and sweep from 1 to 2 by the length of sleeve at hindarm, and complete straight across to the front.

This garment is easy and full, in its general character resembling the fashionable style of Cape, though it has the advantage of being more manage-able in rough weather, the forepart keeping it close to the body. Tabs are generally placed at the front of the wing to secure it to the forepart, and enable the wearer to keep it in its proper place.

Patch pockets are usually placed on the forepart, the position of these being indicated on Diagram 1.

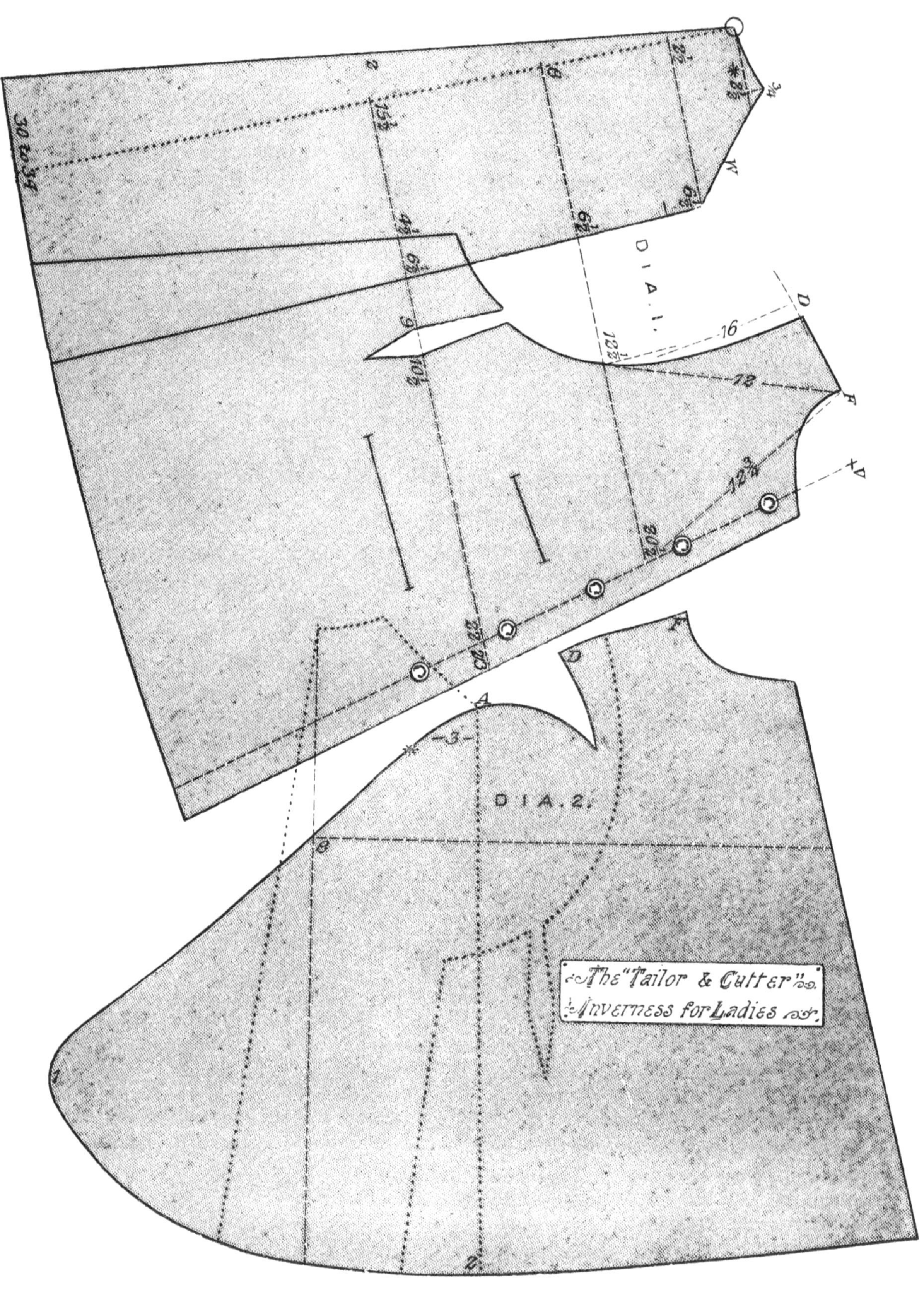

DIA. 1.
DIA. 2.
The "Tailor & Cutter"
Inverness for Ladies
D
F
16
18
12¾
30 to 34

The materials mostly used in these garments are drab Venetian or Melton, and when the wing is lined with a bright check silk lining, it makes a very stylish and attractive garment.

New Style of Ladies' Mantle.
Plates 37.

On one of our Fashion Plates we are illustrating a new style of Mantle which is rapidly acquiring a popularity amongst a certain class of ladies. It resembles to a large extent the Inverness, only it is made to outline the figure closely at the back of waist. The bottom of the back is finished with one box pleat and two side pleats, and thus providing fulness at the bottom of the back skirt. The neck is finished with a Panteen collar, under which is attached a hood. This is generally made detachable, the mode of fastening it being either hooks and eyes or holes and buttons.

The garment is generally made up with large armholes, and consequently no sleeves. This, however, is optional, and if sleeves are desired, a close scye is arranged and an ordinary sleeve inserted. mmThe wing is generally lined with a bright silk, and this material is also used for lining the hood. By these means a brightness is added to the garment.

Diagram 1, Plate 37,

Illustrates the cutting of the body part.

Draw lines at right angles to O.

O to 2½ is one-third neck, mark up ¾ inch, and shape back neck.

O to *2½ is one-sixth natural waist.

O to 8 is depth of scye, to 15½ natural waist, to 30 full length.

Hollow back at waist 1 inch, and from back seams as shown.

*2½ to 6 is width of back.

1 to 3½ is 2½ inches, and complete back.

to 20½ half-chest plus 2 inches.

20½ to 12½ the across chest measure.

Sweep by 12½ from front shoulder less back neck to find F.

Add ¾ inch to this, and sweep again this time from 20½.

Find point D by sweeping by the over-shoulder measure, ½ W.

F to V one-third neck, and draw breast line from V through 20½.

Shape scye as illustrated to within 1 or 2 inches of waist.

Suppress the waist 1 inch between back and sidepiece, and sidepiece and forepart, allow the spring over hips, and complete the forepart, as illustrated on diagram. Cut the various parts out, and chalk round them as a basis for

Diagram 2, Plate 37.

This shows how to produce the wing.

The front, the neck, and the shoulder are drafted the same as the front of forepart of body. A line is drawn from 6 through 8, and the sleeve head is formed as illustrated from 2 to 7. Line 1, 2 is drawn parallel to 8, 12½ from the ordinary back pitch.

2 to 3 is same length as hindarm of sleeve; use 2 as a pivot, and sweep from 3 to 4.

Continue across from 4 to 5 straight.

If more fulness is desired in wing, raise point 8.

In sewing this to the body part, the shoulder is sewn in with the back and forepart.

There is a fair amount of fulness between 2 and 7, and this must be distributed as an ordinary sleeve.

The wing follows the sideseam of the back, and at the bottom the sidepiece is joined in to the ordinary seam, care being taken to preserve the balance.

The Hood. Diagram 3. Plate 37.

These portions of ladies' dress are really intended to be worn over the head, but it is the exception for them to be used in that way, and are really more worn now as an ornament.

In cutting them, both uses have to be borne in mind, so that the practical and the ornamental may be combined.

One of the simplest methods is to take the back and lay it down as per dotted line of Diagram 3, and leaving 1 to 1½ inches behind the centre of back at D. Make A to D about 1 inch less than the natural waist, and D to E rather less, say 1 inch less than A D.

Follow the curve of back neck round from A to B, making it half neck. Make C B about 2 inches, and complete outline of hood as shown. A D would be cut on the crease, D E seamed together, and C E left open, the neck being secured at A B under the collar.

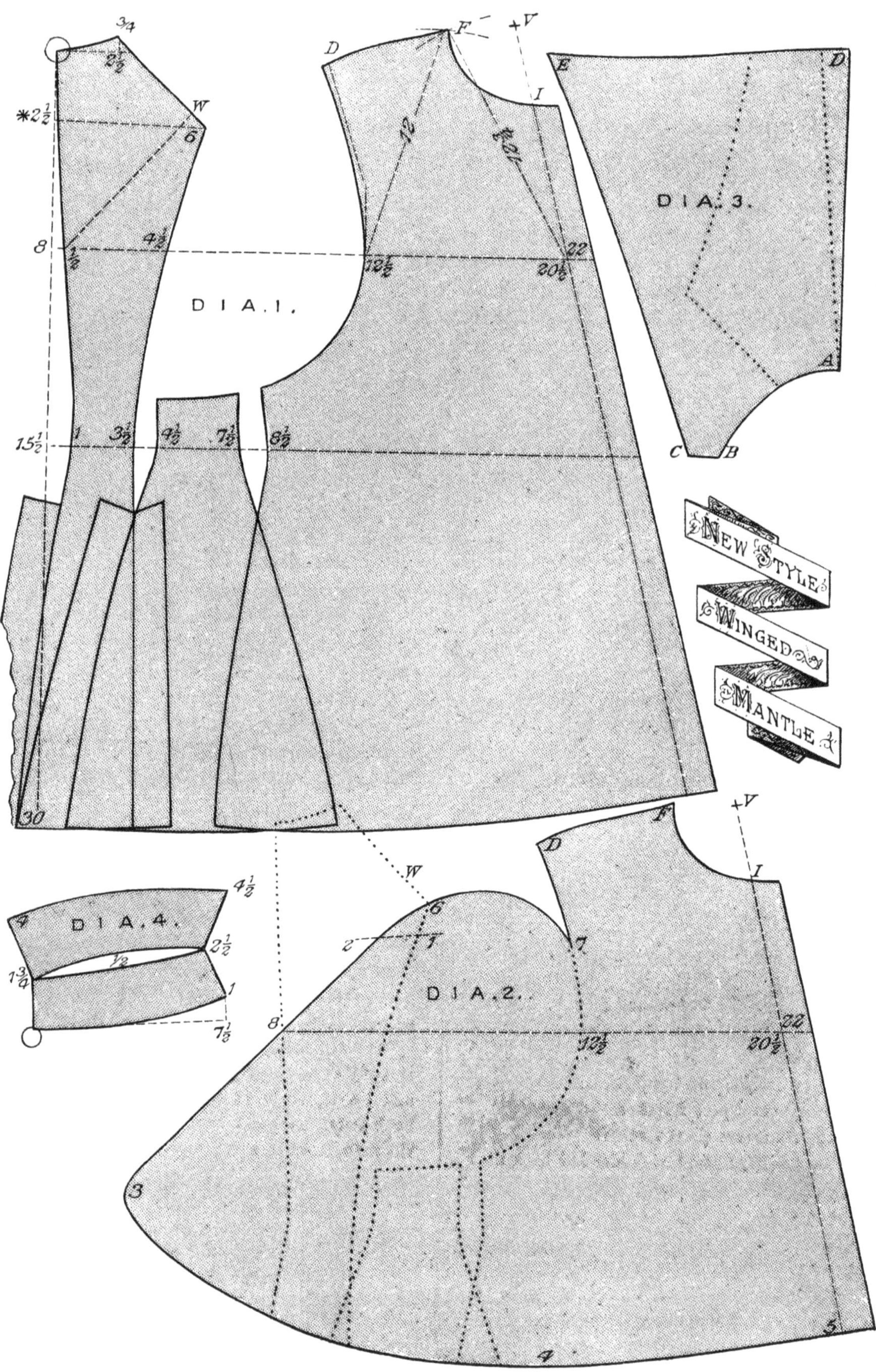

3/4
2½
W
*2½
6
8
½
4½
D I A. I.
15½
1
3½
4½
7½
8½
30
D
12
F
+V
I
R2L
22
12½
20½
E
D
D I A. 3.
A
C
B
New Style
Winged
Mantle
4½
D I A. 4.
4
2½
1¾
½
1
7½
W
6
2
1
D
F
+V
I
7
8
D I A. 2.
12½
22
20½
3
4
5

Diagram 4 illustrates the cutting of the Panteen collar, which, as will be seen, is practically two stand collars, the one deeper than the other, the deeper one being fastened tovthe upper edge of the one secured to the neck of the garment as an ordinary stand collar.

In making up these garments the fronts would usually be made to button through, whilst the wing might either be made to fasten in the same way, or cut away from the front so as to show the body part. In this latter case it will be desirable to attach arm bands to the front, so that the front may be kept in its place should the weather prove boisterous.

Patch pockets are very popular for these garments, but in this every customer must be consulted, as some may prefer not to have any pockets.

SECTION TEN.

Sleeves.
Diagrams 63 to 73. Plates 38 and 39.

The sleeve problem has been so often brought before the trade as an unsolved one, that cutters are well acquainted with the difficulties that present themselves in its consideration. Further, it is more than likely the stern realities of daily practice have brought them experiences other than pleasant, and caused them to think a good many times over the remedies so much required. It is generally acknowledged that, to get a really perfect fitting sleeve, the scye should be located as nearly as possible at the natural juncture with the arm and body. This is imperative at the front of scye and at the bottom of scye; but with the width of back it is somewhat different, since loss of width to back can be compensated for in tlie sleeve; and when we consider the decided preference shown for narrow backs in ladies' garments, the importance of the system being arranged provide for this in its ordinary workings will at once be seen. This, we claim, has been satisfactorily accomplished in the sleeve system we are now submitting. We fully illustrate its working in regard to this feature towards the end of this section; but before our readers can consider

that, it will be necessary for them to acquire the system in its simplicity, consequently we begin with

The Jacket Sleeve

System, as illustrated on Diagram 64. The first thing we have to do is to take the cut out pattern of the body part. (Diagram 63 illustrates the scye of Diagram 1, Plate 4.) We begin by drawing a line at right angles to the depth of scye line, and touching the most backward point of the scye at 11 (see dot-and-dash line), then another line is drawn at the front of scye, and the distance these two lines are apart is the first quantity taken; this is applied to Diagram 58 by making from O to 5½ this quantity. We now wish to get the balance of the sleeve, and to do this we must locate the two pitches; the forearm pitch is always placed ¾ of an inch above the level of the scye, as at B; the hind-arm pitch may be fixed according to taste; a very good plan for Jackets and Ulsters is to fix it at the top of sideseam. The pitches located, we take the square and let either arm rest on a pitch as at A and B; now let the arm at C come forward or backward in accordance with the style of sleeve desired, always keeping the square touching these two pitches, when it will be found the more forward the square is brought the greater the distance will be from E to B, and *vice versâ*. It must always be remembered, in arranging the pitch of the sleeve, that the forward-hanging sleeve will have more superfluous cloth at top of hindarm, though it will give much more freedom than the backward-hanging one. Having arranged the square in position, note the amount from B to E, and apply this to Diagram 64 by measuring back from 5½ to 1½ and square across to 8. Now measure the scye from A to 11, and 22 to B, straight across — not round — the scye; whatever that measures, apply from 1½ to 8; from O to 4 is half this distance, which in ordinary cases finds the top of sleeve head; draw a line from 5½ to 4, and also draw a line from 22 to B of Diagram 63, and whatever the scye is hollowed from this line, as at E, add on that amount of round to the sleeve at ¾. The sleeve head may now be drawn from 5½ to 4 and 8, when the next operation is to mark off the length to elbow and full length. Measure the width of back and apply it to 8, and measure on to elbow, allowing three seams for making up, and on to full length in the same way. For an ordinary close-fitting sleeve, hollow the forearm 2 inches, then measure from 2 to 8, half the size of sleeve desired, plus two seams; in the same manner apply the width of cuff. Get the angle of cuff by squaring across from hindarm, taking the angle from elbow downwards as the guide. Draw the forearm straight from 5½ to 2, and from 2 to C, and on no account hollow it between, as an examination of the arm will at once show it to be round between elbow and wrist, and to cut a hollow to fit it is quite a mistake. Tone down the angle at 2, and the topside sleeve is complete.

To get the under sleeve, measure round the bottom of scye from A to B, and apply from 5½ in the direction indicated by 7; sweep from the elbow at 8 to get the length of hindarm, and finish as per diagram. The amount of hollow required at is got by squaring across from the forearm pitch at right angles from the square when placed to find the balance as illustrated on Diagram 63; and provided the scye is not made too deep for the figure, the amount of hollow may be gauged by the distance between the square line and the bottom of scye.

The Ulster sleeve is practically the same as the Jacket sleeve, though it may be preferable to give it a trifle extra width at the elbow and cuff; but as this is a feature always governed by individual taste, it is impossible to lay down any definite guide in this particular, except actual measurement, which plan the cutter should always adopt in all cases of doubt. The quantities marked on the diagram being the usual sizes for material of ordinary thickness.

Ladies' Bodice Sleeve. Diagram 66. Plate 38.

If our readers have thoroughly grasped the principles involved in the Sleeve System, they will soon recognise they are identical with those employed to cut the bodice sleeve. The width across the scye is used to find the distance from O, 6; the sleeves pitches are located — the forearm ¾ of an inch up from the bottom, and the hindarm, in this instance, at the second sideseam, which may, of course, be varied; but this mode is most in accordance with the views of ladies at present, the topside sleeve being made much wider than half, and consequently it will be noticed a great difference

exists in the quantity on the square when taking the balance of the sleeve; the first amount for this sleeve is 6, the second is 2½, and this, of course, makes the sleeve head very round. In locating point 5, make it rather less than half 3½, 10½; proceed with the elbow as before described, measuring from 2 to 7½* half the size the elbow is desired, plus two seams; then come out from 7½ to 8½ 1 inch, or as much as it is desired the top-side sleeve shall be wider, when, of course, a similar quantity is taken off the under-sleeve, as fiom 7½ to 6½. Point 7½ should be used as the pivot to sweep from 10½ to get the top of hindarm of undersleeve.

Puffed Sleeve Heads. Dia. 66, Plate 38, and Dia. 28. Plate 11.

Have been so very popular for some time past, that no description of a system for sleeves would be complete without an explanation of the mode of producing them. First sweep by the elbow at 8½ from 10½ in the direction indicated by dotted lines 1½ and go out from 10½ three times, or very nearly three times, the amount of puff desired, and add on an equal amount of 1ound to the top above 5, thus: suppose an extra ½ inch of round is desired to the sleeve head, add on 1½ inches as indicated by the dot-and-dash line. Some may consider this an excessive allowance, but when they remember the puff must be provided for on both sides, that is, up and down, they will at once see that twice is the least possible. quantity, and to this must be added an allowance for the hollowing tendency of fulling in the sleeve head; for whenever a part is fulled on or drawn in, the round is apparently much reduced.

Diagram 28, Plate 11, shows one style of forming puffed sleeve heads; in this diagiam the amount has been added on to the top of forearm and hindarm in some of the later diagrams we have made all the addition at the hindarm. This, however, is not very important when there is only a small amount added. mmOn this diagram we give an illustration of how to add on still more puff than is shown on either of the other diagrams.

Here, the elbow is made a pivot to sweep from 9 7; the quantity added varies from 3 to 10 inches, in this case 10 inches has been added, and a corresponding amount of round added at the top; this is perhaps an extreme illustration, but it illustrates the principle.

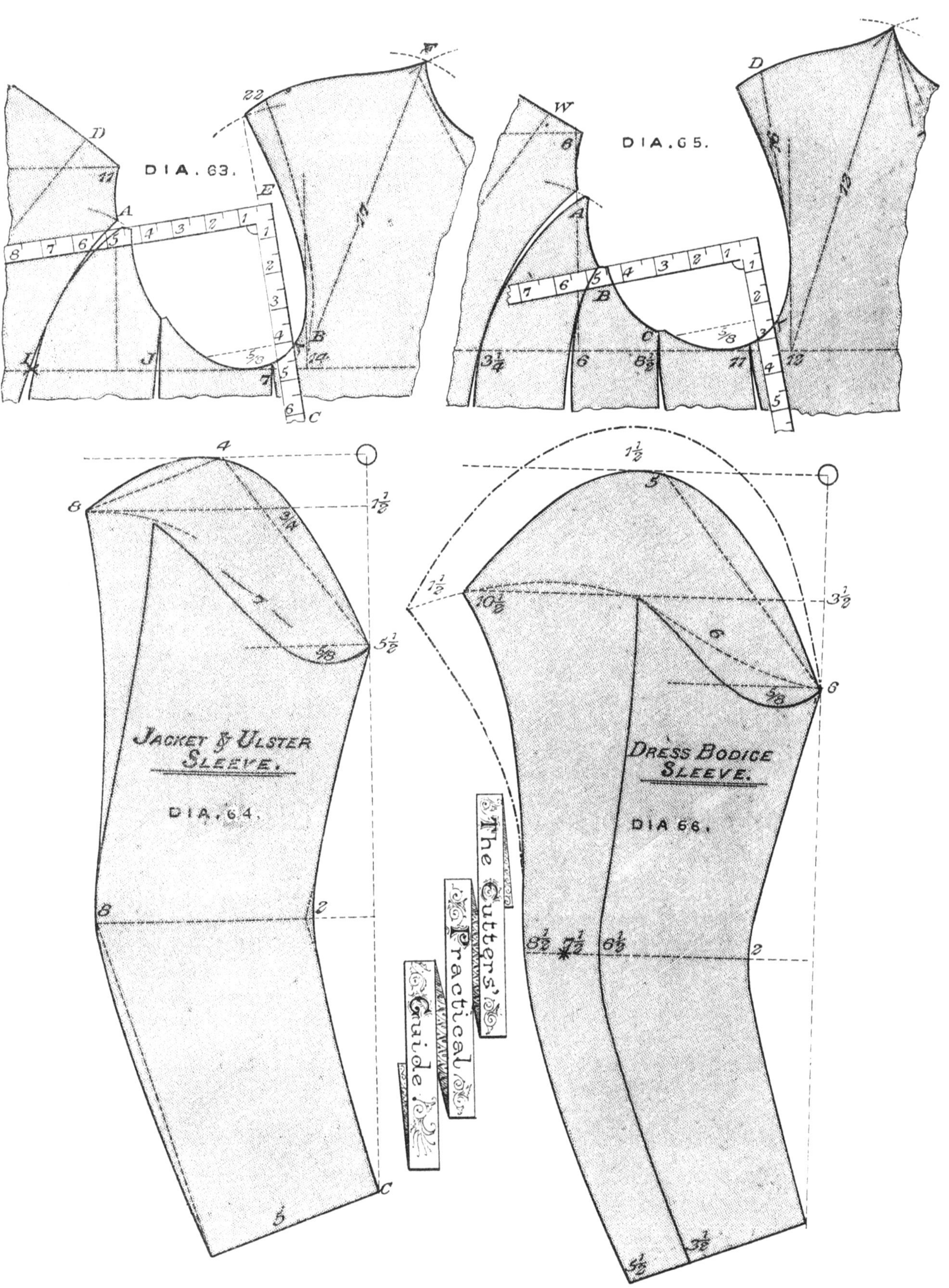

DIA. 63.
DIA. 65.
JACKET & ULSTER SLEEVE.
DIA. 64.
DRESS BODICE SLEEVE.
DIA. 66.
The Cutters' Practical Guide

The amount added, now, for jackets and ulsters is from 3 to 6 inches.

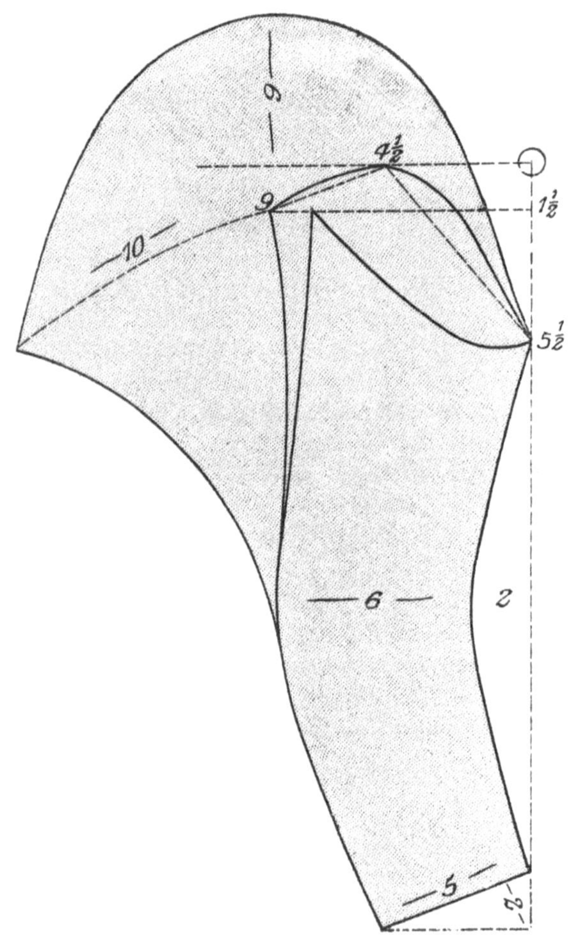

Sleeves for a Large Size Dress Bodice.
Plate 39.

In cutting sleeves for a very large size bodice, such as is illustrated on Plate 39, we should apply the system just in the ordinary way as a basis. But here we should use a little judgment, for we know ladies of this class are usually very square-shouldered and short-necked, so that it would be our duty to keep the fulness of sleeve head as little as possible, in order to prevent anything that would in the slightest degree raise the shoulders; so we should take off ¾ or 1 inch of round from the top of the sleeve head as illustrated by the dot-and-dash lines; this would enable the sleeve to be put in almost plain, and would be quite satisfactory, as the bones of this class of figure do not show any prominence at this part, the surrounding flesh making shoulders comparatively flat.

Diagram 20, Plate 8, illustrates a sleeve suitable for check material. It is produced in the same way as Diagram 64, with the top and undersides grown together at elbow, a fish being taken out under the arm to make it shapely at back. We will now give a few

Hints on Making.

If there are buttons and holes at either fore or hindarm seams, a button stand must be left on that side the buttons are intended to go on. In putting the linings in, always keep them rather long than short, and always flash baste them over the seams. In the case of the Dress Bodice Sleeve, the extra length in the hindarm of topsides must be put on at the elbow in fulness. In putting the sleeve into the scye, keep it close round the back scye as from A to C, Diagram 65, keep it fair round the bottom from A to W, and begin the fulness a little below D, and terminate it well above the forearm pitch.

If there is a moderate amount of fulness to go in the sleeve head, it may be drawn in with a running thread and pressed away before the sleeve is put in; but if there is more than can be successfully arranged in this way, put it in in little pleats, and if the sleeve be desired to appear puffed, do not open the seam at sleeve head, which would press it flat, and so destroy the end in view. A judicious use of canvas or horsehair, or even a little roll of cloth or wadding, will be a great assistance to produce a good puffed sleeve head.

The Sleeve Problem.
Diagrams 69, 70 and 71. Plate 39.

The problem which has puzzled the profession during the past fifty years more than any other is simply this: how to compensate in the sleeve for variations in the width of the back; and though in practice the difficulty has been invariably surmounted, yet when the various processes have been tested theoretically, they have all been more or less deficient in meeting the self-evident needs; and the measure of success their authors have achieved has doubtless been largely due to the elasticity of the material and the judicious manipulation that the workmen have put into the garment.

Let us take a glance at Diagram 69, and see the varying width of backs marked 8, 9, 10. These represent backs of an inch difference in the width — 9 is the normal, 8 the wide, and 10 the narrow. Now it is evident that when the arm rests at the

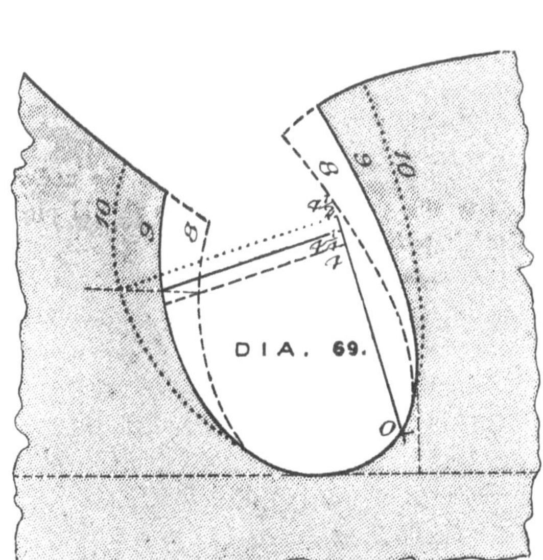

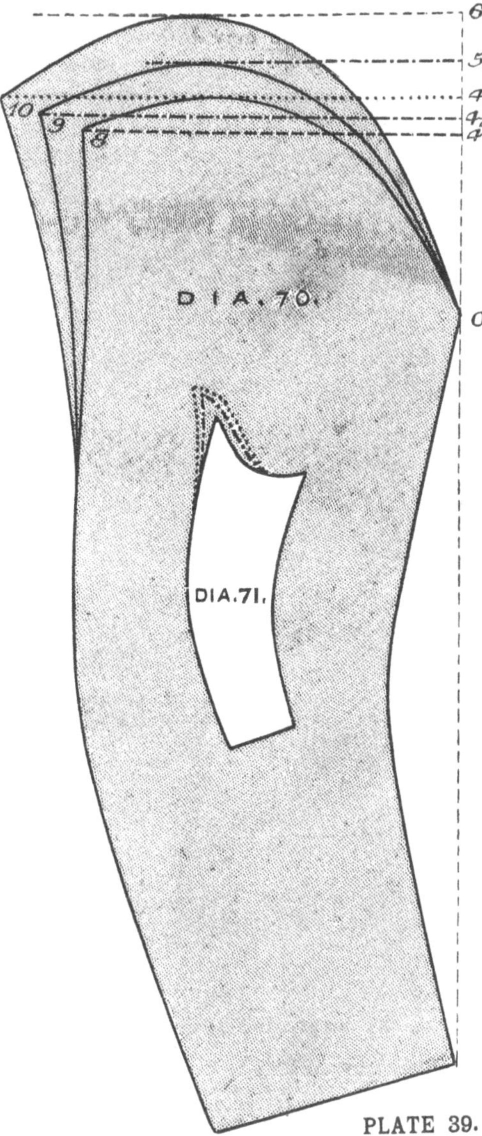

side, this variation is one of width or circumference from centre of back to centre of chest, as well as length from the gorge over the shoulder to the wrist, for a wide or narrow back invariably means a wide or narrow shoulder; but when the arm is raised as it is when the customer is being measured for the length of sleeve, what was circumference becomes at once length; hence whatever is lost to the back must be compensated for in both length and width, and this the system of itself works out admirably, forming the sleeve for the wide back flat, and the one for the narrow back with a lot of fulness; this is a necessity in tailoring wherever applied, if the seam does not go exactly over the prominence it is desired to provide for, hence the various modes of manipulation needed to suit different styles of cutting. It is, of course, too much to expect that garments cut with extremely wide or narrow backs can have sleeves made to fit as nicely as those cut a natural width; the prominence of the shoulder must be provided for, necessitating in the case of narrow backs a much larger amount of fulness; whilst, if the back and shoulders were excessively wide, the sleeve would need to go in plain or even positively tight.

Diagram 70, Plate 39,

Illustrates the three styles of sleeve heads, and it will be very readily seen that as the back is made an inch wider or narrower, the distance across the scye would be that much more or less. This is evidenced as from O to 4½, 5½, 6½, and producing the amount necessary to fill up the round of the shoulder, and as the scye increases in size as the back is made narrower, and *vice versâ*, so the measure from back pitch front is made to vary 1 inch for every inch of difference in the back; the pitch of the sleeve being kept on a horizontal line makes a difference of a 4 inch whenever the back is varied, as in the present case; hence O, 4, 4½, 4½. The topside is naturally the part that is most affected by variations in the back; but the underpart also needs some changes, necessitating the use of the judgment in the sleeve balance as found by the square, in the working of the system, which naturally produces a slightly larger under-sleeve for the narrow back. The variations to be introduced by the aid of judgment are shown as

Diagram 71, Plate 39,

And consists of not hollowing it out so much for the narrow back. The dotted line shows the changes to make for the narrow back, the dot-and-dash line illustrates the normal, and the solid line the wide back. These variations are necessary to allow the arm being brought forward or raised, for it must always be remembered the arm is the freest of all the members of the body, moving backwards, forwards, up and down in a manner which defies the adjustability of the most elastic materials; consequently we have occasionally to err on the side of a little too much material, to permit these movements in garments held closely to the waist, otherwise a grand split would be the result, especially if the scye happened to be a trifle too deep. This is very important in Riding Habits, as the lady invariably lifts her arms well up in the act of mounting; hence a too deep scye and an under sleeve too much hollowed is to be specially avoided. Some ladies, however, are content if their jackets fit nice and clean at the back scye, and do not require to raise their arms, trusting to the elesticity of the material for those occasions when this is necessary. For such, the under sleeve should be well hollowed and made slightly shorter, and strained up to the hindarm of top sleeve when making.

Variations in Style.

The fancy style of sleeve head, which, during the past few years, has been received with so much favour, has made the sleeve problem easier. The slashed sleeve head, the pleated topside, those arranged, with sleeve capes, as well as the high puffed sleeves, all have the same result, though the extreme to which they are carried clearly indicates that the original purpose of merely providing sufficient room for the shoulder has been lost sight of, and fashion has been allowed to hold the reins of fancy.

Variations in the width of the elbow be made equally at fore and hindarms, the preference should be given to the hindarm, to make the larger share of the increase, and the forearm to decrease. Variations in the width of cuff should be made one-third at forearm and two-thirds at hindarm.

"Leg-o'-Mutton" or "Gigot" Sleeves.

This style was exceedingly popular a year or two ago. The easiest way to cut them is to cut an ordinary sleeve with top and underside separate, then put the hindarm seam together from elbow and cuff, and from the hindarm of the underside complete the sleeve head. If this should produce too much puff to the sleeve head, it may be reduced a little by cutting the under sleeve across at the elbow, when the size of the sleeve head is considerably reduced, and still the hindarm seam omitted, and as the underarm would be hidden, the short seam from forearm to elbow would not be noticed.

Very Full Sleeve Heads.

At the time we write these are decidedly on the decline ; but as some may desire to produce them. we supplement our own diagrams by some that appeared in the LADIES' TAILOR, by H. A. H.

Diagram 7 shows how extra width is introduced from the elbow downwards, whilst Diagram 8 shows how to adjust the model patterns so that there is only a moderate degree of looseness at cuff.

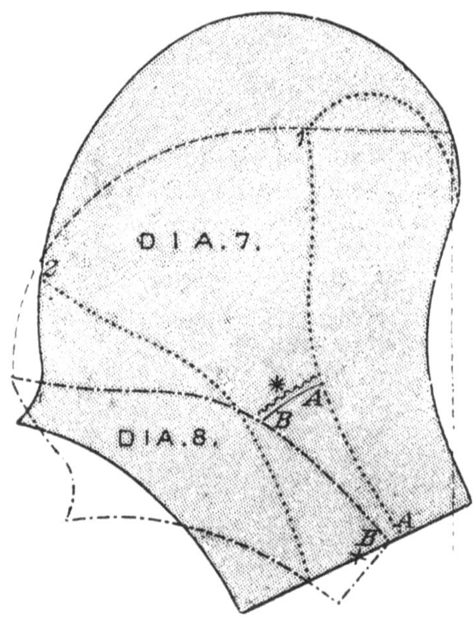

Diagram 9 shows how to cut the Football Sleeve. The ordinary sleeve pattern is taken as a basis, and it is marked out at hindarm as for puffed sleeve. Addition is made for the seams consumed, and the topside sleeve is cut in three or more parts,

reducing the puff at top, and adding on an amount of round about 6 or 8 inches down.

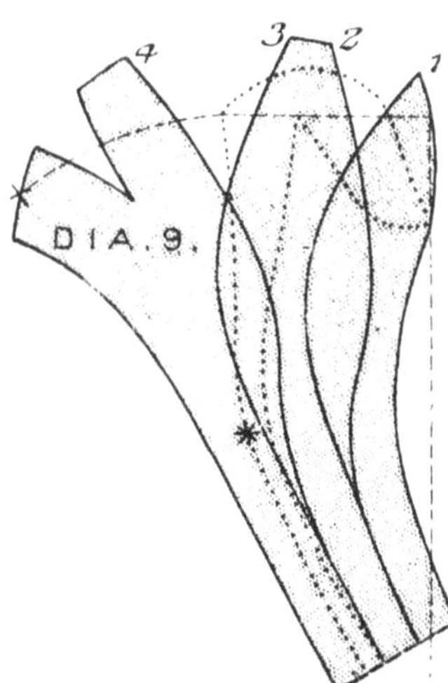

Defects in the Fitting of Sleeves.

This will put our readers in possession of the leading principles, for a very important lesson is to be learnt from a defect, if it is only thoroughly studied and the principle mastered; for in cutting, however perfect a system may be, it is necessary for those who use it successfully to fully grasp the principles involved — for the system is, after all, only the tool which needs the hand, the eye, and the heart to direct and use it to meet all cases satisfactorily.

Creases Across the Top of Forearm.

These very unsightly creases are generally the result of an insufficient depth between the top of hindarm to the top of forearm, or to use another term, incorrect balance; the same might be effected by taking a good fitting sleeve, cutting the hind-arm across, and cutting out a wedge. It is most apparent when the arm is brought forward, as in the act of writing, and almost entirely vanishes when the hands are clasped behind. This effect is bound to exist in a more or less degree in every sleeve, but we should always aim at reducing it to a minimum. If it should be found to exist to a degree which is not only unsightly but uncomfortable, the easiest way to alter is to lower the forearm, which practically amounts to the same as if a wedge had been inserted to the hindarm seam to nothing at top of forearm; though in one case the forearm is shortened, and in the other the

hindarm is lengthened, the relation existing between the two seams is identical in both cases, the length being easily adjusted if a turn up has been left at the bottom of cuff. The opposite defect to this is a dragging from forearm to elbow. In this defect a most uncomfortable pressure is felt when the arms rest at the sides, but plenty of ease exists for the arm being brought forward; there is a lot of foulness and full material at the top of hindarm, and a general tendency for the cuff to stand away from the hand. This latter effect is also produced by a different cause, viz., the forearm cut too hollow between elbow and hand. It should always be borne in mind that the sleeve between the elbow and cuff at forearm should be cut straight. To return to our defect, just as the creases across the forearm are cured by lowering the forearm, this would be remedied by raising it; but as this is not practicable in the made up garment, we suggest what we term a negative alteration, viz., lower the hindarm, which has practically the same effect as raising the forearm, with the exception of the length of sleeve, which may be adjusted at cuff, as previously explained.

Creases in Forearm and Elbow.

Ladies frequently wear very tight-fitting sleeves, and if these are cut too straight there is not sufficient length at the elbow for the arm to bend, which either results in a split at the elbow or a quantity of superfluous length forming in folds at the bend of the arm. To remedy this in the made up garment is somewhat difficult; in fact, if there is no inlay in the forearm, it cannot be treated properly, though it may be relieved by lowering the forearm in a slight degree. In cutting new sleeves, cut your pattern across at the elbow, and insert a wedge to nothing at forearm, which will make sleeve more bent.

Loose and Superfluous Material at Top of Hindarm.

This, too, is necessary, to a certain extent, in order to allow sufficient play in the sleeve for the arm coming forward. Ladies, however, do not require so much in this way as men — they prefer elegance to ease — and in order to avoid this foul material at back of the arm, it will be necessary to clear out the undersleeve at top between top of

hindarm and lowest part of the sleeve hollow, whilst a little may be taken off the top of the hindarm of undersleeve and stretched up. In all these defects the quantity or extent of the alteration must be decided by the degree to which the defect appears. There are many other defects to which sleeves are liable, but those touched upon are perhaps the most important ones.

SECTION ELEVEN.
Ladies' Vests. Diagrams 1 to 8.
Plate 40.

For some few years past, Vests, as a separate garment, have been growing in popularity. They offer plenty of opportunity for the introduction of variety or contrast into a costume, and in this way they are used to relieve an otherwise plain and severe style of costume. Amongst the materials used are fancy worsteds, stockinettes, leathers, silks, washing materials, and such-like goods, and these are frequently embroidered, brocaded, braided, and otherwise ornamented, so that they have a very stylish effect.

For the most part they are made up in a similar style to a gent's vest, *i.e.*, minus sleeves, etc., though sometimes sleeves are added, in which case the ordinary bodice sleeve, cut plain, will be used, and care taken not to get the scye too deep or too forward.

We have on this Plate illustrated the most popular styles, and our readers will agree with us in thinking there is plenty of variety. In dealing with these we will turn our attention first to

The System. Diagrams 1 and 2.
Plate 40.

We take the usual measures as for a bodice, omitting the sleeve measure, but adding the opening and full length. These we apply first to the back, as illustrated on Diagram 1.

From O to 8 is the depth of scye.

O to 15½ is the natural waist length.

Square lines at right angles to 6, 8, and 15½.

From 15½ to 2 make 2 inches, and draw backseam.

O to 2½ is one-third (half) neck measure (7½).

1 to 10¾ is one-fourth breast, plus ¾ inch.

2 to 9¼ is one-fourth waist, plus ¾ inch.

Make 1 a pivot, and sweep from O to W.

Make width of shoulder on back from ¾ to W ⅛ breast, plus ½ inch.

Complete upper part of back by these points.

For the skirt below waist hollow 1 inch, and make skirt about 2 or 3 inches deep.

The Forepart. Diagram 2.
Plate 40.

Draw lines O 8; O 9¾.

Make O 8 the same as 8 to 15½ of the back.

From 8 to 1 is 1 inch, and hollow side-seam as per diagram.

O to 9¾ is one-fourth breast, plus ¾ inch.

9¾ to 2¼ is the average across-chest measure, minus 1 inch.

Sweep for front shoulder from points 2¼ to 9¾.

First sweep is made from 2¼ by the front shoulder measure, minus the width of back neck.

Second sweep is made from 9¾ by the first quantity, plus ¾ inch.

The third sweep is made from 2¼ by the over-shoulder measure, minus 1 W of the back.

F to D of the forepart is made the same as the back, from ¾ to W, minus ¼ inch.

F to V is one-third of the (half) neck.

Breast line is drawn from V to 9¾.

From V to I is the same as F to V.

Add on ¾ inch for button stand beyond breast line.

Reduce waist to one-fourth waist, plus ¾ inch, by the aid of darts, placing the first dart 1½ inch from breast line, and second dart 1½ inch from one.

Measure up the length as usual, allowing ¾ inch for seams. Complete draft as illustrated.

S.B. No-Collar Vest. Diagram 3.
Plate 40.

his is a very popular style just at present; it is made generally to button up fairly close, though this is, of course, a matter of taste. In the more important features it is cut the same as Diagram 2, but for all garments that are to be made without a collar, it is necessary to fill up the gorge about ¾ inch, as indicated at the notch just below F. arranging the notch so that when it is filled in with a small band to go across back neck, there is

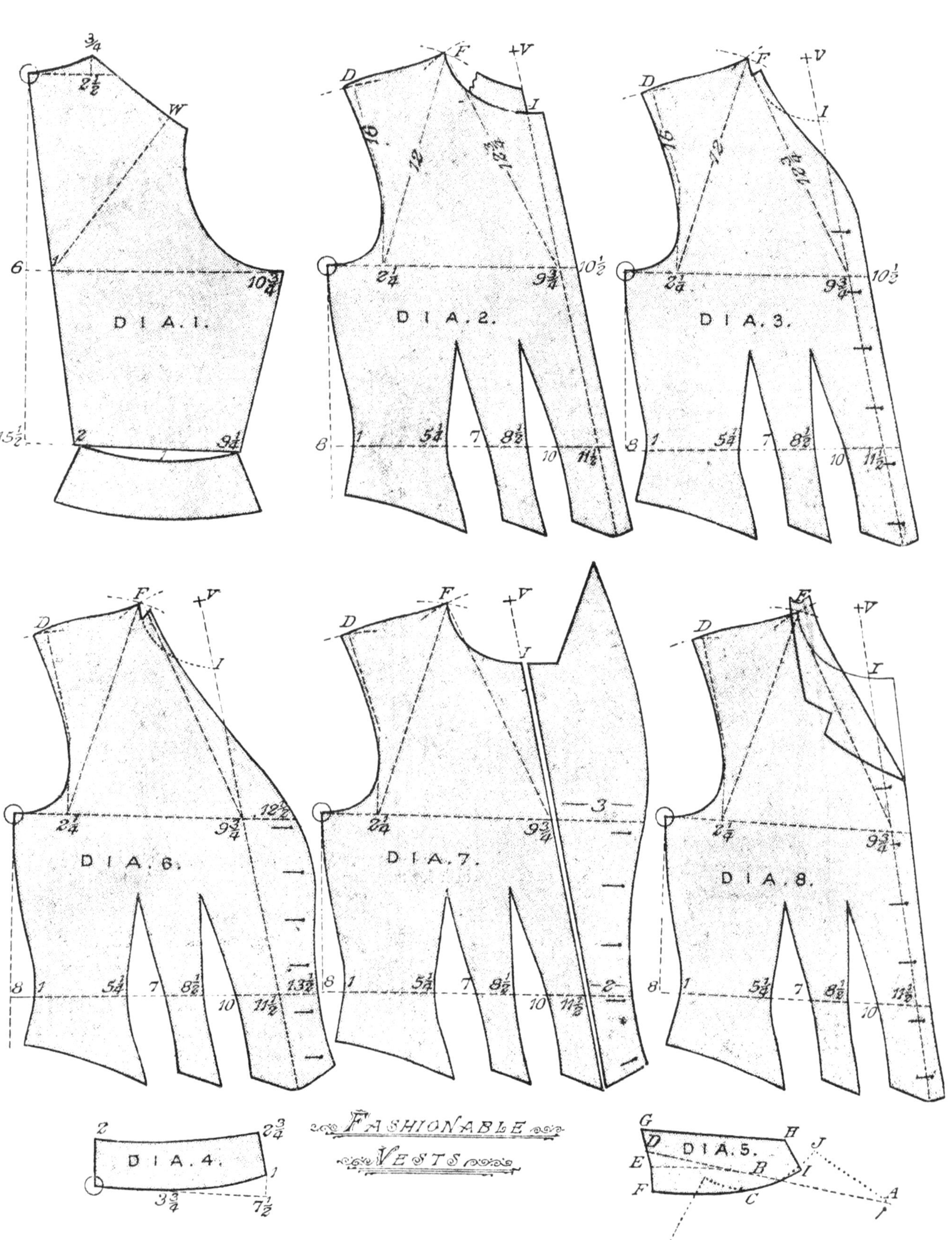

DIA.1.
DIA.2.
DIA.3.
DIA.4.
DIA.5.
DIA.6.
DIA.7.
DIA.8.
FASHIONABLE VESTS

sufficient spring for the neck. A good deal of taste can be displayed in the outline of the opening between the top button and the notch.

D.B. No-Collar Vest. Diagram 6.
Plate 40.

This is the same style as Diagram 3, but made double breasted. The same variation is necessary at the neck as for Diagram 3, but instead of adding on ¾ inch for button stand, the amount beyond 9¾ to 12½ is made 2¾ inches, and from 11½ to 13½ is 2 inches. The amount added on for overlap is quite a matter of taste, and may be varied either wider or narrower.

D.B. Vest with Lapel sewn on.
Diagram 7. Plate 40.

The forepart of Diagram 7 is precisely the same as Diagram 2, minus the button stand, though in some cases it will be well to lower the gorge so that the drawing seam may not be placed too high. The lapel is cut with a straight sewing-to edge, so that a seam up the front is only introduced for style, and may be omitted if so desired. The outline of the outer edge of the lapel is entirely a matter of taste, as also is the width indicated on the diagram.

Step Roll Collar. Diagram 8.
Plate 40.

The principal variation in this diagram is one introduced in the making up: a turn collar has been sewn to the gorge, and perhaps a little more width has been left at top of forepart beyond I. The collar sewn on to the gorge may either form a step or a continuous roll according to taste. Plenty of variety may be introduced in the amount of opening, as well as in the width of collar and turn. Stand Collar. Diagram 4.

Plate 40.

Draw line 0 7½ the half-neck point.

3¾ is midway between O and 7½.

O to 2 is at right angles to O 3¾.

1 2¾ is at right angles to 1 3¾.

Curve sewing to edge as illustrated.

Complete upper edge to taste.

Fall Collar. Diagram 5.
Plate 40.

A is the height of opening.

C B is ¾ inch.

Draw line from A through B to D.

D to E difference between stand and fall of collar.

F is width of back neck from neck point of front shoulder.

E F is depth of stand, and draw line F C I.

E to G depth of fall, or turnover desired.

Complete collar; from F to G being slightly hollowed, and G H to I drafted to taste.

In cutting collars, carefully avoid getting them short.

Hints on Making.

The backs of Vests are usually made up of silesia, Italian cloth, or silk. The lining is made up in pretty much the same way as for a gent's; the best houses use silk, whilst the cheaper ones are content with sateen.

Bones are placed at both breast darts, so as to make them fit as smartly as possible. Slits are generally left at the bottom of the sideseam in order to provide a little freedom over the hips.

Watch pockets are generally inserted either at the breast or at the waist, but in this detail it would be usual to consult the customer's taste. Facings are put all down the front and across the bottom of the forepart, and a pleat is usually placed in the lining at the shoulder.

A buckle and strap is sometimes placed at the waist of back, but more often these give way to strings as being thinner.

Tabs or buttons are often placed on the forepart to fasten the fronts of the jacket to, when the latter is worn loose and open.

SECTION TWELVE.
Ladies' Skirts.

Under this heading we purpose giving illustrations of a variety of Riding Trains, two of which will be reduced models of West End garments, and the third will be given more to illustrate how these may be cut by system, for though we do not generally advise

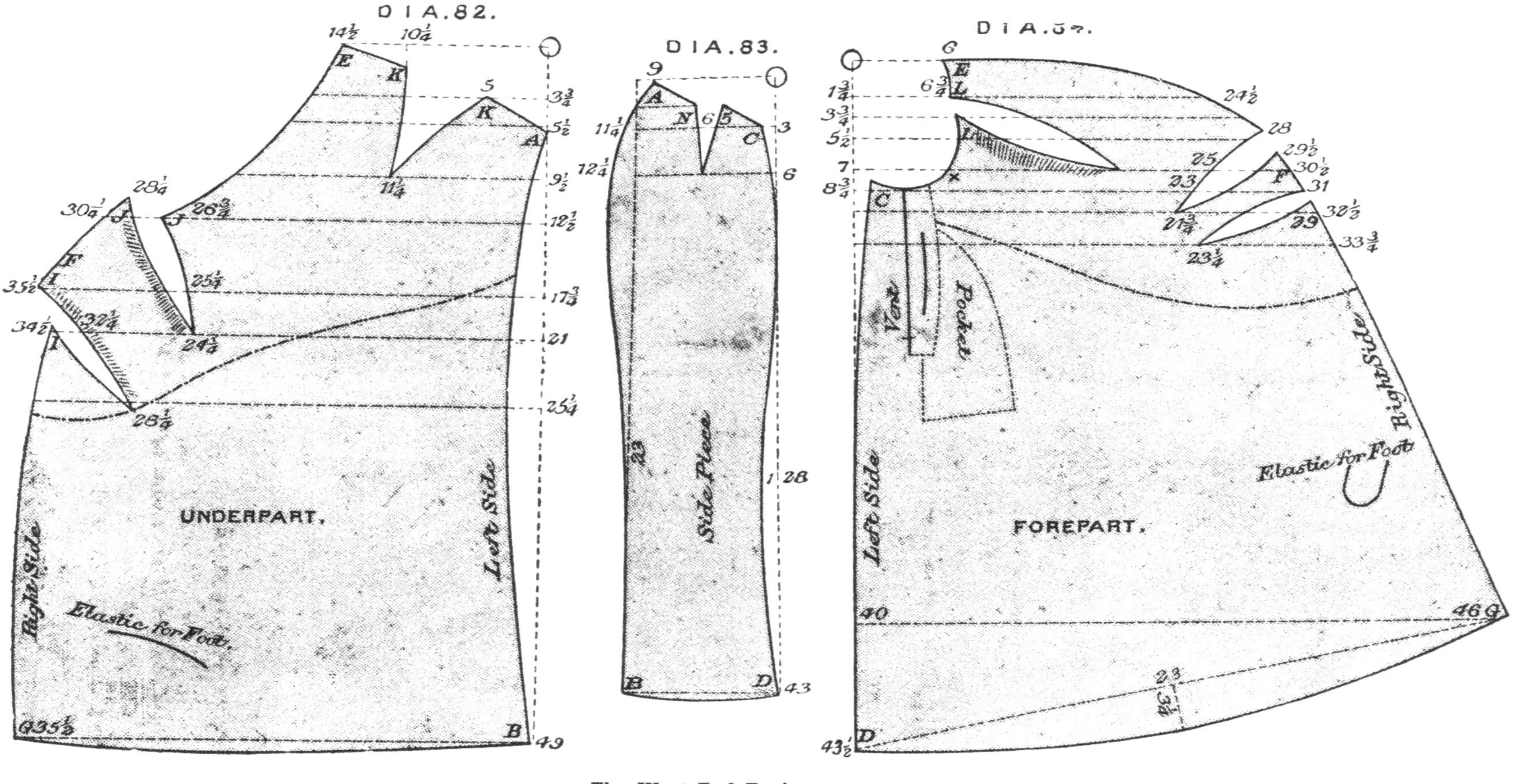
DIA.82.
DIA.83.
DIA.57.
UNDERPART.
Side Piece.
FOREPART.
Right Side
Left Side
Left Side
Right Side
Elastic for Foot.
Elastic for Foot.
Pocket
Vent
The West End Train.

such a method of cutting these garments, yet it is especially useful in cutting for children or any out of the way size. For general purposes,

The West End Train, Dias. 82, 83, 84, Plate 41.

Will meet the requirements of the ordinary run of customers better, it being a pattern that has been carefully tested and tried by a large number, and is now so improved as to leave little to be desired. It is largely used in the West End, as well as the most fashionable hunting districts.

As will be seen, it consists of three pieces, viz., back (Diagram 82), side (Diagram 83), and front (Diagram 84), which are put together exactly as they are placed on the diagram; the right side of the top part being joined to the right side of underpart, as shown by E F G, the corresponding letters going together in each case. The diagram exactly represents the inside of a train with the seam at E F G ripped open. The vent is placed either at the side or front, according to taste, and a pocket is generally inserted in the facings as illustrated. The under part and top part are lined over the seat and knee with Silesia, to take some of the wear caused by the friction with the saddle, the position of this being shown by the dot-and-dash line, and elastic is put on in a suitable position for each boot. That part of the underside as shown by I F J is fulled on to the opposite part of the fish on either side. The topside is also stretched up as shown by marks at L, but at all other parts it is put together plain; the letters corresponding show where the various seams are to be sewn together. The bottom is finished with a broad hem, in which weights of lead are frequently inserted when the material is at all thin. The length is regulated by making the sides as at C D agree with the length from waist to ground when standing, trains being now much shorter than they were in the olden time, when trains merely consisted of so much cloth pleated into the band at waist. They are finished at waist both with and without waistbands; in the former case they are merely bound, and left so for the sake of thinness; but if a band is put on, it is as well to have a point to put at the centre of front as at X, which is a very great assistance to the lady in adjusting its position. Whatever plan is adopted for finishing the waist at top, it should be carefully arranged to agree with the exact size of waist, and hooks should be put on by which to fasten it to tabs fixed at back and sides of the bodice part. Any slight variation in the size of waist may be arranged by reducing the size of cuts in under part of K and of sidepiece at N, but if there is more than 1 or 1½ inches of difference in size of waist, it will be best to enlarge or reduce it throughout by adding to or taking from the parts all down, as at A B of undersides and C D of topsides; whilst all variations in the length must be made by adding to or taking from the bottom.

In Cutting from the Cloth,

Great care must be used to have the face of material right side out, and we think we cannot better explain ourselves than to say: Lay the pattern down as represented in the diagram, *i.e.*, presuming the cloth to be opened out with the wrong side uppermost. Place the pattern of the top part with the side at C D close up to left-hand selvage, standing with the bottom of the cloth towards you. The under part is then taken out by laying it with A B close up to the right-hand selvage, and then taking the sidepiece out from the most convenient part with C D towards the right. These instructions apply to the ordinary style of riding with the right leg resting on the pommel of the saddle. There are a few ladies who ride with the left leg in that position, when these instructions must be reversed; but such cases are few and far between.

A "Try-on"

Should always be arranged, if possible, as the run of bottom is a special feature with those who make this branch a study, and this can only be success-fully arranged by a "try-on", as it is always advisable to consult the ladies' wishes, while at the same time being prepared to advise her upon any point she may desire. The position of the elastics for foot can also be decided in this manner, which will be found more simple and successful than any elaborate calculation of leg length, &c. A dummy horse is kept for this purpose in all the leading ladies' tailoring establishments; but if the firm should not possess this desideratum, it may be safely left in the hands of the ladies' maid and the intended wearer, who will adjust all these little details to a nicety.

The Diagram

Is drawn to the one-twelfth scale, and should produce a garment, when made up, to measure 2½ yards round the bottom for a 24 waist. Full size patterns of this may be obtained at our. office, price 1s. 6d., post free 1s. 7d., which method may be preferred by many of our readers to drafting it out for themselves.

This being such a very important garment we have added the following diagram and description of an up-to-date

West End Train. by H. A. H.,

and which is taken from the pages of "The Ladies' Tailor".

The following is his statement of the subject, and which is well worthy of the most careful study: —

Diagrams 1 and 2.

Like every other garment, the Riding Train has undergone very great improvements in recent years, both as regards cutting and making, which have consequently added to the fit and comfort of that garment when the wearer is in the saddle. The great feature of the present Trains is their fitting perfectly close round the knee, thigh, and seat; almost as clean as a pair of trousers, with very little surplus material anywhere, while the topside hangs nice and straight from the hips downwards. To produce this, the cutting and making of a skirt requires great attention. Considerable care is also required that the thing is not overdone; that is, to get it too tight over the knee, or too little width across from seat to the knee when the rider is in position, or the consequence will be that the skirt will work up and gather into folds in the lap, which is very uncomfortable and unsightly. The great desideratum is to get the receptacle for the knee in the right place. This can only be done by direct measure, as ladies vary considerably in the length of their legs, so that no division of a certain portion is sufficient. To be at all successful with trains, ladies should be placed in a saddle position to be measured, so as to get the exact length of knee.

The measures generally required are — length of Train from hip to bottom, from centre of waist to knee, and size of waist. As will be seen by the

diagram, the important feature of this skirt is that no seam shows. Being only two seams they are well under, and the cuts and darts are so arranged that the underpart which covers the right leg and the pommel fits exactly. The same applies to the hollow of the right leg, between the waist and knee. As will be seen, there is rather a large cut taken out of the bottom, which helps in cleaning the loose stuff from there.

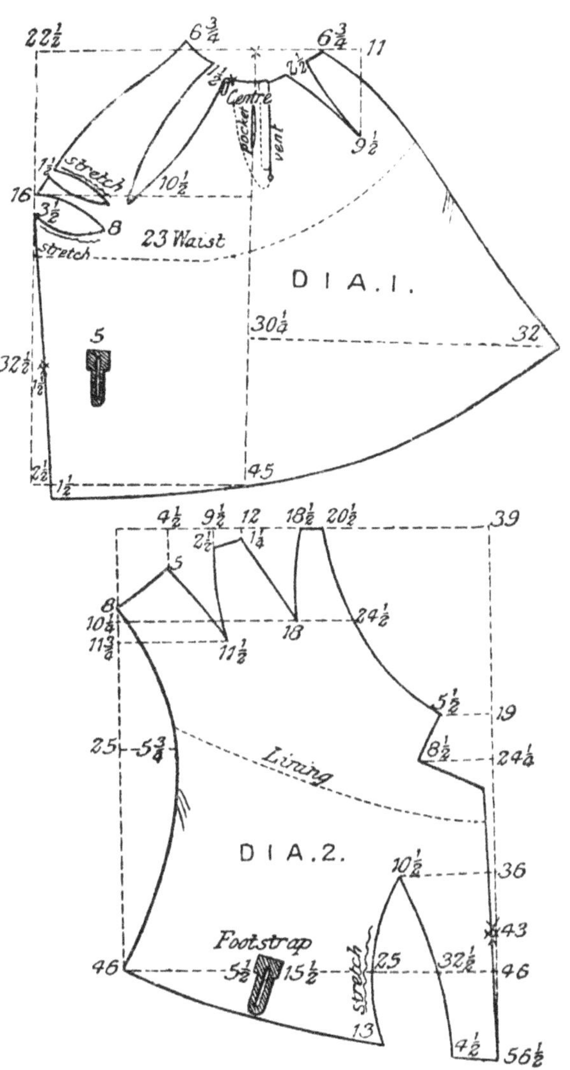

As this diagram is all laid down in plain figures, very little description is needed, as ninety nine out of every hundred trains are cut from a pattern; so that the greatest difficulty in regard to the fitting of a Train is the try-on, and the most important thing wanted when trying on is judgment. Before proceeding to try on, I shall just explain the way they should be basted. All seams should be basted outside, the V's only cut down the centre, so that if necessary after the first try-on, they can be moved either backwards or forwards, as the case may be. When ready and on, help the lady to mount. Be careful to note that the skirt is in the centre, and that no surplus stuff is gathered under the seat when seated.

Let me say here that it is impossible to fit a Train without either a dummy horse or a saddle stand. The latter can be had for the small sum of 50/-, which would answer the same purpose as a dummy horse costing £50. Now you can proceed with the try-on. The main operating seam is the basting seam, and with the same basted outside you can pin and re-pin *ad lib.*, until all the creases and wrinkles have disappeared. While fitting, see that the foot-straps are in the position, also that the cuts at the knee are in the right place.

Now just a few words about the

Making of a Train.

When the Habit is cut, it is the rule of every cutter to mark which way the parts go together. If this is done while the Train is being cut, it saves a great deal of trouble both to the cutter himself and the workman. If the sewing part, the most important seams are the darts, which, while being sewn and pressed, it should be borne in mind what they are placed there for. For instance, the knee cuts should always be pressed so as to work up a receptacle for the knee, and the same for the pommel. The same applies to the other cuts. When all the seams are sewn and pressed open, it is ready for what we may call the internal work, the first thing being to turn up the bottom. I may state here that it is a rule to leave a 4 or 5-inch hem round the bottom. Attention should now be directed to the top. On the left side of the Train a slit is made about 10 inches long, and to this a facing is sewn so as to take the pocket and buttons, and the slit is fastened down with a fly. (See diagram.) Then the tops should be lined with fine linen as marked. Elastics should be placed where marked, or the place it is thought right when fitting the train. These are two in number; one is placed on the underside for the left foot, and another for the right. The elastic should always be of the best silk and 1 inch wide.

It is advisable to well stay where the elastics are fastened, as there is a great strain on them at times. The top should be finished off by binding, the same

as trousers, as it is thinner in the waist than a waist-band. The great thing in making the train is to see the round of the knee is well formed by pressing, and that all the darts and cuts are nicely pressed off at the ends, so that no lumps are left. There should be four hooks placed on the top, with corresponding eyes, made on small tabs placed on the Habit; these can be fixed in the course of the final try-on. These are very necessary, as they keep the Train from creeping down, and they have also the effect of keeping the Habit from creeping up.

The New Safety Train. Diagrams on Plate 42.

Many accidents to ladies thrown from their horses having been very much aggravated by their Habit Trains catching in the saddle, has induced some of the inventive minds to prepare a Train in such a style as would not offer the least resistance to the complete fall of the lady from her horse. We have recently had several of these through our hands, and the diagrams on Plate 42 is a reduced

model of one of these, and which, if our readers will reproduce by the ordinary tape, will be suitable for an average lady of 24 waist and 40 side length. We shall not go over the diagram point by point, as it would serve no purpose, especially as these are seldom cut by system; indeed, we believe we shall be right in saying ninety-nine cutters out of every hundred engaged in the best ladies' trade cut their Trains out in this way; though for those who prefer

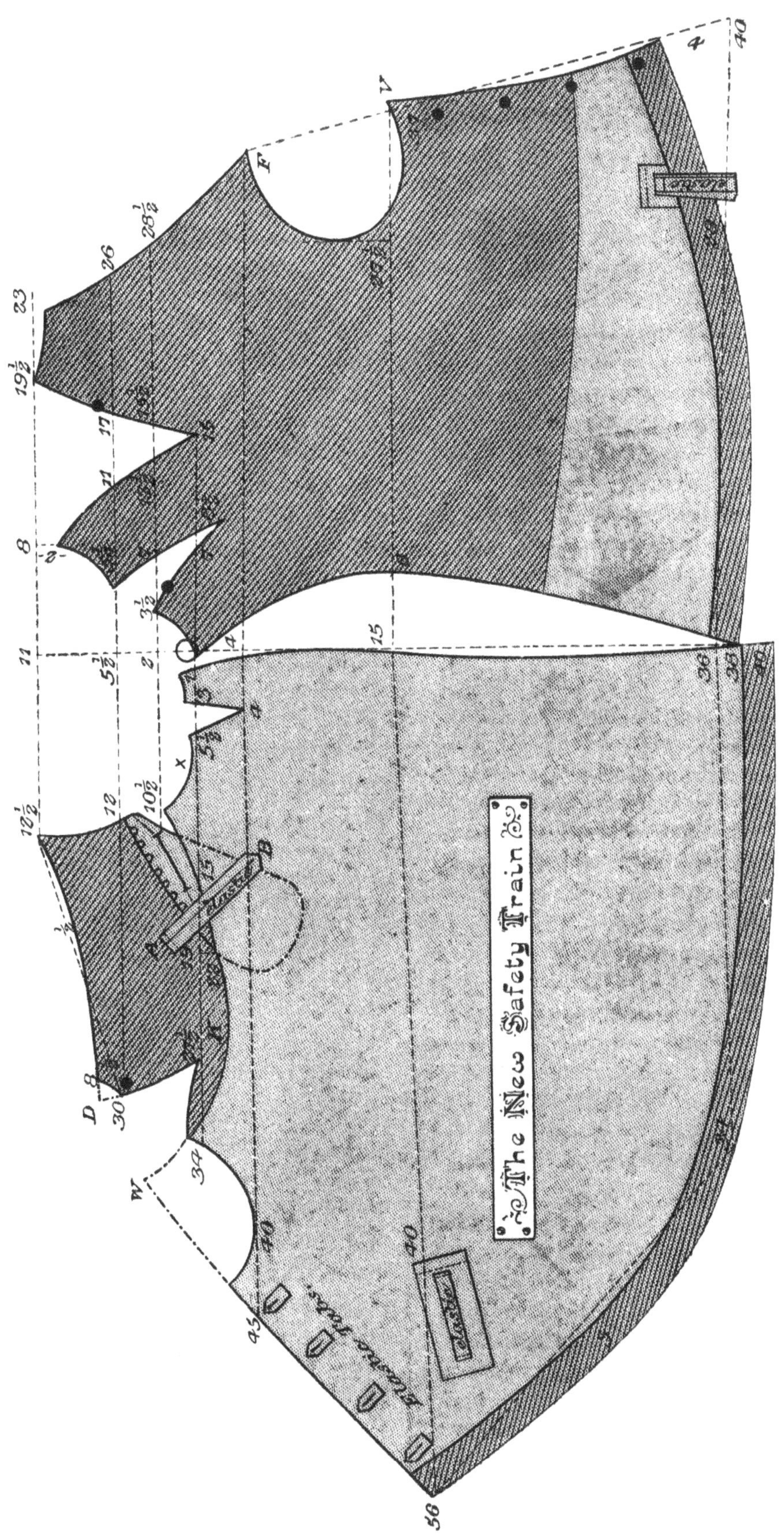
The New Safety Train

a system, we give one on page 108, so that our remarks on this New Safety Train will be more of a practical than a scientific nature. Variations in length should be made at the bottom; but if the side length should show a great increase, it would be well to lower the V for the knee, as at W D, so that the distance from 12 to K agrees with the measure taken on the customer. Variations in the size of waist alone may be made by enlarging or reducing the V's; whilst for ladies larger or smaller, both in seat and waist, the variation should be made through from O to 40, by merely adding to or deducting from, as the case may require. Care must, of course, be taken to get the pattern cut the right way, as previously described for the West End Train.

The Special Features

of this Train are, first, it being left open from D to 56, there a large hole is cut, as illustrated at W D of topside, and F V of underpart, so that the usual surplus material between the knee and the pommel is avoided, and in case of accident there is plenty of room for the Train to free itself from the saddle. A double strip of elastic about 9 inches long is sewn on at A, and a button placed at 3 O, so that the elastic may come under the knee and secure the lady at that part; and in order to avoid any possibility of the elastic becoming unfastened, a short loop of *twisted* cord is put at 8 close to the button, which is put over the button after the elastic is fastened to it, so that if the elastic should work itself free of the button, it is still held by the loop; this loop is also useful to hold the skirt up when walking, when it is fastened to the button at 17 of undersides. Below the opening it will be noticed there are four elastic loops, which are fastened to the buttons on the under part; neither of these are stayed with linen, as the object of having it open is to allow the weight of the body to break away these tabs or buttons from their place in case of the lady being thrown from her horse, and the train catches on the pommel. As some of our readers may desire a Train without this safety arrangement, we have outlined at W and D the amount to be filled in of the topside, and from 33½ to V of the underside, when it will be made up in the ordinary style, closed all round.

A Few Hints on Making.

The shaded parts of top and underside are lined with linen or silesia, the stays for the footstraps are covered with Italian cloth, and the opening is bound with Prussian binding or leather, a waist band is generally put round the top, and may either be of Melton or Italian cloth, the latter being often preferred on account of thinness. The cuts or V's are usually taped, and the opening for putting on or off is either made at the side, forming a continuation of the V at 5½, 3 and 4, or it may be arranged at front as at 12, 10½, in which latter case it is fastened together with hooks and eyes placed about 1 inch apart; and in the former it is fastened together with holes and buttons and a fly. A pocket is usually inserted in the opening, the outline of which we have illustrated by the dot-and-dash lines. A broad hem, say 3 inches, is left round the bottom, and in cutting an inlay is usually left down the sideseam. In cutting it from the cloth special care must be used not to cut it inside out, an error many beginners make. If the pattern is laid down as it is placed on the Plate, the face of the cloth should be uppermost.

The quantity of material required will be 3 yards of 56 inches wide material; but if it should not run quite so wide, a wheelpiece can easily be put on the topside at 56.

Complicated as this garment looks at first sight, a closer examination will show it to be really of a very simple nature, and such as any tailor of ordinary experience might make easily, the principal feature being to locate the knee accurately, and avoid all surplus material, whether at seat or lap. The length is generally made to just cover or show the golosh of the boot of the stirrup foot Various methods are adopted to hold the Habit and Train together, hooks and eyes, or tabs and buttons, being the two most frequently employed. We have placed buttons on the diagram, one at the side just below 7½ on line 2, and one just above 17 on line 5½, which seam would come as nearly as possible down the centre of back, the centre of front being fixed midway between 5½ and 10½ and should be marked by a little white cotton on the waistband to assist the wearer in adjusting it properly.

These are the principal points to be observed in making this train. We have previously dealt with trying them on, and many other hints of a general character, and which our readers will doubtless remember. Should any point in the diagram not be quite clear, it is drawn to the one-twelfth scale, and may be found accordingly. We may also add that patterns of this style of Train can be had from the TAILOR AND CUTTER Office, special reference being made when ordering to the New Safety Train.

Patent Safety Trains.

In addition to the style we have illustrated, there are quite a number of patent Safety Trains, a few of which we proceed to illustrate. On the accompanying figure will be seen an illustration of Messrs. Thomas & Sons' patent skirt, which consists of very little more than an apron, the whole of the under side being cut away. At first sight this would suggest a most unsightly garment when out of the saddle, but this is not so bad as may be supposed, for by a judicious arrangement of loops and buttons it can be brought round in such a manner as to be very little more unsightly than the ordinary train when the wearer is standing.

The Busvine Safety Train.
Diagram 1.

In this skirt, a side opening *b* is made in the side of the skirt next the horse, through which the pommel passes, from the bottom upwards, and is closed partially or wholly by a gore of weak elastic material lightly attached by sewing, fastenings or adhesive material; or the openings may be closed by lacing, as shown at kkckk. A knee sleeve *d* is attached to the inside of the skirt, and also a shoe for the foot; or there may be two sleeves for the right and left leg of the rider.

Hohne's Patent Safety Skirt.
Diagram 2.

The skirt covers the lower parts of the rider's legs on the outside only, and the front part is attached to the right leg by the strap *a* passing round above the knee and fastened to the tab *b*, by buttoning, and also by the loose flap of material *c* encircling the leg below the knee. After the skirt has been thus attached, the part between the dotted line *d d*, or thereabouts, and the edge *e* becomes wrapped round the lower part of the rider's right leg.

The following is the inventor's own description of it: —

"When the rider is mounted, the front part of the skirt is attached to the right leg by means of a strap passed round the right leg above the knee and secured to a strap stitched to the inside of the skirt, and also by a sort of garter, formed by a loose flap of material attached to the inner side of the skirt, which encircles the leg below the knee, and is secured by buttoning. The buttons are situate on the inner or left side of the right leg, and not next the saddle, so as to avoid all liability of chafing the rider. An elastic loop is also provided near the lower part of the skirt, in which the right foot is placed, in order to keep the skirt in its proper position. When this portion of the skirt is thus attached, the edge becomes partially wrapped round the rider's legs, and thus prevents any interruption of the continuity of the skirt being visible when viewed from the near side. Another elastic loop is attached to the back part of the skirt, and is passed over the left foot, to keep the rear part of the skirt in place, and this also becomes partially wrapped round the left leg. Before dismounting, this semi-skirt may be converted into an apparently complete one by detaching the fastenings from the legs and feet, and buttoning together the edges of the opening, when a loose flap, expressly provided for the purpose, completely conceals the slit."

This is a riding skirt with a leg aperture suitably cut and formed in one piece with the skirt. The diagram shows an inside view of the skirt, and the way in which the leg aperture C and opening for

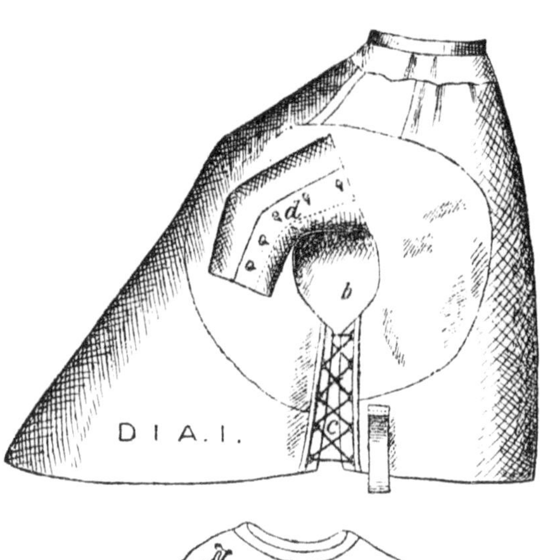

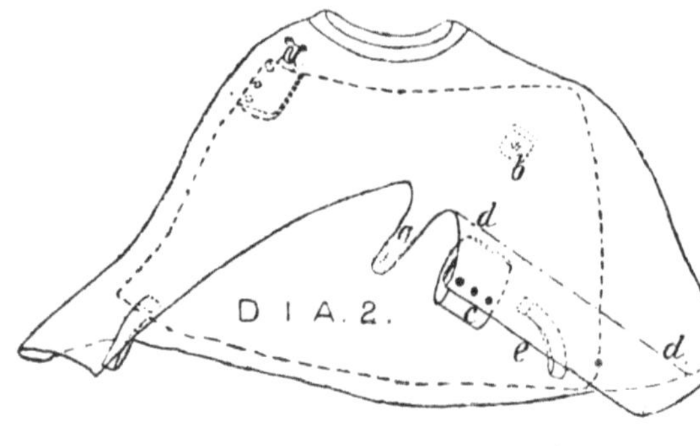

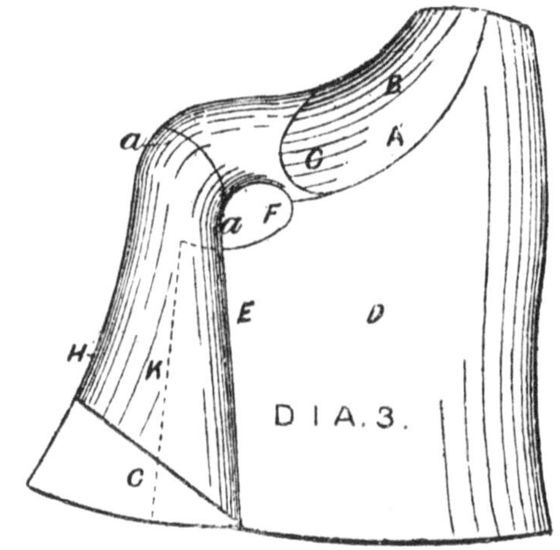

the pommels are formed. The pieces and patterns A, B are cut to form part of the upper portion of the skirt. The lower part of A, extending to the seam *a a*, forms the upper part of the aperture C

for the rider's right leg. The lower part of the passage C is formed by turning in the lower part K of the skirt and suitably folding and joining to the outside seam H. The piece D is cut to form the flap E, which is brought over and tacked lightly or run together upon the leg-piece K, leaving the aperture F for the pommels. The flap E will break away should the rider be thrown.

**The Cutter's Practical Guide Riding
Train, by System.
Diagram and Figure on Plate 43.**

It is generally acknowledged that the majority of cutters produce their Riding Trains from block patterns, and we are not going to dispute the efficacy of so doing, as we believe it is one of the best of methods of producing the general run of Trains; but there are times in the experience of most cutters, whose business lies to any extent in the ladies' trade, that orders have come for very out-of-the-way sizes. Most probably this comes in the shape of the little girl who is just beginning her career as an equestrienne, and as her form is altogether different to that of the normal figure, for the cutter to use his ordinary block pattern would be found not only inappropriate but almost certain to lead to failure. It is for such cases that a system, based on what we believe to be sound principles, is of especial use, and the one we now lay before our readers for the first time will, we feel sure, be equal to all such cases. Systems such as this one are only arrived at after much study and extended experiments; indeed, this which we now lay before our readers, occupying but a page of this work, has taken years of study in its development; and though we do not claim perfection for it, we have every confidence that it will produce a good fitting Train, and be especially useful in those out-of-the-way sizes above referred to, as well as forming a foundation for others to elaborate and perfect.

The Measures

Required at side, waist, seat, round seat, and knee, with right leg raised as in the act of riding (this latter may be omitted, but is decidedly preferable); they would probably stand 40 side, 24 waist, 40 seat, 64 seat and knee. The application of these measures is as follows: Draw line A B C; A to C is the side length; A to B one-fourth side, and square across to

THE CUTTERS
PRACTICAL GUIDE.
SYSTEM FOR
RIDING TRAINS.

D L P; B to D is one-fourth seat; and D I corresponds with the forked quantity of trousers, viz.,
one-third B D; I J is the same as D I; J to L is
one-fourth side, which will be found about equal to
one-third of the leg length; L P is half-knee circumference ; thus the total distance from B to P is
made up; this may also be obtained by measuring
off B to P half seat and knee circumference, plus
1 inch; and point L found by measuring back from
P half knee circumference. Come up from L to M
from 1 to 1½ inches, and draw line J M*; make M
a pivot, and sweep from R to P. We now turn to
the upper part; square line D E at right angles to
D B, and mark from E to G one fourth waist plus
1½; hollow from E to F about 1½ inches, or an
amount equal to one-sxth of the disproportion of
waist in the reverse way as followed for corpulent
trousers, taking the ideal as waist 6 inches less than
seat; take out 1 inch in a V at H, and terminate it
about 4 inches down; this is often used to form the
opening. Square line F K at right angles to F J,
and make F K one-fourth waist plus ½ inch, and
continue the run of waist across as shown, and connect K R as shown; take out two fishes of about 1½
inches as shown, so that they will come just over the
knee. Continue below P by coming down from L to
O 1½ inches, and squaring at right angles to O P;
shape the side by springing it out about 1 inch at C,
and slightly round it as illustrated, and the topside
is complete.

The Underpart

Is got by lying down the cut-out forepart, and
sweeping from A to X, using C as a pivot, and
making A to F 4 inches, and draw side of underside
from X to C. Now make star a pivot, and sweep
from K to S, and mark off 4 inches; draw a line from
X to S, and reduce to the size of the waist by means
of V's as illustrated, making T U V W about 1 inch
above line S X. Come out from R to Y from 1 to 2
inches, and take out V to correspond in quantity
with the two fishes from the forepart, taking out
the surplus length from M to Y in a V upwards,
as illustrated by dotted line at M. Complete
the outlines of undersides by the topsides, making
it rather hollower at the bottom, as shown by
the dotted lines. A fish may be taken out of
topsides, as illustrated by dot-and-dash line from I,
if a very clean-fitting lap is desired. If more room
is desired over the seat of undersides, increase the
quantity from A to X and K to S, which will have
the same effect as an increased seat angle would to
trousers, the principles involved in this Train being
very similar to those employed in trousers cutting
generally. Care must be taken to locate the knee
correctly, and, if found possible, it will be as well to
take a measure from waist to knee when in the
saddle, and then apply it from I to M, which may
increase or reduce the distance from M to I. The
same hint we have previously given for the making
of Trains will apply with equal force to this, so that
it will be quite unnecessary for us to again repeat
them here.

Cycling Skirts. Plate 44.

The popularity of cycling has created quite a
large demand for suitable garments, and whilst the
controversy on the subject of knickers and skirts
has raged in a portion of the Press, the trade has
done well to design suitable cycling skirts. The first
step in this direction was to arrange a series of
pleats at the sides with the view of providing plenty
of scope for the movement of the legs; but the
weak point was not so much there, as it was found
the average skirt allowed plenty of freedom is
the material was properly distributed, and many
attempts were made to do this. Some placed
elastic straps to the sides of the skirts to fasten
them to the legs, but that was not enough, and
after repeated experiments a skirt was designed
with a fork at the back forming a seat, and consequently a division at the back; but as this was
hidden in the folds of the pleats when walking it
was in no way objectionable, and it had this great
advantage that it distributed the material on either
side of the wheel, and so obviated many defects
that exist in the ordinary skirt.

There have been quite a host of these placed on
the market, many of them have been registered and
patented, but we have seen none to beat the skirt
designed by Mr. J. C. Hopkins, of Birmingham, to
whom we are indebted for many of the following
hints: —

The System.

Measure required, length, usually about 6 inches
from ground, or to taste.

Waist and seat, latter taken about 7 inches below
waist.

Front width, Diagram 1, draw line O 37, O to 7.

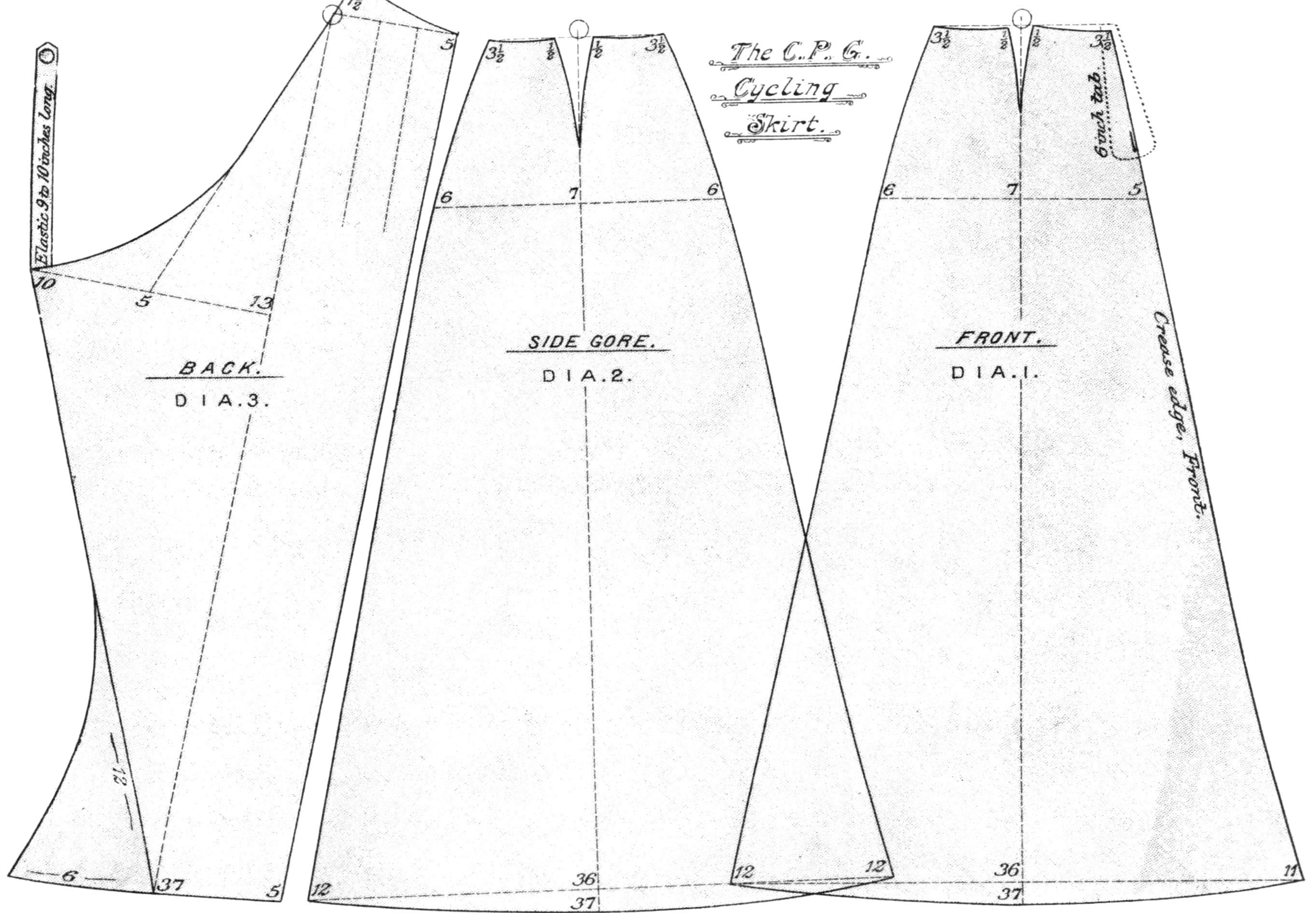
The C.P.G. Cycling Skirt.
BACK.
DIA.3.
SIDE GORE.
DIA.2.
FRONT.
DIA.I.
Crease edge, Front.
Elastic 9 to 10 inches long
6 inch tab

7 inches; O to 37 length, plus 2 seams. Take out V of 1 inch at O, and make from 1½ to 3½, one-eighth waist nett, on either side. From 7 to 5, one-eighth seat, and 7 to 6 one-eighth seat, plus 1 inch.

36 to 11 one-fourth seat, plus 1 inch, draw line of front from 3½ to 11.

36 to 12 one-fourth seat, plus 2 inches, and complete as shown.

Side width, Diagram 2, draw line O 37, the length of side. O to 7, 7 inches.

Take out V at top of from 1 to 2 inches, as from O to ½ to 3½ is one-eighth waist nett.

7 to 6 one-eighth seat, plus 1 inch on either side.

36 to 1½ one-fourth seat, plus 2 inches. Complete as shown.

Back width, Diagram 3, draw line O 37. O to 13, one-fourth seat, plus 3 inches. 13 to 5, one-eighth seat, 13 to 10 one-fourth seat.

Draw line from O to 5, and curve fork out to 10. Raise back at top 1½ inches. O to 5, and 37 to 5, 5 inches.

Draw line straight from 10 to 37, and add spring gusset about 12 inches deep by 6 inches wide, as shown.

The width of the back to the right of construction line is formed into pleats, and may be increased if thought desirable. Cycling skirts, however, are best made without any great amount of superfluous material.

As thus described, the skirt consists of five parts: 1, the front width cut on the crease; 2 and 3, the side gores; 4 and 5, the back widths. This may sometimes be reduced to three with advantage, by cutting the back and side gores in one piece. This, however, will necessitate a little reduction being made at the front of the side gore, taking off say 2 inches all down the side, and adding the same amount to the side of the front. This re-adjustment enables the skirt to be taken out of the ordinary 54 inch material advantageously, but for narrower widths goods the original plan is the better.

Hints on Making.

Line the front with glissade or some, slippery material; it will prevent the skirt riding up.

Arrange the placket holes on the left sides about 10 inches deep; put the pocket in the corresponding position on the right side.

The seat seams should be very strongly sewn; indeed, it is a good plan to put braid over it, and stretch on either side.

Finish the top with a waistband, slightly fulling the sides on to this. Put a mark at centre of front on waistband to enable wearer to adjust this.

An Italian cloth tab is placed inside front about six inches deep, as indicated on diagram, and in this a buttonhole is worked.

From back fork (point 10) a piece of thick elastic about 10 inches long is sewn, and on this is secured a button, which, when fastened to the tab, securés the fork of back part in position.

The bottom is finished with a turn up of about 3 inches, unless a facing is sewn on, which is decidedly the best course when more than 3 inches is desired to be turned up.

The bottom is sometimes faced with leather.

The Divided Skirt.

We herewith place before our readers a diagram and system for the divided skirt.

The Measures

required are: waist, seat, length of front or side, and length of body. This last measure may be obtained by asking the customer to be seated on a chair, and then take the length from the waist to the level of the seat. The measures of a normal figure would appear as follows: Waist 24, seat 42, front length 40, body length or rise 11. The width at the body may be made to the directions of the wearer.

The following is the method of drafting the pattern: —

Draw the straight line O 40, which is the front length.

O to 11 is the body length.

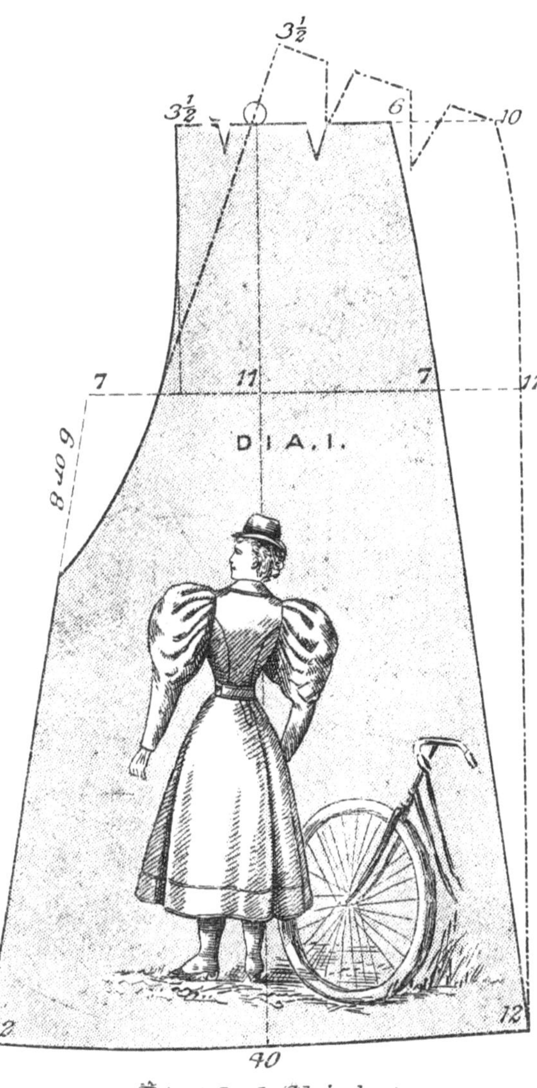

Divided Skirt.

Draw lines through 11 at right angles to O 40.

From 11 mark out to 7 one-sixth of the seat.

Mark out half that quantity (3½) from O, which finds the centre of front.

O to 6 finds top of sideseam 1 inch less than 1 to 7.

Mark out 12 to 15 inches on each side of 40.

Square lines from 7 to 12 on each side.

Form fork by starting at 3½ and curving line down to a point 6 or 8 units below 7.

Make the lengths from 7 to 12 the same as from 11 to 40, and gently round the bottom.

The waist is reduced to the size by taking out V's, and by curving line in at top of sideseam.

The Underside, Diagram 1,

is represented by the dot-and-dash lines.

Take the pattern of the topsides, and lay it down on the material and mark down the legseam from the fork point to the bottom.

Make a pivot of 12 at bottom of sideseam, and sweep out from 6 on waist line.

From fork point draw a line through O, which finds the seat line.

Mark out from O to 10, and from 11 to 11.

Then join 10, 11, and 12, which completes the sideseam.

The height of the back is marked 3½ up from O.

The waist is reduced to size by taking out V's, and by curving in the top of side-seam to harmonise with the topsides.

Making, &c.

The Divided Skirt is made on similar lines to trousers. The darts are sewn up, and the fulness pressed away from the bottom. A piece of linen is then basted in the fork and round the seat, and the edges turned in and felled. As the skirt opens, either at the back or the sides, a fly should be made to fasten on the sideseams of the topside, and a fly catch on the undersides; or if the opening should be placed at the back, it may be arranged as the usual placket hole. The opening should be at least 10 inches long. The back part is not fastened into the band, being only buttoned on to it so that it falls at the back in the same way as men's trousers fall to the front. The bottoms are faced with the same material, and usually bound with leather. A few of these skirts are lined with silk, but the greatest number are unlined, unless for the linen round the fork and seat.

———

"The Ladies' Tailor" Cycling Skirt.

We next give our latest style of cycling skirt, which has the advantage of doing away the fork point and at the same time provides ample room for the saddle. It will be found an excellent skirt, and our readers may recommend it with confidence.

The system for drafting is as follows, the measures necessary being the length, and the size of seat and waist.

Diagram 1.

Square line O 36.

Mark down 7 inches to find seat line.

Square out from 7 to 14¼ of seat plus 4 inches.

Mark out 1/6 of waist to 4 inches.

From 4 to 6, 2 inches.

Raise ½ inch at 6 and ¾ at 10, which should be of waist from 6.

Mark out at 36, 26 inches.

Measure side length from 10, to 26 (generally half inch longer).

Make length of fish about 7 inches and complete sword flap as Diagram.

Diagram 2.

Square line O 13 and O 36½ the side length.

O to 2 two inches which provides for the prominence of hip.

Mark up from 13 to 4½ on to 6.

From 6 to 1½ is one and a half inches.

Draw line from 1½ to 2 inches and hollow one inch.

Complete waist measure by making from 2 to 4 four inches (two fourths on front and the other on the side.)

From 7 to 14 one fourth of seat plus 4 inches. Mark back to 9, 5 inches.

Draw line through 5 to 22 and also 10 to 27, which forms pleat.

From waist seam to 27 is the side length, 36½.

Curve 14 to 13 on to 4½.

Diagram 3.

Measure round numbers 4½, 13, 14 and 27 on Diagram 2. Make from O to 36 the same.

O to 12 the body rise. This measure is obtained by asking the lady to be seated, then measure from waistband behind to seat of chair (usually 12 inches).

O to 14 is 14 inches.

Fix 7 halfway between, which will give you the centre of back and crease.

It will be noticed on Diagrams 1 and 2 that the front and half side from 2 to line 5, 22 from the waist and seat measure, beyond this being the amount for pleats, viz:

5 inches on side and 7 inches on back.

Therefore on the single we have 24 inches to form pleat and provision for saddle.

O to 14 would have to be increased in accordance with size of seat (the same as underside of trousers). If we increase the width and keep the rise the same then more seat angle or provision for seat would be the result.

Diagram 4.

The putting together of this skirt is very simple. It will be noticed on Diagram 4 that the extra piece added to side at waist is a continuation of back. The straight line of back from O to 36 is sewn in to curve of side (Diagram 2). Other particulars may be gathered from Diagram 4.

Fashionable Walking Skirts.
Plate 46.

There are five measures necessary for an ordinary Walking Skirt, and they are as follows: — 1, Size of waist; 2, size round waist; 3, length of front; 4, length of side; 5, length of back.

The waist measure is taken tightly round the hollow part of the waist, and if over the bodice deduct 2 inches. The seat measure is taken easily round the widest part of the hips, usually 7 inches below the waist. The front length is measured from the hollow of the waist in front to the instep. The side length from the hollow above the haunch. to the ankle. The back length from the hollow of the waist to the heel.

In this instance we shall start with a normal size, the measures for which are as follows: — Waist, 24; seat, 40; length of front, 40; length of side, 41; back, 41½.

The New Lacing Skirt

Is at present the most popular for ordinary wear, and it is customary to begin with the forepart. mmIn order to simplify the method of dividing the various parts, take half the waist measure and half the seat measure as the working scale. The waist scale is 12, and the seat scale 20.

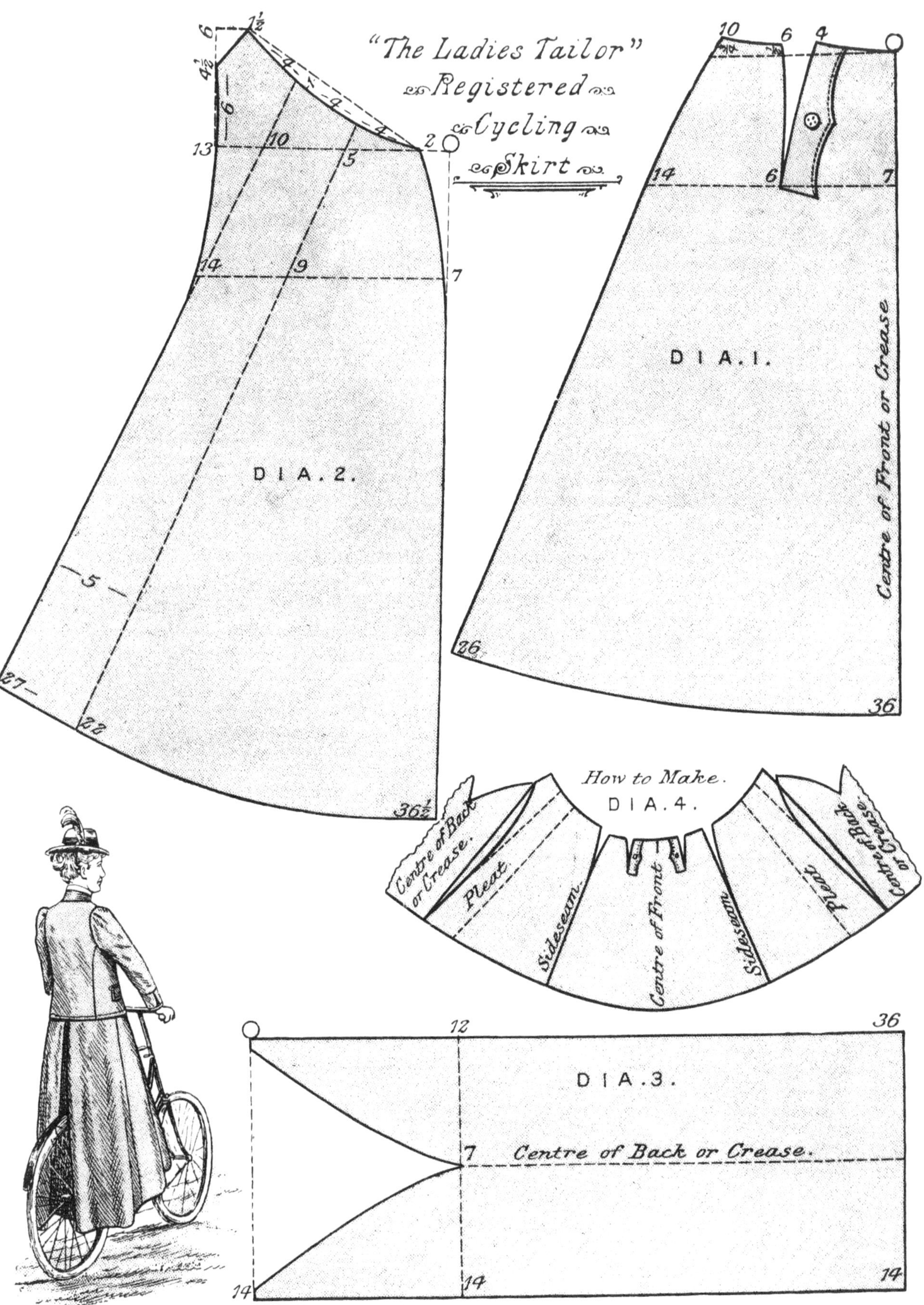
"The Ladies Tailor"
Registered
Cycling
Skirt
DIA.2.
DIA.1.
Centre of Front or Crease.
How to Make.
DIA.4.
Centre of Back or Crease.
Pleat
Sideseam.
Centre of Front
Sideseam.
Pleat
Centre of Back or Crease.
DIA.3.
Centre of Back or Crease.

Draw the straight line O 40 length of front.

O to 7 is the length from the waist to the seat line.

O to 3¼ is a fourth of the waist scale and one seam.

From 7 to 5 is one-fourth of the seat scale.

From 40 to 10½ is half of the seat scale and ½ inch.

Draw the sideseam from 3½ through 5 to the bottom at 10½. Hollow the line slightly so as to throw some spring over the foot and bottom.

Lower the centre of the front ¼ inch at O, and form slight curve from O to 3¼.

The Side Piece.

Draw the straight line O, O.

Square a line across top at right angles.

Mark on each side of O one-fourth of waist scale, and ¼ inch for a seam; that is, 3¼ on each side.

Hollow waist line 1 inch in the centre, then mark off the side length from O to O at the bottom.

From 1 to 7 is the distance from the waist to the seat line.

Mark out on each side of the construction line one-fourth of the seat measure; 5 on each side, 10 inches altogether.

The width at the bottom may be made to match the width of material, except for very large sizes.

Mark from O on each side from 12 to 14 inches, the former quantity for a short figure, the latter for a tall figure.

Draw a line on each side from 5 through to bottom, also curve sideseams from 3¼ to 5, and mark off the side length and back length. Hollow seams as shown on the diagram.

The Back Part.

Draw the straight line O to 41.

Mark out 1 inch from O, and curve from 1 to 7.

From 1 to 4¼ is one-fourth of waist scale and a seam.

From 7 to 5 is one-fourth of the seat measure.

Draw a line from 4¼ through 5 to 15.

Mark down 10 or 12 inches from 4¼ so as to form placket hole or opening. Leave on 8 inches for a single kilt, or 12 inches for a double kilt on each side.

Measure off the width from 41 to 23.

This style of skirt fits perfectly close round the seat, and is fastened at the back with a fancy silk cord put through eyelets, while a kilt pleat is formed below the opening.

Another feature of this skirt is the absence of any darts in the waist.

The Ordinary Costume Skirt.

If your customers do not wish to follow in Dame Fashion's wake, the second style of skirt will be found very useful for ordinary purposes.

The measures may be taken in the order indicated in an earlier part of this lesson. Begin as usual with

The Forepart.

O to 40 is the front length. O to 7 fixes seat line.

Square across the top from O to 7, and at the seat line from 7 to 10.

O to 3 is one-fourth of the waist scale, then take out a dart of 1 inch; from 4 to 7 is also a fourth of the waist scale.

From 7 on front line to 10 is one half of seat scale.

In order to obtain the width at the bottom, mark out 16 or 18 inches from 40; or mark down 1½ inches from 7, and place one arm of the square resting on 8½ and the other at 10, and square through to the bottom.

The Sidepiece. Diagram 2.

Draw the straight line O O.

Square a line across the top, mark down to 7, and square the seat line at right angles to O, O.

O to 4 on each side is one-third of the waist scale.

From 7 to 5 on each side is one-fourth of seat scale.

Take a dart of from 1½ to 2 inches out the side-piece at O, and curve line from 3-to 5 on each side. The width at the bottom is usually half the scale, or a trifle more on each side of the construction line, or 21 to 25 inches.

Join lines as indicated by the diagram.

The Back Part.

Draw the straight line O 41. O to 12 provides for a double kilt pleat.

Hollow the line from O to 12 to the extent of ¾ inch.

The width at the bottom is usually made the same as the width of material from 25 to 27 inches.

Complete the outlines of the diagrams as set forth.

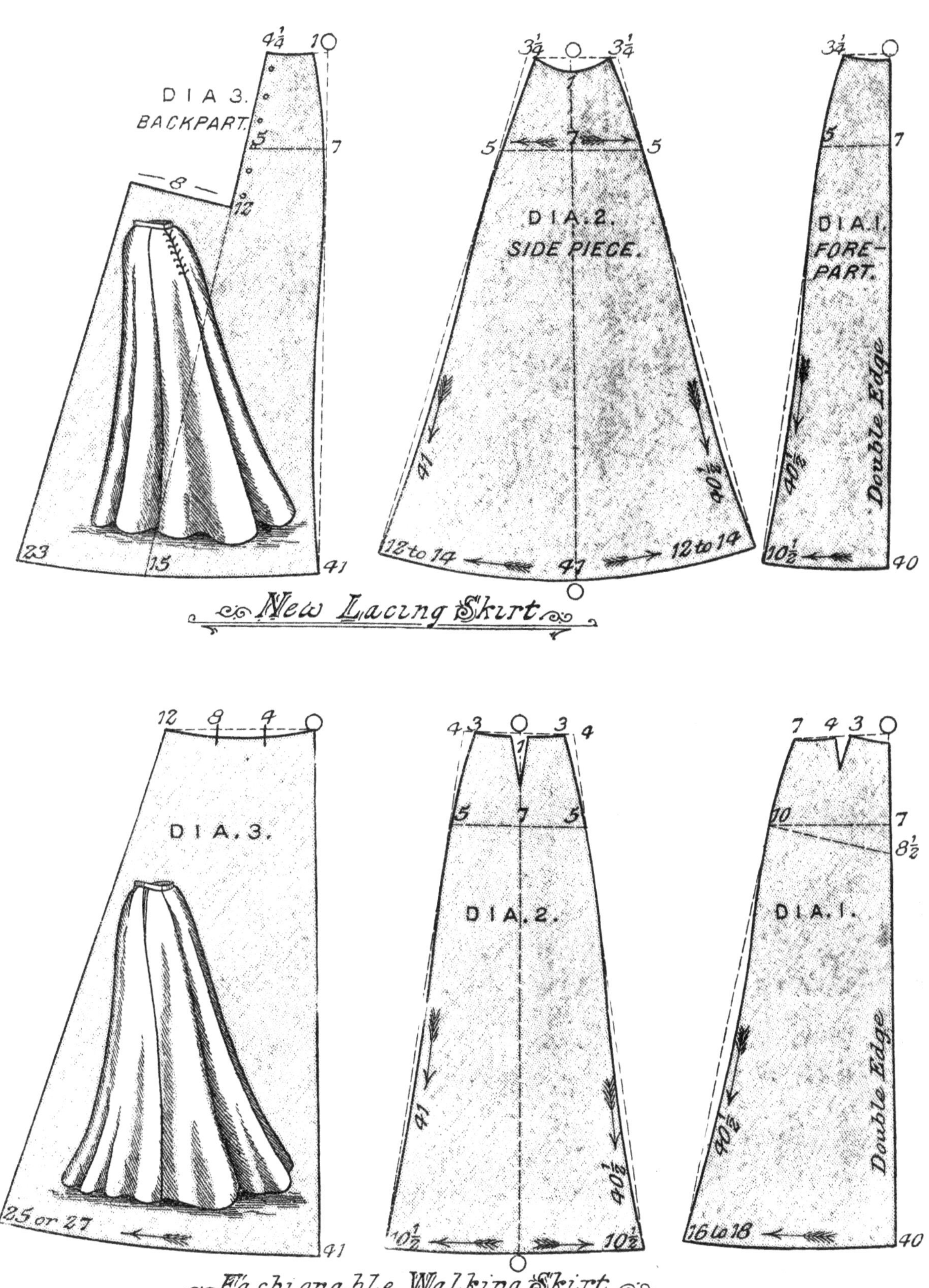
DIA 3.
BACKPART.
New Lacing Skirt
DIA. 2.
SIDE PIECE.
DIA. I.
FORE-
PART.
Double Edge
DIA. 3.
Fashionable Walking Skirt
DIA. 2.
DIA. I.
Double Edge

New Styles of Skirts.

The long reign of plain skirts has now been broken, and other styles with an abandance of frill and wavy folds round the bottom, are being made in the high class firms in the West End and Paris. It was one of the most natural things to expect that Dame Fashion would one day return to a former love, and frills and flounces once more become chief favourites.

change of style, however, has not produced a revolution in the method of cutting these skirts, and anyone possessed of an ordinary plain skirt pattern, can, by a little judicious manipulation, produce one of the new styles from the old Model. But in order to facilitate matters we have prepared some diagrams showing how the various styles can be produced from an ordinary Model.

Diagram 1

Is the forepert of an ordinary skirt to the following measures: — 24 waist; 40 seat; front length, 40 ; side, 41 ; back, 41; the waist scale is 12, and the seat scale 20.

Begin by squaring the lines O 7, and O 40.

O to 7 is the distance from the waist line to the seat line.

O to 40 is full length of the front.

Square across from 7 to 10, and make the width one-fourth of the total size round the seat, or half seat scale.

Place the square resting on 9 at front edge, and 10 on seat line, and square line through 25 to bottom.

O to 3 is one-fourth of the waist scale.

A vee of 1 inch is taken out of the forepart from 3 to 4.

Make from 4 to 7 also one-fourth of the waist scale, and join 7 and 10 with a gentle curve.

Adjust the front and side lengths, and join across the bottom.

Diagram 2. Sidepart.

Square the lines O 7 and O 7 at right angles to each other.

Mark in 1 inch at O, and square line through 7, 9, and 25 to bottom.

From 7 to 9 is 2 inches; then mark out on seat line seat line from 7 to 10 half of the seat scale.

Place square resting on 9 and 10, and square line from 10 through 21 to bottom, which is 41 long.

From 1 to 3½ is one-sixth of the waist scale and ½ inch extra, while a V of 1 inch is taken out between 3½ and 4½.

Make 4½ and 7 also one-sixth of the waist scale and ½ inch extra, then join 7 and 10 with a gentle curve.

Diagram 3. The Backpart.

Square line O 7 and O 41 at right angles to each other.

O to 41 is the length of the back, cut on the double edge of the material.

O to 7 is the width at top of backpart for a double box-pleat. The width at the bottom is made 25 to 27 inches, then square from 7 through 21.

When shaping the waist, hollow the top of the forepart ½ inch at O, and also the backpart from O to 7.

The next operation is to make the alterations from the ordinary pattern, which may be done as follows: —

Cut the forepart across by the curved line from 28 to 25, the sidepart by the line from 25 to 21, and the backpart from 21 to 13.

This will give you three sections represented by the Diagrams 4, 5 and 6.

In order to make these into a frill for the bottom, mark each diagram at two places on the top edge, as shown by A B, Diagram 4, E F, Diagram 5, and I K, Diagram 6.

Draw a line from A to C, and from B to D, then cut along the lines, and open out the pattern at C and D to any extent required, generally about 4 to 6 inches. This will give greater width across the bottom, and yet leave the top edge the same size as the original forepart from 28 to 25.

The other two diagrams may be treated in the same manner, but with a slight increase in the size of the wedge inserted at L and M.

The Second Style. Diagram 7

Of skirt is also produced from the ordinary model pattern. Take the forepart, sidepiece, and backpart of the ordinary skirt, and place them close together, as shown by line O to 21 at waistband.

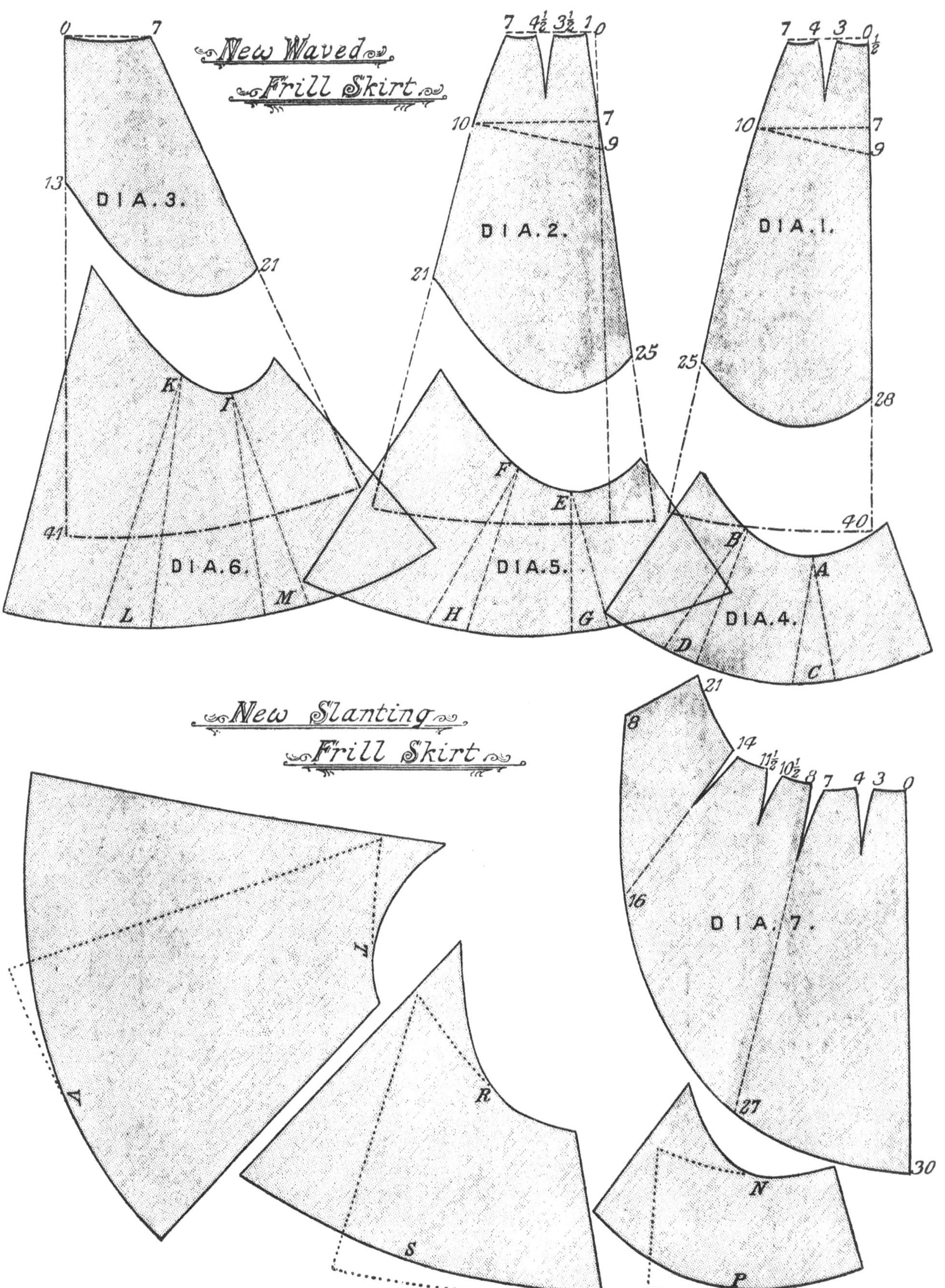
New Waved Frill Skirt
DIA. 3.
DIA. 2.
DIA. 1.
DIA. 6.
DIA. 5.
DIA. 4.
New Slanting Frill Skirt
DIA. 7.

O to 30 represents the double edge of the front.

Curve the line from 8 through 16, 27 to 30, which may be cut in one piece. It is not absolutely necessary that the same quantities should be used, as a fair amount of originality may be introduced into the design without losing individuality of the style.

The lower parts of the skirt are represented by the Diagrams 8, 9, 10.

The dotted lines represent the original sections cut from the model pattern; but in order to give the wavy or frilled effect round the bottom, a wedge has been inserted in each diagram at N P, Diagram 8; R S, Diagram 9; and T V on Diagram 10.

The result is a more hollow sewing-to edge, as shown by the hard lines, while the fulness round the bottom has been increased, or may be increased to any extent.

Braided Skirts.

Braid is always a favourite style of ornamentation with the high-class ladies' tailor, and, when nicely done, and the braid of good quality, it needs nothing else to stamp the garment as high-class production. Braid is generally arranged on symmetrical designs, that is, the one side is an exact repetition of the other, only in reverse. When the ladies' tailor has to braid a skirt, he either has to get a ready prepared design that can be transferred to the material with a hot iron, or has to design one himself, which, if he has any idea of drawing, is a very easy operation. Let him take a daisy and a few leaves, or any other flower, and then blend them together, and he will soon get a very pretty design. Having got this, he folds his paper over and pricks it through with a good-sized pin; this gives him the other half of his design of the same pattern as his original drawing but reversed. He then places this pricked design on his cloth in the position he desires the braiding to be, and sprinkles some white powder over it — finely scraped pipeclay will do, but it is rather coarse, and French chalk is preferable. Having carefully gone over every pin-hole with this, he removes the paper design, and then proceeds to fill in his design in a more substantial way. Take some flake white and mix it with a little gum and water, and mark round the designs indicated by the spots with a quill pen, any part that may not be quite distinct being easily obtained by a reference to the design. Having got the outline distinct, the putting on of the braid is a very simple process, always trying to arrange the stitches so as not to show. If possible, a strand of the braid should be used for sewing. Use care, be patient, and the result will reward you. The braid mostly used is a narrow Russia, though some very artistic results are got by using different kinds of braid, some of which are of a very ornamental character, and show up a decided contrast to the narrow Russia, and in this way are useful in working in designs of leaves and flowers. Very much more might be written on this subject of skirts and skirt drapery, but we have already

Set of Braiding for Ladies' Costume.

extended our remarks somewhat, this being a subject that is not so well understood as other branches of the tailoring trade, but a little practice and a little experiment on the lines we have suggested will soon simplify what may appear a difficult matter, and pave the way for success. Indeed, of all the branches we treat of in this work, there is none that depends more on practice to attain proficiency than the art of draping. We will now conclude this section by a few hints on

Draped Skirts.

At the present time it is very unusual to drape skirts; but should this fashion be revived again, it may be well to state here that such skirts are generally made up on a foundation of linen, Italian cloth, silk, or some similar substance, and on this the material is arranged to form in folds and fulness as desired. Skirt Draping is an art that is best acquired by practice. Very much depends on the material used for the effect. The following general principles may prove an assistance.

Vertical folds, such as kilts, consume width.

Horizontal folds, such as tucks, consume length.

Diagonal folds consume length and width.

The foundation is placed on a dummy, and the material is pinned up in such a way as to form the sweep and folds. Unlimited scope is thus offered. The drapery may be arranged in folds of any kind; the material may be on the straight or the bias, or there may be a variety of materials.

SECTION THIRTEEN.

Ladies' Trousers, Breeches, and Gaiters.
Diagrams 77 to 80. Plates 48 and 49.

We now come to what may be looked upon as the more unusual garments, and which, perhaps, causes the young cutter more worry and nervousness than any other garments. This may very easily be avoided. The first operation is, of course, measuring, and on this we will give a few hints. First measure from the waist to the full length of side desired, in the usual way as for gents. To get the length of leg there are three very good ways; the one most generally practised is to ask the lady to sit down on a chair, and then measure the distance from waist to the chair; this gives the length of the body, and if this be deducted from the side, the accurate length of leg will be the result. Another way is to measure from waist to hip bone, and place the fork on a level of three inches below this. The third method of getting the leg measure is to

measure from centre seam of back on to the bone of wrist, as for a sleeve, and a quantity will thus be obtained which coincides wonderfully well with the length of leg. Though, of course, it is highly advisable to get the length of leg correct, yet it is always preferable to get it short rather than long, as the former causes little inconvenience owing to the position occupied when in the saddle, being so different to gents, who ride astride, and consequently require their Riding Breeches to come close up to the fork, with plenty of length from fork to knee. For the same reason, gents require a far more open style of cut than ladies. The remaining neasures of waist, seat, size of knee, and bottoms are easily taken as far as Trousers are concerned; but with Breeches it is quite different. In those firms that make these garments a speciality, they ask the lady to take a seat, and lift the skirt over her knees, and take the tight knee, small, and calf in the ordinary way. It will be for our readers to decide whether they will follow this plan, or ask the lady to forward them herself. For our own part, we can see no reason why any objection should be raised, provided the operation is done in a businesslike way. In all these things it is not so much what you do, as how you do it. A judicious tact will soon enable the cutter to get over these somewhat delicate operations with ease, and overcome that nervousness which betrays a want of experience. We will not dwell further on these preliminary remarks, but proceed to deal with

The Trousers. Plate 48.

At one time it did not matter much how these were cut, so long as they were made big enough, but now that the trains are made so very closefitting, it will readily be seen how great is the necessity for their fitting perfectly. Trousers are not so much worn as they were at one time, breeches and leggings, or breeches and top boots, being largely patronised by the leaders of society; but inasmuch as the customers our clients are likely to have to cater for, not being composed entirely of that class, we think it preferable to give diagrams of both Trousers and Breeches. The materials from which these are mostly made are stockinnette and elastic cloths.

One of the leading West End firms makes a speciality of dressed deer skin, which allows of the desired form being imparted with the utmost nicety.

This firm generally makes garments of this class to fasten quite close below the knee, and supply leggings; or top boots are worn with them. We have heard many rumours that ladies are patronising the knickerbocker breeches with the Devon knee bands, as now worn by gentlemen, the material selected for these being of the most masculine patterns. These, however, have not yet become very general.

The System.
Diagrams 77 and 78. Plate 48.

It is not necessary for us to point out the positions of top, leg, or bottoms, as our readers know these are found in the usual way, though it may be as well to mention that the legs are 1 inch longer than the measure for fulling on over the knee. E H I is the centre line of the legs; from E to B and E to D are both one-third of the seat, C is midway between E and D; O to F may be made 1½ inches, O to G the half waist and 3 inches, the waist being reduced to size by means of V's, as illustrated. The width of the legs is equally divided on either side of H I, the usual widths for trousers being about 16 knee, 15 bottom. In drafting the undersides, come up from C to J 1 inch more than from C to E, and square the seat seam from J by letting the other arm of the square rest on B; make up the size of the seat at the side by allowing 2 or 3 inches for seams and ease, continuing the sideseam to the top pretty straight, and reducing it to the necessary size by means of V's.

Hints on Making.

It is of the utmost importance that the position the lady occupies when in the saddle should be borne in mind, as that is the only position in which they should be worn, hence it will be necessary to manipulate the sides differently.

The topsides should be fulled on at the knee, quite 1 inch for the leg that goes over the pommel (usually the right leg), and the underside fulled on a like amount at the seat. All those made from cloth have a considerable portion of the seat and legs lined with chamois, to prevent any possibility of chafing; they are generally finished with fly fronts, the fly extending to the leg seam; eyelets are placed at the back, so that they may be adjusted to the exact size of waist; others are made with flys at the side, but this is by far the older plan.

The V's taken out at the waist must all be neatly finished, either by covering with galoon or some other similar method. Waistbands are never put to the trousers, the whole aim being to keep everything as thin as possible. The waist band lining is invariably silk, which makes a nice finish to the top.

Breeches.
Diagram 79. Figure 45. Plate 49.

The material from which these are mostly made is a kind of Stockinnette for the Breeches, and the Leggings or Gaiters are made from the same material as the Train, &c. Not unfrequently, however, the Breeches are made entirely from chamois leather, and even when Stockinnette is used, the legs and seat are lined with chamois.

The Measures

Require a little explanation, as they will probably cause the young cutter a little anxiety at first. Those required are to all intents and purposes the same as for a gent, though the method of taking them must necessarily vary. First of all, measure the lady from waist to knee; the position of the knee can easily be fixed by asking the lady to bend her knee. The small can be fixed at 2 inches below the knee, and the calf at 4½ to 5 inches below the knee; so the next measure will be the full length of Breeches at the side. Now, in order to get the relative length of leg, ask the lady to be seated, and measure from waist to the seat of the chair, and by this means get the body length, the remaining portion of the side length giving the leg length. Now take the waist (tightly) and seat (easily), and then it will be found necessary to get the tight size of knee, small, and calf. We have previously referred to the method of taking the size of leg, though in the West End trades, where these garments are made a speciality, ladies are kept, so that should the cutter have any hesitation in taking these himself (which does not often occur), he can call the young lady assistant, and direct her what measures to take as he retires. In provincial trades the ladies' maid must take the place of the young lady assistant, and so it will be necessary to request the lady to forward these measures.

The System, Diagram 79, Plate 49,

Of cutting these is as follows: A to B is the body

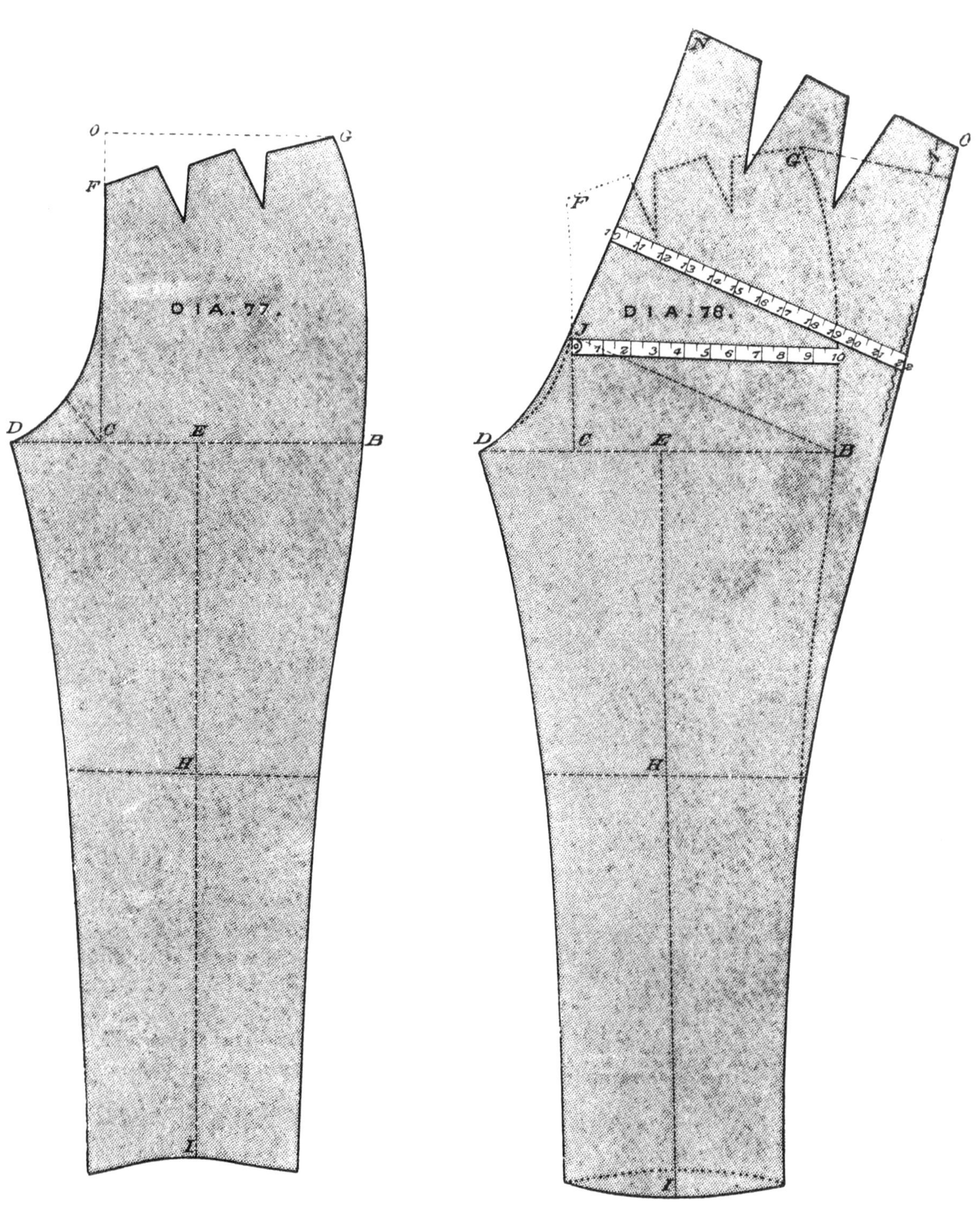
O
G
F
DIA. 77.
D
C
E
B
H
L
N
O
G
F
DIA. 78.
J
D
C
E
B
H
I

length, and line B C D E may be drawn and made the first construction line. B to C is one-sixth seat, B to D one-fourth, and B to C one-third; lines are squared up and down from C and up to K; K to A is one-fourth waist, plus 2 inches, and the fronts are lowered at K, 1 to 1½ inches. V's are taken out of the front to reduce it to one-fourth waist, and the hip is rounded from A to M. From C to * is one-twelfth seat, and C to F is 9 inches; F to G is to 1 inch, the amount varying according to the degree of ease it is required to give in the stride; C to H is the length of side to knee, less the body rise, but plus 1 inch; continue in like manner to I and J, the length to small, calf, and full length, plus 1 inch; on either side of these points place one-fourth size of leg at that part, adding ¼ inch for seam on either side, and complete topsides as shown. For

The Undersides,

Come up from D to L ⅛ seat, and draw seat seam at right angles to L B; measure up the size of seat, plus 2 inches from L to M and N to 6, and make the undersides 1 inch longer than topsides at top; draw the sideseam straight, or only slightly curved, from Q C to knee, and reduce to size of waist by means of V's. The undersides are 1 inch short at the leg, so that the knee of topsides may be fulled on, the extra length given to the undersides being intended for fulling on over the seat. The buttons on the right leg are placed on the inside at knee, the object being to prevent any chafing which might arise from the saddle and the buttons, if placed at the sideseams. The fronts are usually finished to button through up the front, the opening extending to the legseams. The tops are usually bound and finished with waistbands as for gents' Trousers. We have previously mentioned the chamois leather lining of leg and seat, but as this is a very important feature we repeat it here. These garments are often made to come down to the ankle, in which case it would only be necessary to carry line H I J down to the desired length, and divide the size of leg equally on either side.

The Leggings. Diagram 80.
Plate 49.

Whilst many ladies patronise top boots, there are also a large number who wear Leggings and Gaiters. The mode of cutting Leggings is as follows: Draw

a straight line R T U V S; R to S the length; T marks the calf; T to S divided into three equal parts; and T to 7; U to 5¾; U to 4½; and S to 4⅞ are all half the leg measures at those parts, plus seams; 4⅞ to W is half the size of bottom (fashion width); Z to * is the run of buttons, beyond which a button stand of not less than 1 inch is added; X Y is as much in front of R W as Z * is behind it. The Leggings may now be completed as per diagram.

Ladies' Cycling Knickers and Bloomers.
Plate 50.

Although known as Cycling Knickers, these are not confined solely to this sport, but are equally useful for walking and golf; in fact they now form quite a necessary accompaniment to ladies' under-clothing, and are worn in lieu of the underskirt, effecting a better hang to the outer skirt, yet retaining the warmth and comfort desired. The Bloomers are used exclusively for cycling by the younger and more enthusiastic adherents to the cycle, and, doubtless, are preferable to the Knickers and Cycling Skirt. The measures are as follow: — 1. Waist, taken tightly over the bodice, deducting 1 inch; 2. Seat measure, taken tightly, folding over the superfluous drapery at back in order to obtain a more accurate measurement. 3. Measure from the hollow of waist at side to small below knee, which can easily be ascertained by pressing the dress closely to limb below the knee; 4. For the length of body rise, ask the lady to be seated, arranging the drapery of her dress to one side, then measuring the distance from the waist to the level of the chair; 5. The size of gaiter, which may be obtained from the lady, or while she is still seated, ask her to raise her dress, then take the measure tightly over the necessary part of the leg.

Draw line A B, leg length, which is obtained by deducting the height of body rise from the length at side taken.

B to 7, one-sixth of seat measure; 7 to 10½, one-twelfth of seat measure; 10½ to 14, the same amount. Square front line 10½ D for height of body rise, less width of waistband, at right angles to B, 10½.

From D to C ¼ of waist measure, plus 3 inches, lowering the fronts at top from D E, 1 inch. Draw centre line from 7 parallel with side construction line B A. Now draw line AF at right angles to A B, marking down below from 4 to 6 inches overlap below knee.

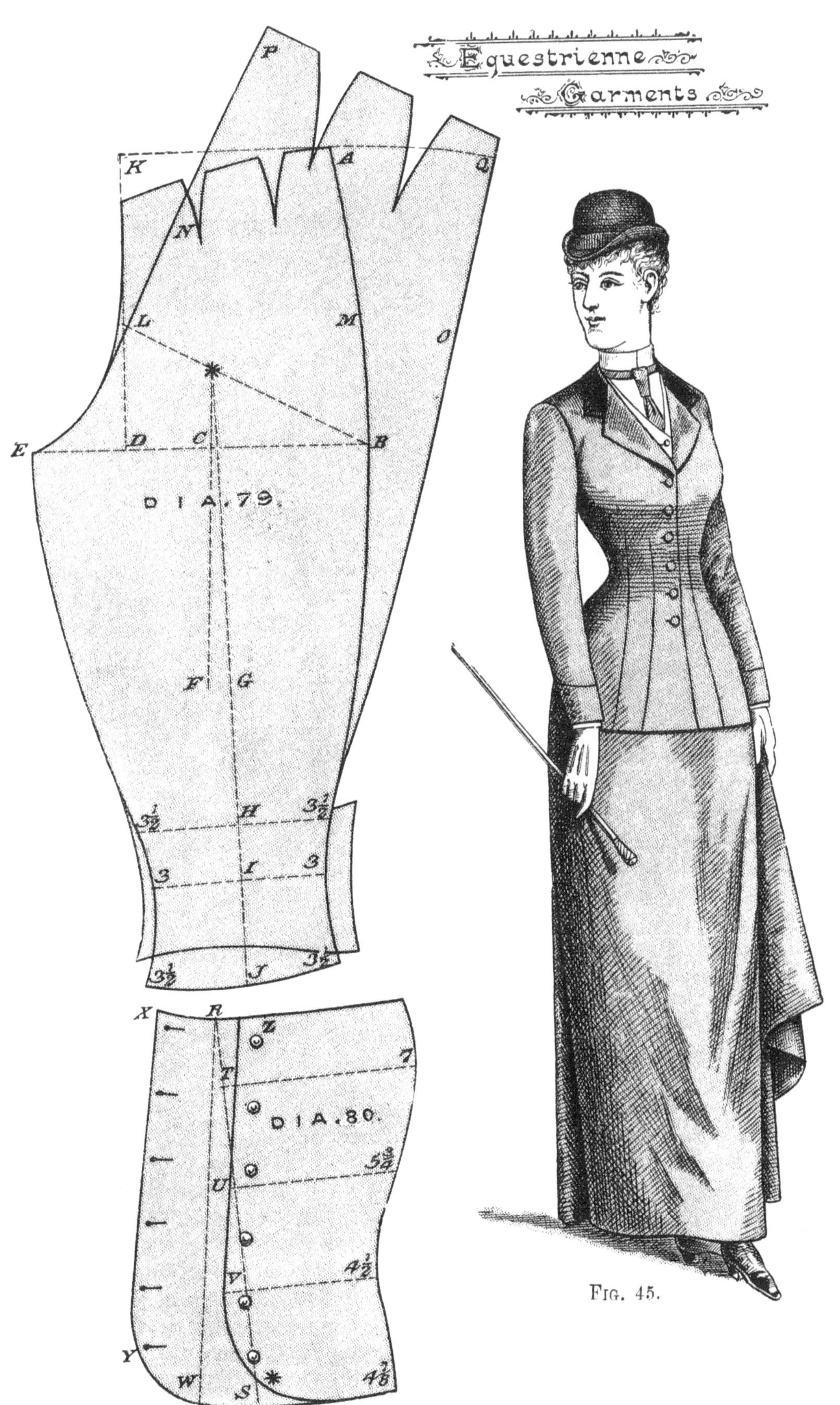

Equestrienne
Garments
DIA. 79.
DIA. 80.
FIG. 45.

The width of topsides at knee from F to G may be made to taste, a guide for a medium width being to make them 2 inches more than ¼ seat, plus seams. Arrange the width of bottom according to the amount of fulness or gathering required in the band or gaiter, although the quantity marked will be found a fair average for the length of band below. Now draw sideseam from C out from B according to taste, and width on to G through to point marked at bottom. Next the legseam, from 14 through F to bottom, slightly rounding from legseam and sideseam as illustrated. To reduce the width of topsides at waist, to measure mark from E to H one-twelfth of waist, taking out 1 inch from H toI; I to J, one-twelfth of waist, taking out 1 inch from J to K. Thus the distance from E to C is of ¼ waist, plus 1 inch for the seams of the darts. For Bloomers add to the side width from 5 to 8 inches, fulling in to the band at waist with a couple of pleats at the sides as depicted. An addition is made at the legseam also, starting from the fork and gradually increasing to the bottom. Having cut the topsides, we place them in a convenient position to mark the

Undersides.

Measure up from 10½ to T one-eighth of the seat measure, which allows for plenty of ease when the body is in a stooping or bent position. The seat seam T L is then drawn at right angles to B T, and continued down to 14 by the fork of topside. Now mark out from sideseam opposite point T 5 inches, and draw sideseam of underside from R Q to point G at knee to bottom, obtaining the correct length of underside by using G as a pivot, and sweeping from C to Q. Place the square on the seat seam L T, and square across to Q, with the opposite arm of square resting on seat seam. Now place the width of topside (6 in.) at L, and measure to Q, allowing 1 inch over for seams, the remainder to be taken out in darts, From L to M is one-twelfth of waist, M to N is half the surplus quantity to be taken out; N to O one-twelfth of waist, and O to P the remaining quantity to be taken out. For Bloomers add to side width the same amount as at topsides, pleating the surplus into pleats as marked. The waistband is cut as illustrated, with a round sewing-on edge, and is cut to nett waist measure. They are invariably finished with a fly at the sides, with pocket located on the right side just in front of tlie buttons, at the bottom catch, as in the Habit Skirt.

The bottoms are sometimes finished with an elastic band, when all that is necessary is to allow a sufficiency for the hem. An alternate method of finishing is with a

Band

Which is cut as follows: — Draw a straight line as O 15, one inch more than small of leg. Make the width of band to taste; in this instance 4 inches. Measure in from 15 three-quarters inch, and marking up the same amount. From O at the opposite end mark down ⅜ inch, dropping down at point 4, ⅜ inch. Now mark in 1 inch for button stand, and complete draft as shown.

Gaiters. Diagram 4.

The annexed diagram is well-tested models of Ladies' Gaiters and Spats, and if reproduced by the ordinary inch-tape, will ensure a pattern suitable for the majority of ladies, as they vary little in the lower part of the leg which these cover. If more width is desired, add on down seam at back; but if a longer tongue is required over the boot, that addition must necessarily be made at the front. A gaiter strap, or stout elastic is arranged to go under the boot to keep them in position, the exact location of the strap being easily determined on trying one on.

SECTION FOURTEEN.

Blouses, Shirts, and Combinations.
Plates 51 and 52.

In reviewing the previous sections to see what garments have not been treated of, we especially noticed those which form the subject of this section.

Amongst the many special garments the tailor who caters for the fair sex is called upon to make, the Shirt and Blouse are perhaps the garments that are mostly worn, being suitable for all kinds of outdoor exercise, be it boating, lawn tennis, or the latest development for ladies — cricket; but probably the larger share of the orders the tailor receives will be for boating costumes in flannel or similar materials.

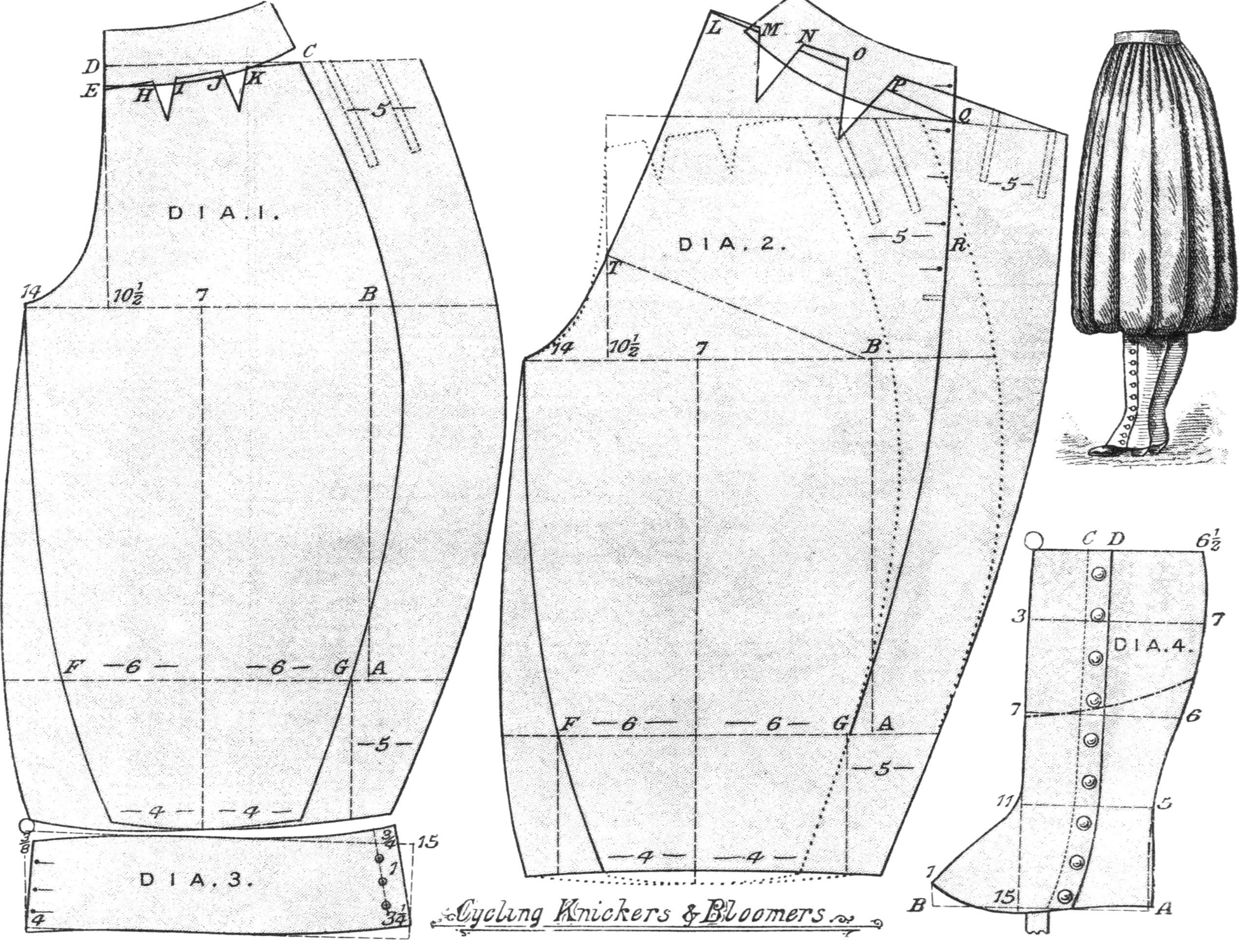
DIA. 1.
DIA. 2.
DIA. 3.
DIA. 4.
Cycling Knickers & Bloomers

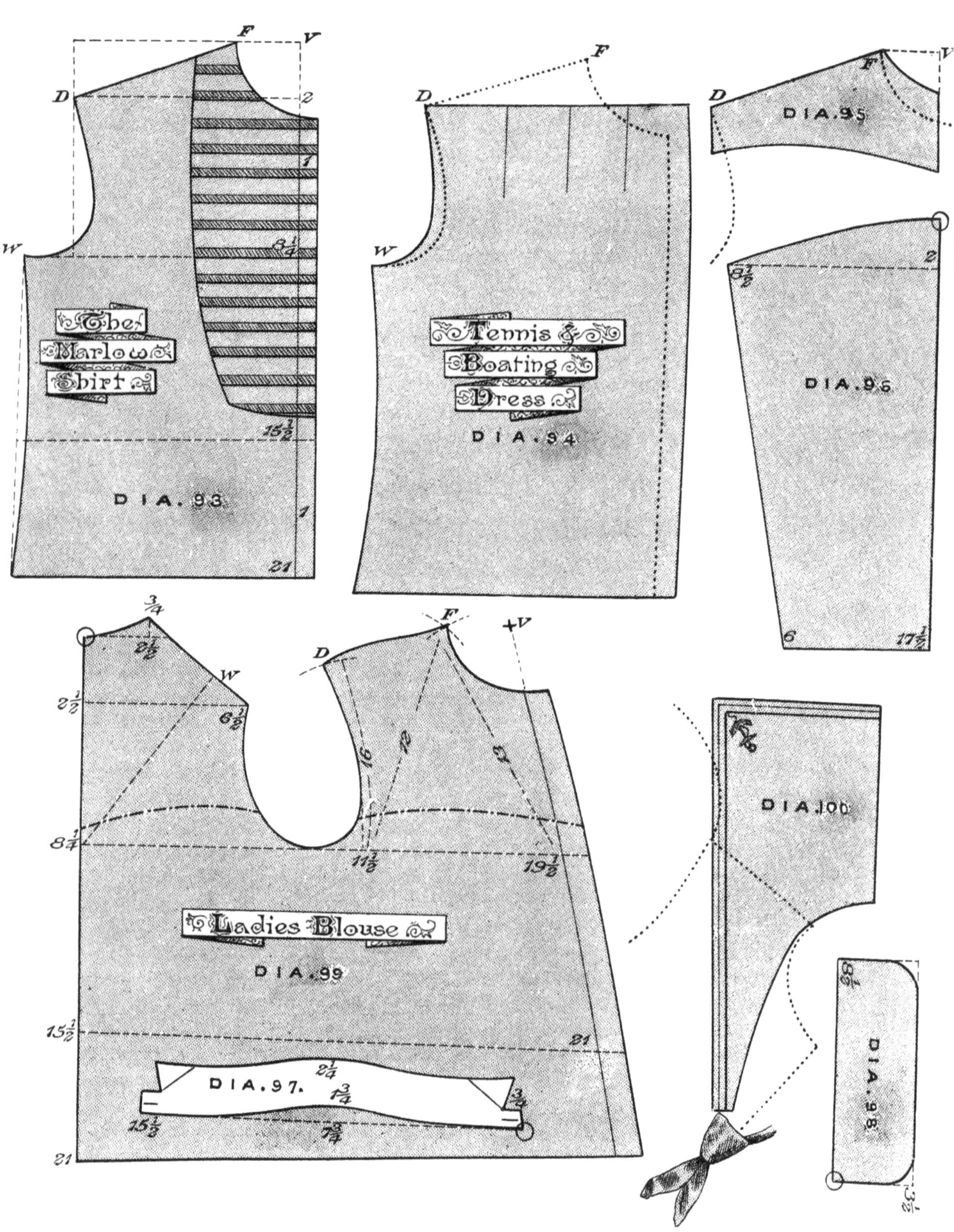
F
V
D
2
1
8¼
W
The
Marlow
Shirt
15½
DIA. 93
1
21
F
D
W
Tennis &
Boating
Dress
DIA. 94
V
F
D
DIA. 95
2
8½
DIA. 96
6
17½
¾
2½
W
2½
6¾
8¼
F
V
D
16
12
C
11½
19½
Ladies Blouse
DIA. 99
15½
21
DIA. 100
DIA. 97
2¼
1¾
15⅔
7⅔
¾
DIA. 98
8¼
3½
21

These are, of course, mostly made from cambric, and got up in the same way as a gent's shirt, the front being inserted of a different width stripe, or the front may be the only part striped, the body part being white. If our readers look at a gent's shirt, and see how it is made, they will have a capital guide for making these. There is, however, one important difference, they are left open all down the front, and only extend to about 5 inches below the waist. That part is generally worn under the Skirt, a fancy waist belt being worn over the waist band of the Skirt. A tape is placed at the waist, and a drawing tape run through it, thus enabling the fulness to be equally distributed all round the waist, or as may be deemed the most effective. This garment is very popular amongst the frequenters of the Thames Valley in the summer time, as well as at those fashionable seaside resorts such as Brighton, Hastings, Eastbourne, &c.

The System. Diagram 93. Plate 51.

Square lines V 21, V F; from V to F is one-sixth of the neck, as also is the bottom of the gorge, in fact the gorge is swept by point V; from V to 2 is one-eighth of the natural waist; to 8¼ is ¾ inch less than one-fourth of the breast ; to 15½ is the natural waist length, below which it is continued to taste; from 2 to D is one-fourth breast, from which a line is squared down as shown, and a line drawn from F to D, which finds the slope of the shoulder; from 8 to W is 2 inches more than a fourth breast; the scye may now be drawn, hollowing 1 inch in front of line D; the side is drawn at right angles from W, and the waist hollowed ½ inch or more; a button stand is left on down the front of about 1 inch, and the front is complete.

We now take the front to cut the back, and lay it down as per dotted line of Diagram 2; fill in the back scye 1 inch, as in diagram; draw a straight line across from D, and add 1 inch beyond the extreme edge of front, so that there will be about 2 inches to full on or pleat into the yoke on either side.

The Yoke, Diagram 95, Plate 51,

Is cut also by the forepart, which is represented by the dotted line, the shoulder seam is cut the same; but to find the back seam, come up half way between the bottom of gorge and V, give a little extra width below D, and shape the remainder to taste. This style is very popular. We now pass on to

The Sleeve. Diagram 96. Plate 51.

From O to 2 is 2 inches, or whatever is allowed over the fourth of the breast when drafting the forepart from 8¼ to W; continue on to 17½ the length of sleeve desired; make from 2 to 8½ the half size of scye, plus any allowance that may be desired for pleating on the shoulder, and make the width to taste. The bottom of the sleeve is put into a cuff, the outline of which is illustrated on Diagram 98.

Diagram 97 shows one of the many styles of collars worn on these garments, and which it is unnecessary for us to describe further, as the only variation necessary to introduce is the length.

Ladies' Blouse. Diagram 99. Plate 51.

This is probably one of the simplest garments it is possible to cut, as it is really only the outline of a Bodice, minus any waist suppressions. They may be worn in a similar manner to the Shirt described above, and the fulness arranged above the Skirt at the waist. The dot-and-dash line across the back and front illustrate the place adopted when a yoke is desired, the lower part being often fulled on this line, in which case about 2 or 3 inches must be added on beyond the outline of both back and front, according to the degree of fulness desired.

The Sailor Collar. Diagram 100.
Plate 51.

These are often worn with Blouses, sometimes separate, sometimes fastened to them; being generally of a contrasting colour, they add much to the effect. They are very simple to cut, the system being as follows: Take a forepart and back of the size breast desired, and place the shoulder seams together, mark down the back seam for the centre of the collar, and then round the back neck and down the front as low as desired; the length and width being quite a matter of taste, we can only refer our readers to the diagram as a guide, which is but an example to be varied from as desired.

Either the sleeve shown on Diagram 96 or an ordinary sleeve are suitable to be worn with a Blouse, but whichever style is adopted looseness must be a marked feature, otherwise it will not be in harmony with the body part; for that reason, perhaps, Diagram 96 style of sleeve would be the most suitable.

Combinations.
Diagrams 101 to 104. Figure 51. Plate 52.

This garment has become very popular during the past few years, and is used for many kinds of athletic exercises, under short-kilted skirts, whilst in addition to this they are largely used for ordinary wear; so that no work on ladies' garments would be complete without it. They are made in so many different materials that we shall have to leave our readers to arrange these details, so at once proceed to describe

The System. Diagram 101. Plate 52.

Draw line A N; A to C is one-eighth natural waist; A E one-fourth breast; A H natural waist plus ½ inch; H J one-fourth seat plus 1 inch; J N length of leg desired. A to B one-sixth neck; C to D one-fourth breast; E to F 1 inch less than one-fourth breast to find front of scye; E to G one-fourth plus 2 to 2½; H to I one-fourth breast; J to K one-fourth seat; K P drawn at right angles to J K or parallel to J N; P to O width of leg desired; J M half K J, or one-eighth seat; L is midway between M and J. Take a fish out of forepart to make it fit close at waist, as per dotted line. If intended to fasten down the front, add on a button stand of about 1 inch, and the forepart is complete.

The Back. Diagram 102. Plate 52.

Take the cut-out forepart and place as per dotted lines; from H to T is 1 inch; F to S is 1 inch; A to R is ¾ inch. All the other points are as for the forepart. It is customary to arrange them to fasten at the waist behind, when an extra inch should be left at bottom of back, to allow of the undersides overlapping.

Diagram 103, Plate 52,

Illustrates the underpart of the lower portion, the dotted lines illustrate the forepart; H to O is 3 inches. Draw line from M through U, measure up seat, and generally allow 3 inches beyond seat measure (if desired very easy, allow more), and draw sideseam straight through from P X to W; draw line H I across to W, and so get the length of side; place the square on the seat seam Y U V, and square across to W. The undersides may be cut all in one with the top, by merely letting the undersides overlap ½ inch at P and X.

Diagram 104, Plate 52,

Is the sleeve. 1 to 2 is 2 inches, 2 to 3 is the length of forearm desired, 4 to 5 is the same, 2 to 4 is half size of scye, and 3 to 5 is the width of sleeve desired. These combinations are frequently cut low at the neck, but our readers will readily be able to do this, as it only needs cutting as much as is desired from R B of back, and C B of forepart.

Ladies' Knickers.

The system as here laid down can be used for Knickers; cutting the topsides, as illustrated by dotted line from Q to I, which is got by arranging the square one arm on H L and the other resting on I. These garments are almost invariably made without sideseams, which can be arranged as before described for Combinations. The waist is reduced to size when putting them into a waistband.

SECTION FIFTEEN.

Collars. Plate 53.

The collar forms such an important part of every garment, that it would on no account do to omit it from any work that aimed at completeness; and as we anticipate this volume going into the hands of many novices, we shall treat of them rather fully; and if perchance we go into the smaller details too much for the more experienced, we crave their indulgence on behalf of the novices.

Stand Collar. Diagram 105. Plate 53.

This is the simplest form of collar possible to put on any garment; it is illustrated on Figures 19 and 20, Plate 14. A little examination of the neck

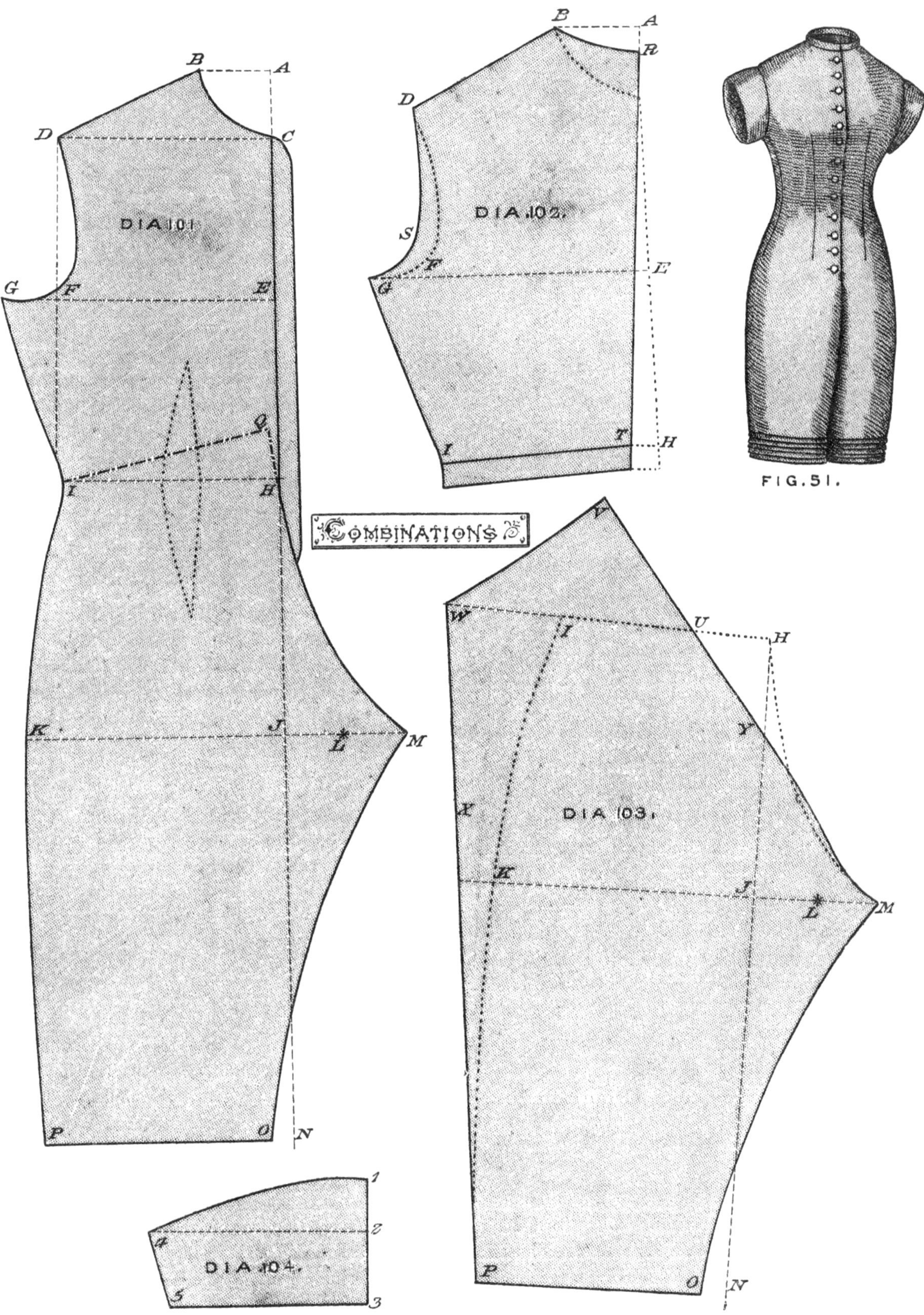
B A
D C
DIA.101
G F E
Q
I H
COMBINATIONS
K J L M
P O N
DIA.104.
1
2
4
5 3

B A
R
D
DIA.102.
S
F
G E
I T H
FIG.51.

V
W U H
I
Y
X
K C
DIA.103.
J L M
P O N

will show it must be longer round the sewing-on edge than at the top; this is provided for by cutting a round sewing-on edge; and it may be as well to state that the rounder the sewing-to edge, the shorter it will be on the top, and consequently fit the closer. The system for producing these is as follows: — Draw line W D F, and make W toF the half size of the neck; come up from F to V 1 inch as a standard (more if a very close fit round the top edge is desired). D is midway between F and W. Draw curve from V to D, and continue on to W. V to 2* is drawn at right angles to V D, the height also to taste. W 2 is at right angles to W D, the height also to taste; W 2 may be cut on the crease or not, as fancy may dictate. In making it is interlined with a good stiff buckram, and in putting this in it should be put in rather shorter than the outside, as the position it occupies on the wearer being a decided circle, renders it imperative for the outside to be the longer. We will not describe the putting on of this collar, as it is done in the same way as is described below, when dealing of Diagram 115, so we pass on to deal of

The Panteen Collar: Diagram 106.
Plate 52.

This is illustrated on Figure 26, and may be best described as a double-stand collar, as it is cut exactly the same as described above, with a second collar cut deeper, as illustrated by dotted line below W D F. In making, the stand collar is put on first, and then the other is sewn to its top edge by its lining, the outside being arranged to come about ½ inch over the top; the lining of the stand collar coming over the top of this is neatly felled in the ordinary way. This is a very popular collar, and has a much smarter appearance than the plain stand collar, which it resembles so much. It is worn on almost all garments: Blouses, Bodices, Jackets, and Ulsters all have this style of finish at the neck occasionally.

The Shakespeare Collar, Diagram 107,
Plate 53,

Is really only a variety of the Panteen, the fall half being cut much narrower behind, and with a long point in the front. It is mostly used on Blouses, &c., in place of that illustrated on Diagram 97.

The Medici Collar. Diagram 108.
Plate 53.

This is illustrated on several of the figures, and, as our readers are well aware, it is, at the time we write, a very popular finish for all garments at the neck. It is really a stand collar cut with a hollow sewing-to edge, and consequently a very full or long top edge; indeed just such an effect as would be produced by taking an ordinary stand collar and inserting V's all along the top. The excessive size on the top edge allows it to be worn much deeper than it could be in any other way, and consequently this commends it to those who are exposed to inclement weather; indeed, it has been called the storm collar. The system for producing this is as follows: W D F at right angles, W D the height of collar desired, W to 1½ 1½ inches, D to F half neck measure minus ¾ inch, F to V 3 inches. Draw D V with a gradual curve, and outline the top part to taste; and as these may be finished square, pointed, or curved, there is considerable scope for the designer. The system as here laid down will produce a good average style; if more fulness is desired round the top, increase the quantities from F to V and Wto 1½ In making, it is, of course, interlined with buckram; and, as the inside of these show, the lining is generally of silk or some bright material, but whatever is used in this way it should be nicely and neatly finished.

Prussian Collar. Diagram 109.
Plate 53.

This is not so much worn now as it was at one time, but in order to describe all kinds of collars, we give it a place. The system is as follows: W D half neck, D F 1 inch, draw curve of sewing on edge from W to F, W to V and F to ½ is the stand, below which, as from V to I, is the fall. In making, the sewing to edge must be well stretched in the hollow. In style this much resembles the Panteen collar, but it is not so deep in the stand at front, and is cut all in one piece, though it is nothing unusual to find the under collar arranged with the stand and fall cut separately. Especially when it is made of very thick material, as it frequently is for Box Coats and Driving Capes, such as ladies are now wearing for driving, &c.

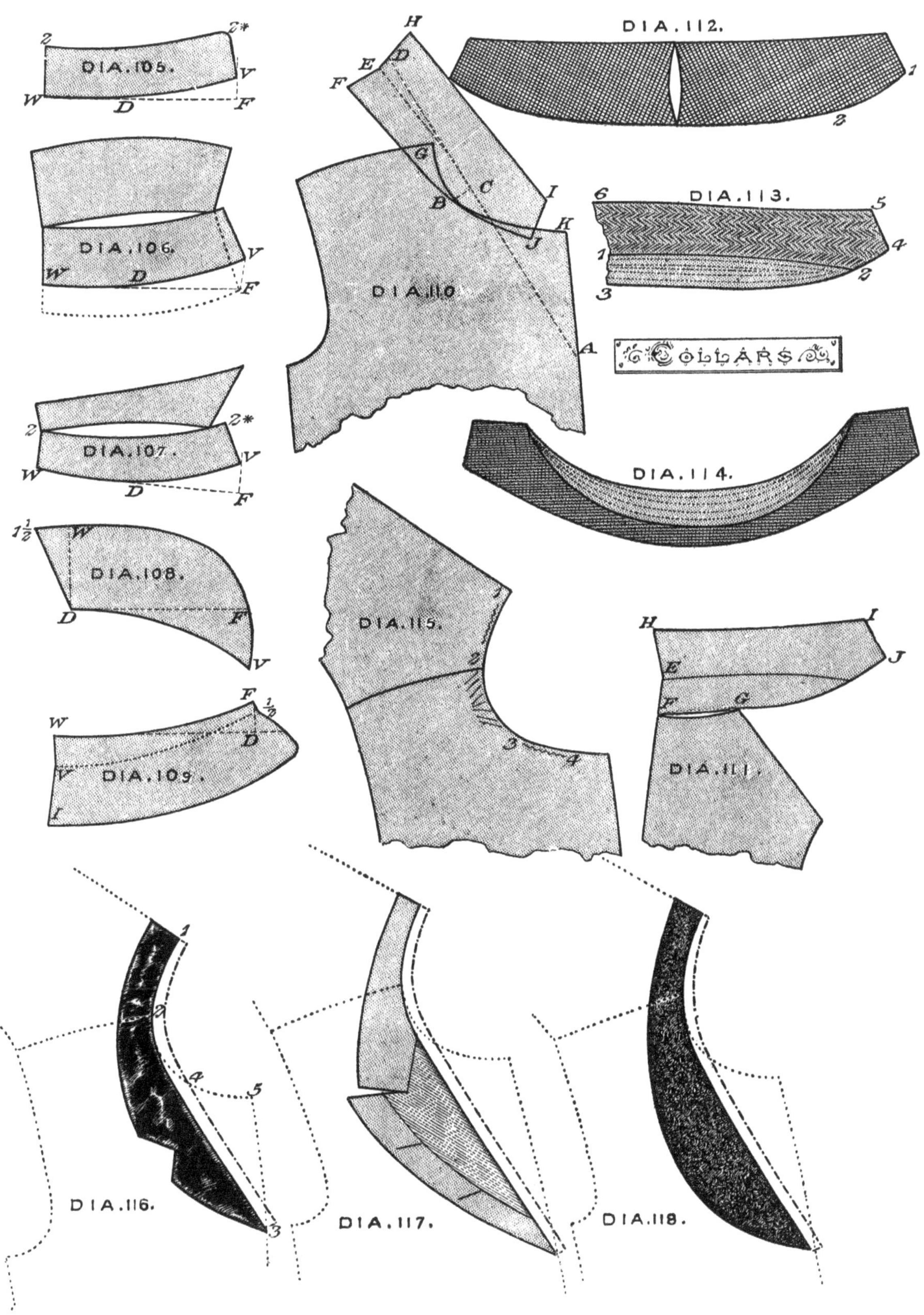
DIA.105.
DIA.106.
DIA.107.
DIA.108.
DIA.109.
DIA.110.
DIA.112.
DIA.113.
COLLARS
DIA.114.
DIA.115.
DIA.111.
DIA.116.
DIA.117.
DIA.118.

Stand and Fall Collar. Diagram 110. Plate 53.

This is illustrated on many of the figures. This collar is perhaps the most, difficult of all to the novice; but as it is a very important one, we will endeavour to describe all about it in detail, and begin with the system. Begin by taking the fore-part of the garment it is intended to go on; decide where you wish it to turn, as at A, Diagram 110; mark up from B to C a trifle less than the depth of stand desired; having previously decided that the depth of the stand or the upcome on the neck above the collar seam should be 1¼ inches, and the fall 1¾ inches; the fall is that part which turns over from the crease. Both these quantities are fair average. For such a collar come up from B to C. 1 inch, and draw a line from A through C to D. Get the length of the collar by measuring from G to F the width of the back neck, as from 1 to 2 of Diagram 115, allowing about ½ inch extra length. Now come down from D to E the difference between the stand 1¼ and the fall 1¾, viz., ½ an inch. The object of this is to give more relative length from H to I as the fall gets deeper, a very necessary arrangement. Draw line from E to C slightly curved — this is the crease edge on the part where the collar folds over; from E to F measure down the depth of stand desired, in this case 1¼ inches, and connect F to B, and continue on to J, letting the collar overlap at J about ¼ inch. E to H is the fall behind, and J to I the same in front; and as this is to a large extent a matter of taste, no more definite rules than we have laid down can be given. With regard to back of collar from F E to H, it may be as well to illustrate, as a want of proper attention at that part frequently results in a collar standing away behind.

Diagram 111, Plate 53,

Illustrates how this should be arranged. Place the collar on the back neck, as shown at F G, when F to E should form a continuation of the back seam, and above this it should be sprung out, so that when it is turned over at the crease row it will have sufficient spring to go over F. This completes the cutting as far as the system is concerned, and what we now give is more of

A Practical Explanation.

We will assume the pattern of the collar has been cut out in paper, and we now proceed to cut the inside collar, as that is really the collar that produces all the fit and style. This is sometimes made from different material to the garment, especially when the cloth is very thick, in such cases a thin Melton of as nearly the same colour as possible is used, the advantage being that it is thinner and more easily worked up; but we do not advise this except when the cloth used for the garment is very thick and unyielding. In cutting the inside collar from the material, cut it on the bias; and on no account cut it from the lengthways of the material. It is far preferable to join it in order to get it on that bias, as the joins are out of sight. It is well understood that cloth on the bias is very easily stretched or shrunk, and consequently is more easily manipulated. If there is any face or way of the wool to the material, it should run from H to E to F, Diagram 111. Now join the collar at the back, either by taking a small seam or, if the material will stand it, by stoating. This done, the next step is to arrange the collar canvas.

Diagram 112, Plate 53,

Shows how it should be put in, the cross marks representing the threads of the canvas. The canvas should be shrunk by being well wetted and dried without the use of the iron before cutting, and in cutting it out sufficient should be left for working in. It should always be cut in two halves alike, the one end having the threads, otherwise it is impossible to get both ends running in an altogether different direction to the other when cut whole, and consequently the effects are seen in the collar when made up. If cut as illustrated on Diagram 112, the straight thread will run from 1 to 2. Join it by letting the two ends slightly overlap each other, and we next baste the collar lining and canvas together. The fall of the collar should lie flat on the canvas, and then a row of basting put along the crease row, and then the stand part of the canvas being on the bias can be easily stretched to fit the stand of the collar lining. The first step in the stitching and padding of a collar is to stitch along the crease as from 1 to 2.

And in doing this the hand should be pulled fairly tight, so as to draw in that part in accordance with your customer's requirements; a stooping figure with head forward requires it drawn in more than the normal, whilst the erect or head-backward type require less. The stitching of the stand comes next, and the object of this is to make that part of the collar firm and stiff, to stand up. This is usually done about four rows to the inch, and may either be done by hand or machine. If by hand it should be a short fore-stitch, so that the collar lining would represent the appearance of Diagram 113, as from 1, 2, 3. For the fall a padding stitch is required. The object of padding the fall is to get it to curl in well, which effect is produced by curling the canvas over the finger, and so getting it on longer than the collar lining. But as most of our readers will understand all this we will not describe it in further detail, but pass on to

Diagram 114. Plate 53,

Which illustrates the pressing process. The object of pressing is to model the collar into the required shape, as well as to press the sewing that has been put into the collar. This is best accomplished by the aid of a thoroughly hot iron, and the collar pressed until it is quite dry. The shape when this operation is finished should be somewhat after the outline of Diagram 114, the stand being represented as turned over, whilst the effect of the padding will now be seen by the curling of the fall. Now smooth over the outside collar on the double, as cloth always shrinks more on the double than the single. By smoothing we do not mean stretch it, but merely smooth it, though it is no detriment for the kkstandkk portion to be slightly stretched. Next fit the collar to the neck, to see the collar ends harmonise with the turn, as well as to see that it breaks at the right point. Having corrected the collar in any detail that is necessary, we proceed to cover it. Let us suppose the edges of our garment are to be bound. Lay the fall of the outside collar quite flat on the sleeve board, and on this place the fall of the collar lining, and put a basting thread along the crease row, and then the fall is basted from the outside, the collar being slightly bent to allow of the outside being a trifle the longer, then turn the collar over and put in a

row of stitching about three-eighths of an inch from the crease; this keeps the stand in its place. The collar is then bound and sewn on. To illustrate this latter process we give

Diagram 115. Plate 53.

Across the back from 1 to 2 it should go fair, or, of the two, very slightly tight; from 2 to 3 the collars should be fulled on about ½ an inch; and from 3 to 4 commence by putting it on tight up to the break, and beyond that fair or plain. Now press open the seam, and serge the neck, and in front of the break of the collar canvas and the forepart canvas should be drawn together edge to edge over the collar seam. It only remains now to turn in the collar and facing, and draw the collar seam; the turn in should be as small as possible, and exactly on the top of the collar seam, as by these means it gives a much cleaner and flat appearance to the front. The only remaining touch is the pressing off, and our collar is complete. We will now pass on to deal with

Cape Collars.
Diagrams 116, 117 and 118. Plate 53.

These are collars laid on the garment, and are cut by the shoulder seams of back and forepart, being placed together as per dotted lines, when the outline of the lapel desired is marked; 3 is the bottom termination of it, and the sewing to point is marked from 1 by 2 to 3, beyond which a seam is left as illustrated by dot-and-dash line; this is made up independently of the garment, and then sewn in the position desired from the back, and turned over, with the result of the shaded part of 116. Diagram 116 is the S.B. style of turn, and is often used for ladies' Bodices, when the part outlined by 3, 4, 5 would have the appearance of a Vest. Our diagram represents this lapel of velvet, from which material these are often made.

Diagram 117, Plate 53,

Illustrates the D.B. style of lapel with silk facing. This may be produced as a Cape collar, as previously described, though it would more likely be used for Jackets. There should only be the smallest possible space between the top of the lapel to the collar end. The silk facing is brought to the end of the holes, and carried over where the drawing seam of the collar would be, or even higher; the aim should be to give the collar the apperance of being the same width all way round as far as possible. The silk mostly used for this is a bright satin faced fine twill; and when used on some of the dull or rough material now so popular, has a very stylish appearance. Before quitting this diagram it may be as well to state that the holes in the turn should run with the top of the lapel, and in like manner the silk should follow the outline of the side of the lapel. Great care should be exercised in putting on this silk, as, being used for ornament only, the effect would be spoilt if it was not put on artistically. Every possible effort should be used to get both sides alike — a result which is not so easy to achieve as may appear at first sight.

Diagram 118, Plate 53,

Illustrates a roll collar laid on; this is cut exactly as previously described, with the exception of the outline of the roll, which must, of course, be run to taste. Fur Collars of this kind are frequently put on Winter Jackets, and undoubtedly gives them a very stylish appearance. In cutting fur it should be done with a knife, and the pile or nap arranged to run the wrong way, which remark also applies to velvet, as it then presents a much richer appearance. In ordinary collars the velvet is always cut on the bias, as that is the only way by which anything like a satisfactory result can be obtained; but with these cape collars a rather wider sweep of material is required than ordinarily, and, as very little working up is needed, it is not of so much importance. mmThis, we think, exhausts the subject of Collars, and if we have gone into detail rather too minutely for some of our more advanced readers, we can only plead the importance of the subject.

SECTION SIXTEEN.

DEFECTS AND REMEDIES.
Plates 54 and 55.

Although this is really outside the scope originally intended for this work, we have little doubt a few hints on the various defects generally met with will prove of service. Let us take first the defects that arise from

An Incorrect Balance. Diagram 119.
Plate 54.

Too long a front shoulder produces a fold, or series of folds, all across the front, as from E to H; the remedy is shown by dot-and-dash line 7, 8, 9. Too long a back balance produces folds all across the back, as from A to B, showing more especially at B. Remedy as per dotted line 1 2 3. These are good illustrations of too much length producing horizontal folds.

The reverse of these defects, viz., a too short back balance, would produce the garment too low at back neck, owing to its fitting close at waist, and thus being dragged down; whilst, if it was worn unbuttoned, it would hang away from the waist behind. The easiest way to remedy is to either pass the back up on the sidebody, and readjust the scye, or, if there is plenty of length about the waist of the garment, shorten the front shoulder and deepen the scye, producing extra relative length of back. A too short front shoulder produces tightness of scye, fulness at top of sideseam, creases down front shoulder, &c. If you have an inlay on shoulder, let it down; if not, reverse the suggested alteration to the back, viz., deepen the scye and shorten the back.

Creases from Blade to the Underarm,
Diagram 119, Plate 54,

As illustrated from C to D, are caused by a too straight sideseam, or insufficient receptacle for the blades. The remedy is illustrated by dotted lines, 4, 5, 6.

Diagonal Creases below Waist,

As from K to L, are produced by too much being added on the one side below the waist, and not enough on the other, so producing a drag from K to L; the remedy is to let out from 14 to 15, and, if necessary, to reduce the hips to their original size; take in from K downwards.

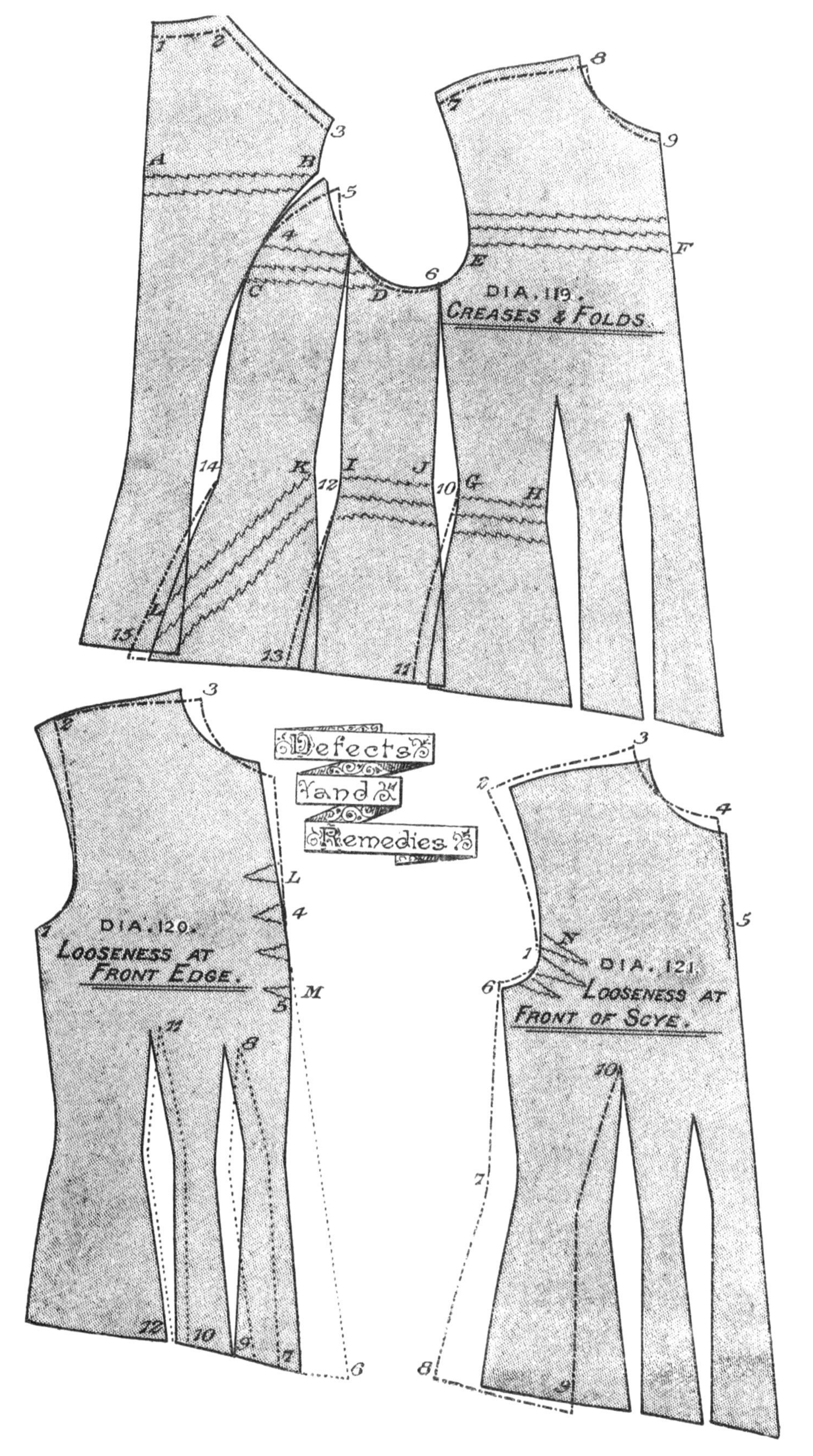
DIA. 119.
CREASES & FOLDS.
Defects and Remedies
DIA. 120.
LOOSENESS AT FRONT EDGE.
DIA. 121.
LOOSENESS AT FRONT OF SCYE.

Creases at Waist, Diagram 119, Plate 54,

As at I, J and G H, have two principal causes — (1) linings put in too short; (2) too tight over the hips. In either case, remedy accordingly. All linings should be put in very long over the waist. (See our remarks on making up in previous sections.) If it is too tight over the hips, the remedy will be to let out, as from 10 to 11, and 12 to 13. Each part should be stretched on the outside, as at K, I, J, G, H, and shrunk in the middle. The bones should also be put in very long.

Looseness of Front Edge, Diagram 120, Plate 54.

As at L, M is produced by a too round front edge as our readers will have gathered from the preceding pages; the front edge should be straight, or if cut round, every bit of round drawn in and worked back over the breast. If this defect exists in a made up garment, the best way to alter it is as per 1, 2, 3, 4, and then draw in the front edge to work the fulness back.

In cutting a fresh garment, the remedy is illustrated by 5, 6, 7, 8, 9, 10, 11, 12.

Looseness at Front of Scye. Diagram 121, Plate 54,

Is produced by an insufficient provision for the busts. One remedy is to alter as per 1, 2, 3, 4, 5, and draw in the front edge; but that is not nearly as good a remedy as illustrated by 6, 7, 8, 9, 10, viz, let out under the arms, and take in at the dart, but a reference to Diagram 121 will, we think, make this quite clear. If there is any difficulty in pressing away the

Fulness at the top of the Darts,

Put a trifle of wadding about the size of the fingernail, and then try to press it away. If this is not sufficient, the darts have not been taken high enough. Remedy accordingly.

Creases in Shoulder.

These rank amongst the most troublesome defects, and, like all others, may arise from various causes; such, for instance, as a shoulder of the wrong shape, a short collar, badly put in linings or canvas, etc. The most general cause of this defect is an insufficient distance from A to B, and too great a distance from B to C; it arises from what many term a too crooked shoulder. On the diagram we illustrate two ways of remedying, one by the dot-and-dash line, the other by the dotted line. These alterations apply only when the defect has been caused by a defective form; but if, as often is the case, they arise from faulty manipulation, the remedy must be found in that direction.

Creases round Neck. Diagram 123, Plate 55.

These most frequently arise from the lining being put intight. The shoulder being hollow, requires the linings put in very wide over the shoulder; and in many cases this defect can be remedied by giving more width to the linings, etc. Some, we know, apply the remedies in a negative way, *i.e.*, they narrow the outside, which practically amounts to the alteration illustrated by the dotted line at neck.

Loose in Back, and Tight in Front. Diagram 124. Plate 55.

This is a defect frequently met with by cutters who take insufficient measures, etc. Everyone will at once agree upon the wide difference there may be in the form of ladies' figures of the same size chest. One lady of, say, 34 breast, will have a well-developed chest and prominent bust; the other will have no figure at all; hence it is evident that to cut the same shape garment for both must end in failure. When this has been done, to remedy is a somewhat difficult matter; indeed, it would require either new foreparts, or a Vest inserted down the fronts, unless very large inlays had been left all over. The alteration shown on Diagram 124 will probably be more useful when cutting a fresh pattern, though, of course, the variations shown are the alterations required in the made-up garment also, viz., a piece taken off sidebody from A to B, and sidepiece from C to D, the front being advanced at E F, and so giving the extra width to the chest needed. Do not give a round front to this figure, as the busts being prominent there is the greater depression between them, and consequently the greater need of shortness down the centre of front.

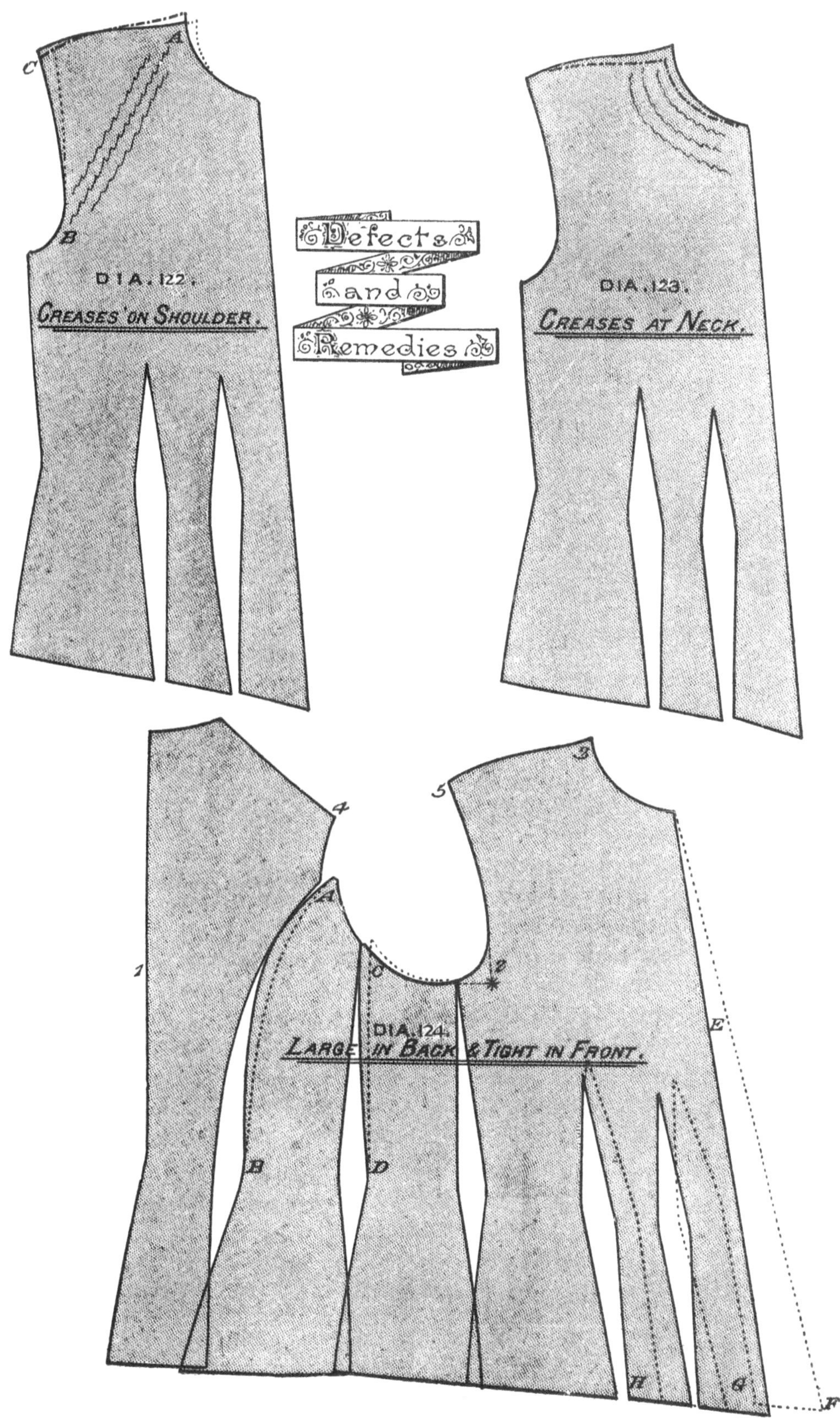
A
C
B
DIA. 122.
CREASES ON SHOULDER.
Defects and Remedies
DIA. 123.
CREASES AT NECK.
4
5
3
1
A
C
2
B
D
E
DIA. 124.
LARGE IN BACK & TIGHT IN FRONT.
H
G
F

We have now dealt with the principal defects usually met with in body garments, and we have treated of sleeves in the section devoted to them. In suggesting remedies, we have not laid down any quantities, as such must be decided on the merits of each case.

SECTION SEVENTEEN.

MISCELLANEOUS.

In getting up a work on Ladies' Tailoring, there are many little things which, though useful themselves, cannot be properly classified under any of the previous sections, so we purpose dealing with such in this section. We take first

Swiss Belts.
Diagram 125. Figures 52 and 53. Plate 56.

These are very popular at the present time, many of them being made much deeper than our illustration, but, as far as the cutting is concerned, it is ths same. The ordinary close-fitting Bodice or Jacket pattern is taken, as illustrated by dotted line, and the outline of the Belt is then marked above and below the waist as may be desired; care must be taken to avoid getting it too hollow at top and bottom of the various parts, or there will be a peak at the seam. The aim must be to get it to run true when cut. These Belts are made up with bones under the various seams as for a Bodice, which will also necessitate the lining being put in extra long. It will be noticed there is only one dart taken out, which will be found quite sufficient. Figure 52 shows the front laced up, but this is not necessary back and front, so that, if desired, the front may be cut on the crease, as it is quite straight, though the introduction of a seam frequently adds to the effect. The next detail we will notice is

Dovetail Tacks.
Diagrams 126 and 127. Plate 56.

Dovetail tacks make one of the nicest finishes possible for box pleats, the ends of pockets, etc., though perhaps it is open to the objection that it is rather showy. Very great care is necessary to execute it nicely, one of the chief points being to keep the threads very regular. Another very essential feature is that all three sides shall be exactly equal. See

Diagram 126. Plate 56.

Commence by chalking on the cloth a triangle of the size you desire the tack to be when finished. This, although a very simple matter, has been a bit of a puzzle to more than one of the workmen we have seen attempt it; and as it is a very essential point to have this very exact, we will give minute instructions how to draw it. Draw line B C, and make a mark exactly in the centre between these two points, and square up at right angles to it to point A. Having decided on the size you wish it from B to C, measure across from B towards A the same amount, and make a mark where it touches this line, when it will be found C to A will be the same distance, and thus you will have an equilateral triangle, i.e., all the sides are equal. Now proceed to bar these three sides with twist in the same manner as you would for a bar tack, i.e., about two or three times, but be careful to keep the corners very true ; and having thus barred from A to B, B to C, and C to A, you are now in a position to proceed with the tacking proper, which you do by bringing your needle up as near point A as possible at 1, and take twist across and prick needle through at 2 as near point C as you can, bring it back at 3, also as near C as possible, and carry it across to 4, up again at 5, and across to point 6, which will complete the first stitch; and you come to your second in the same manner by coming up at 1 as near the other stitch as you can, across and down at 2, up at 3, across and down at 6, and so on till you have finished it, when it will present the appearance of Diagram 2; and we think there are few features which add a more artistic effect to a ladies' Ulster or Jacket than this, especially when applied to the top of a box pleat, for which part it seems especially suitable.

How to take the Pattern of an Old Garment.

This is essentially the dressmaker's method, who makes not the slightest claim to scientific knowledge; but it has also to be resorted to by the best of cutters; so that although extremes meet, yet there is a marked difference in thair methods of doing the same things. The former slavishly follows the run of every seam,

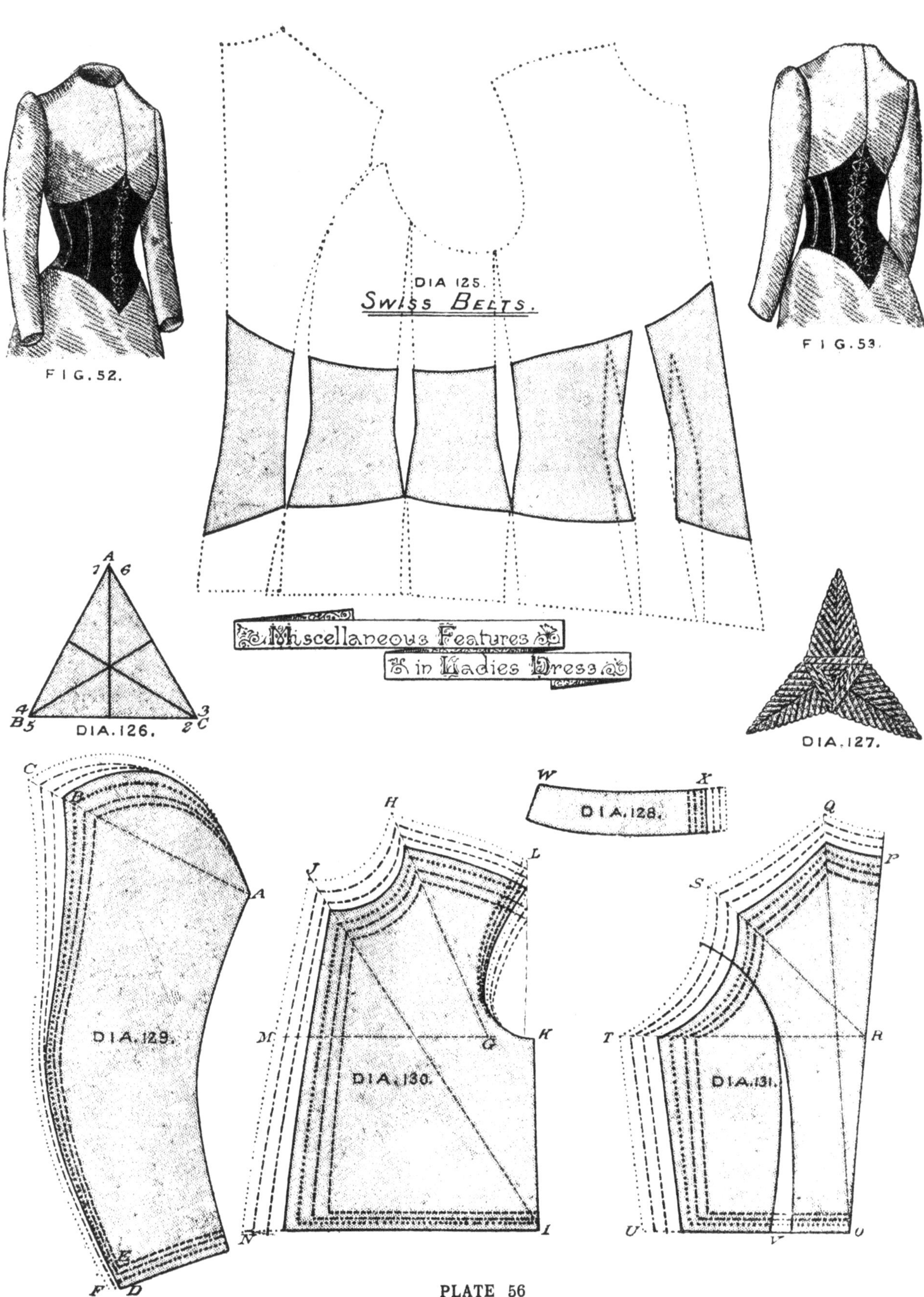
DIA 125.
Swiss Belts.
FIG. 52.
FIG. 53.
A
1 6
4 3
B 5 2 C
DIA. 126.
DIA. 127.
Miscellaneous Features
in Ladies Dress
C
B
A
DIA. 129.
F D E
H
J L
M G K
N I
DIA. 130.
W X
DIA. 128.
Q
S P
T R
U V O
DIA. 131.

whilst the cutter merely takes the essentials of fit from the old garment, and then goes to work to infuse as much art as he possibly can, so as to, as far as possible, bring out the points of beauty, or tone down those prominent features which would detract from the grace of the garment on the figure. The exact method they each use, however, is as follows : The dressmaker takes her pattern garment and pins paper on each part, and by placing it over her knee she is enabled to get the exact shape, and then by allowing seams on all sides, she can thus produce a *fac simile* garment; and it would be idle for us to say the method is not successful, as we have seen some first-class results produced in this way. Some of them go to the trouble of ripping one side of the whole garment, and tracing with a wheel through exactly where the seam was sewn; and having done so, to re-make the garment. That, however, is generally the result of a want of experience of the other way, and which is equally good if done carefully. In contrast to this, however, we will now describe a plan which we think is decidedly in advance of either of the above modes, and which we will designate.

The Tailor's Method,

As adopted by a well-known West End tailor, as follows: Whenever a garment was ordered which he was unable to measure the lady for, he would send the old garment to a firm of bust makers to have a dummy made to fit the Bodice, by which means he would be able to successfully cater for the wants of that particular customer without a try-on, even if she were in the Antipodes; as he would, for all practical purposes, have her duplicate to try on as many times as he could wish. This method, of course, entails an extra cost (about 10s., we are informed) on the first order; but the after result certainly justifies the outlay, and as the bust would always be ready for use at any time, the first cost would be the only one, and would be of use for every kind of garment. Having once obtained this, it only remains to follow his usual method; but all tailors cannot follow this plan on account of the expense, so they usually fit the old Bodice on a dummy or figure as near the same size and shape as possible, and pad it up to the Bodice wherever the figure is lacking. Another method is to lay down the garment so that each piece lies flat, and take a tracing of it by means of a pricker in a similar manner to the dressmakers' method; but this requires practice to do it successfully.

We now pass on to another method of cutting, viz.,

Grading. Diagrams 128 to 131.
Plate 56.

By this method a pattern which has been found to fit satisfactorily is used as a starting basis, and which may be taken as the shaded pattern in the diagrams. Now draw lines as shown above P, continuing it above also from O to Q, and from R (which is level with the bottom of the armhole) through S, and from R to T.

Vary for every 2 in. in the size of breast at P ⅜ in.
Vary for every 2 in. in the size of breast at Q ⅜ in.
Vary for every 2 in. in the size of breast at S ½ in.
Vary for every 2 in. in the size of breast at T ½ in.
Vary for every 2 in. in the size of breast at U ½ in.

Whilst in the small sizes it will be as well to shorten the waist as at O, V, U, say ¼ inch for every 2 inches in the total size of the breast. Turning to

The Forepart,

Draw the line from L to K in the true perpendicular from G, which is at the front of scye, to H, from I to J, from K to M, and from I to N, and

Vary for every 2 in. in the size of breast at L ⅜ in.
Vary for every 2 in. in the size of breast at H ½ in.
Vary for every 2 in. in the size of breast at J ½ in.
Vary for every 2 in. in the size of breast at M ½ in.
Vary for every 2 in. in the size of breast at N ½ in.

The same variation in the length of the waist to be made as was done with the back. For a sleeve, draw a line as from A through B to C, and vary ½ an inch for every 2 inches in the total breast; vary the width at the elbow about ⅜, and at the cuff ¼ inch for every 2 inches total breast, whilst the length may be shortened, say, ½ an inch for the small ones at the cuff, in addition to the variation in the length produced by the grading at the top, which latter will be found quite sufficient for the large sizes. The collar only requires varying ⅜ at the back at X, Diagram 128, the front at N N being left the same, a trifle narrower at W being perhaps needed for the small sizes. This, then, constitutes the method of grading, and where it is desirable to reproduce a given style of pattern with special characteristics, it will be found a very effective method, and is specially suitable for manufacturing trades rather than the artist tailor who caters for the wants of every customer on separate lines, so as to obtain the highest results, rather than to produce a set of patterns with the same characteristic running throughout the whole set.

There are, of course, many other features and details associated with ladies' tailoring, but which the scope of this work, large as it is, will not permit of being treated here. These will be found, from time to time, in our monthly journal, the LADIES' TAILOR.

Conclusion.

Ere we lay aside our pen, we will only state, by way of conclusion, that we have aimed at the production of a work that should supply the young cutter with all he may require to fit him for the post of a ladies' tailor. Such has been our aim; our readers will judge whether we have succeeded in carrying out that aim to a practical issue. We desire to instruct, to improve, to encourage; and it may be that even in the defects of our work, others may take courage and persevere midst adverse circumstances and innumerable difficulties till a successful issue results.

THE AUTHOR.